"Coach Owens certainly has been a great supporting piece for me. We talk a lot, not specific X's and O's, more general philosophy. He knows the game and, even more than that, he knows people. He reads people well, and it amazes me how much he appreciates practice, how much he appreciates the simple things."

— Bill Self, University of Kansas basketball coach

"He gave me an opportunity to coach at one of *the* programs (KU). Coach Owens always handled himself with class. Whether we won or lost, he was just a classy, upstanding gentleman. And he did it at a hard place to coach, but a great place to coach. I will always be indebted to him, and Coach Owens knows that."

— John Calipari, voluntary assistant, University of Kansas, 1982-83;
University of Kentucky head coach

"I am beyond blessed to have a father who loves me endlessly. It's amazing that a little boy from Hollis could grow up to have such an impact on so many lives."

— Taylor Owens O'Connell, daughter

"The most important thing to my dad today is his meaningful relationships with his players. Every July 16 when 7 a.m. hits, Tommie Smith calls to wish him happy birthday. Shortly afterward, David Magley will call, or Bud Stallworth, or Roger Morningstar or Al Lopes. They call every year, never missing his birthday, because he loved them and believed in them. He continues to do so, and anytime they achieve something he always calls me and updates me on their success off the court." *— Teddy Owens, son,*
administrative coordinator of men's basketball, University of Nebraska

"Of all the lives that Coach Owens has touched over the years, I have to believe that I am the most fortunate. He taught me how to compete. He rewarded me and encouraged me when I earned it. He showed me how to be a champion with grace. All of this is well beyond the call of duty for any coach, and for that I sincerely love him." *— David Magley, University of Kansas, forward, 1978-82*

"The bottom line is I would run through a brick wall for Coach Owens."

— Riney Lochmann, University of Kansas, forward, 1963-66

"Coach Owens was always open to sit and talk with individuals about how to be a better player and a better team. He wasn't concerned about players approaching him to talk about the team. To me, he was a great coach—always sincere, honest and open with all of us. I absolutely adored the man and my time at KU."

— JoJo White, University of Kansas, guard, 1966-69

"What I first noticed was that Coach cared about his players beyond just playing sports. He was more like a parent, wanting his players to be more than successful basketball players. He emphasized that we had to be well-rounded on the court and even better people off the court."

— Bud Stallworth, University of Kansas, guard, 1969-72

"Coach Owens is a man of integrity, he is a sincere, honest person who treats everyone with a great deal of respect—which is something that I've carried with me throughout my life on and off the basketball floor. Coach Owens has had a great impact on me as a person and a coach. To this day, every time Coach Owens is around it seems that a memory is made."

— Scott Brooks, Fresno Flames, guard, 1988;
and Oklahoma City Thunder head coach

"Frankly, most of us were not too impressed at first with this new coach, Ted Owens. He wasn't much older than we were and was also from a small farming community in southwest Oklahoma. What were his credentials? Could he coach? Would we like him? Would we win games? What we didn't know then was that he would take this bunch of green kids and build a basketball team that, in our second year, would gain national recognition, win 28 straight games, set the record for the best season in the school's history and enable most of us to earn follow-up scholarships to four-year universities."

— Gerald Hertzler, Cameron College, forward, 1956-58

"When we won, you bet he'd be wearing the same suit, blazer or jacket for the next game. Well, we won often, and yes, those suits repetitively appeared as he paced back and forth along the sideline like a caged lion."

— Nancy Owens Wilde, daughter

"My wife and I talk about Coach Owens all the time. I remember how tough he was on me, but as I look back, it was a wonderful and memorable experience. He respected me enough and cared enough, over the years, to stay in touch."

— Walter Wesley, University of Kansas, center, 1963-66

"Coach Owens is more than a coach. He has been a part of my life since 1967. Our relationship has grown strong over time. I look back now and understand so much more about what went on at KU than I did when I was going through it. He has been there through 42 years of my marriage. He has watched my kids grow up and I have watched his kids grow up. This type of thing does not happen very often. We have a very special friendship that continues to grow as we both get older."

— Dave Robisch, University of Kansas, forward, 1968-71

AT THE
HANG-UP

SEEKING YOUR PURPOSE,
RUNNING THE RACE,
FINISHING STRONG

Ted Owens
with Jim Krause
and Jesse Tuel
Foreword by Bill Self

Requests for permission should be addressed Ascend Books, LLC, Attn: Rights and Permissions
Department, 12710 Pflumm Rd., Suite 200, Olathe, KS 66062.
10 9 8 7 6 5 4 3 2 1

Printed in the United States of America
ISBN- 978-0-9889964-4-1
ISBN: e-book 978-0-9889964-5-8

Library of Congress Cataloging-in-Publications Data Available Upon Request

Publisher: Bob Snodgrass
Publishing Coordinator: Beth Brown
Editor: Cindy Ratcliff
Dust Jacket and Book Design: Rob Peters
Sales and Marketing: Lenny Cohen and Dylan Tucker

All photos courtesy of Ted Owens unless otherwise indicated.

Every reasonable attempt has been made to determine the ownership of copyright. Please notify
the publisher of any erroneous credits or omissions, and corrections will be made to subsequent
editions/future printings. The goal of the entire staff of Ascend Books is to publish quality works.
With that in mind, we are proud to offer this book to our readers. Please note, however, that the
story, the experiences and the words are those of the author alone.

Printed in the United States of America

Special thanks to:

www.ascendbooks.com

Table of Contents

"It is not what you have now that matters, but what you have at the hang-up."
— **Homer Owens, father**

"At the end of the day in our cotton fields of southwest Oklahoma, my dad would challenge me and my two brothers to see who could pull the most cotton. As we finished the rows, we would hang our sacks on the scale at the wagon. We called it the 'hang-up.' We often thought we had beaten Dad, but he always had us beat at the hang-up. His message has stayed with me my whole life, in business, in sports and in life. Whether we are encountering difficulties or experiencing success, we should never lose sight of our ultimate goals and purposes."
— **Ted Owens**

When a cotton farmer would weigh a bag of cotton at the wagon at the end of the day, it was called "the hang-up."

Dedication

I dedicate this memoir to Homer and Annie Owens, the best parents a son could ever have; to my brothers, Quentin and Fred, my first real-life heroes; to my wife, Michelle, who has been at my side through some great times and some tough times; to my precious children, Nancy, Kelly, Teddy and Taylor, and their spouses, Charlie, Ashley and Nick; to Arthur and Layton, the best grandsons ever; to all my coaches and mentors, including but not limited to, Joe Bailey Metcalf, Bruce Drake, Jerome "Shocky" Needy and Dick Harp; to my assistant coaches and other staff members, too numerous to name; and to the players I had the honor to coach and with whom I have shared the joys and rewards of being a member of a team. Finally, I want to thank the many friends who have supported me and strengthened me and made this life such an incredible journey.

Most importantly, I dedicate this book to God for blessing me with His presence since that wonderful day in the wheat field so many years ago.

I was 15 years old in this picture with my brother Quentin (left), who was in the Army Air Corps, and my brother Fred (right).

Foreword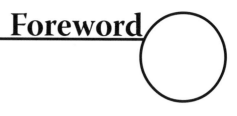

by Bill Self

University of Kansas basketball coach,
2003-present

On April 22, 2003, right before my press conference to be announced as the eighth head basketball coach in University of Kansas history, I had three phone calls to make. I called the only three living coaches who have sat in the same chair—Roy Williams, Larry Brown and Ted Owens. I have coached against Coach Williams, worked for Coach Brown and played against Coach Owens. All three are legends in my mind, and to sit in the same chair was quite a privilege.

Coach Owens and I do have some common points throughout our lives. We both grew up in Oklahoma and attended state institutions there, and both of us were head coaches at Oral Roberts University. We had become friends throughout the years, and during that phone call in 2003, he made me feel so proud and honored to be a part of such a special history.

Let's be very clear: Coach Owens has accomplished many things in his life and has done so in several places, but he loves the University of Kansas. Very few would enjoy the success of a program more than Coach enjoys seeing his "old" program win. This is a man who won big at KU, reached two Final Fours and won a slew of games, and now he is the honorary coach to a program he was in charge of for 19 years. He gives me many ideas of how to "coach 'em up better," and I always listen.

I posed with KU coach Bill Self at the great Royal County Downs golf course in Northern Ireland in August 2013 just before it kicked both of our backsides.

I always thought that Coach was a great recruiter, even if he didn't recruit a slow, average shooter from Edmond, Oklahoma, in 1981—but he did recruit many great ones. I've always thought that a coach impacts and changes lives. No one has done that better than Coach. He takes great pride in the lives of his players and has done a remarkable job of staying in touch and letting them know how he feels about them. He gets it. He knows it is a coach's job to influence young people, but he also realizes the significant role they have played in his life. Every ex-player, coach and manager is one of his boys, and to them he will always be Coach.

Coach still lives life. I've been on golf trips with him, have been his roommate and have had the opportunity to get to know him very well. He is so competitive. He is in great shape, and we have walked probably 15 different courses together, from St. Andrews to Pebble Beach. He hates to lose and usually rigs the bet on the first tee to ensure he doesn't.

He is a very interesting man who has seen a lot that life can offer. He loves his family and extended family so much. I am proud to be his friend. I can only hope my impact in the world can rival the impact of Ted Owens.

I'm proud of you, Coach, for becoming an author. I'm sure everyone reading this book will enjoy hearing your life experiences and enjoy learning more about the man who is loved and respected by so many. Congratulations, Coach—but on the next golf trip, I'm getting strokes, and please don't feel you have to get up at 6 a.m. every morning to do your exercise. I could use the extra shut-eye!

Acknowledgements

In writing this book, I wanted to tell the story of my life. The endeavor was a remarkable journey and I think that I learned some valuable lessons along the way. I certainly did not complete this project alone, and I would like to thank *my teammates* who participated in this extraordinary experience. I was most proud that Bill Self, the University of Kansas basketball coach, agreed to write the foreword—and do so in the middle of the battle that was the 2012-13 basketball season.

First, thanks to Dr. Jim Krause and Jesse Tuel for their guidance. Jesse, an editor at Virginia Tech and a native of Lawrence, Kansas, did all of the finite editing, providing valuable insight and allowing me to tell my story within the word count established by the publisher. Jim, a sports consultant and former basketball coach who authored *Guardians of the Game: A Legacy of Leadership*, not only motivated me to stay on task and meet my deadlines, but also collected perspectives from coaches and former players.

I would like to say a special thanks to the following contributors to the book: Nancy Owens Wilde, Kelly Owens Fischer, Teddy Owens, Taylor Owens O'Connell, Walt Wesley, Scott Brooks, JoJo White, Dave Robisch, Riney Lochmann, Gerald Hertzler, David Magley, Ron Franz, Joey Graham, Stephen Graham, John Calipari, Dr. Bud Sahmaunt, Bud Stallworth and Charlene Prock. They were kind enough to offer their thoughts for the book, and their quotes appear throughout the story. The relationships that I have developed with former players over the years mean so very much to me, and I am delighted to be able to share their perspectives, because they know me well.

I want to thank my family for their patience while I have been committed to the completion of this book. Taylor has been extremely helpful in securing quality photographs for use in the book. Technology is not one of my strengths, so her efforts were greatly supportive. Teddy, Nancy and Kelly offered assistance with selecting a subtitle, and their suggestions were incorporated into the final selection. Last but not least, Michelle has endured me during the years it has taken for me to write this material, offering many great ideas along the way.

I am grateful that Ascend Books took a chance on an old coach who had a story to tell and agreed to publish my memoir. Thank you, Bob Snodgrass, Cindy Ratcliff and Beth Brown, for your support, guidance and patience.

I want to thank ONEOK Chairman John Gibson and Vice President Dan Harrison and all the terrific people at ONEOK for their support of this work. If the book comes close to the quality of your great company, I will be pleased.

Thank you to all of the great folks at the University of Kansas, including Joanie Stephens, Jim Marchiony, Chris Thiesen and Candace Dunback, who supported my efforts and provided all of the pictures, statistics and background information that were needed to complete the project. Thanks also to Mike Houck at the University of Oklahoma; James Jackson and Herb Jacobs at Cameron University; and Gary Bedore of the *Lawrence Journal-World* for providing similar support.

I want to thank my friends in Hollis and Harmon County, Oklahoma, who have helped bring back wonderful memories of growing up in a community where we depended on the love and support of neighbors and friends to survive the tough times and enjoy the good times. The late Dr. Bob Metcalf, along with Judge Mike Warren, Don Matheson, Edith Royal, Charlene Prock, Betty Motley, Bill Cummins, Don Fox and many others provided valuable information and insight.

Finally, thanks to Jim McGary, Brent Luettel, Wilfredo Pochoco De La Rosa, Matt Tumbleson, Eric Lindsey, John Read and the people at National Association of Basketball Coaches archives for their support, which enabled me to complete the book on time and in a professional manner.

To all those above, I am forever in your debt.

Preface

Coach's Life Lesson: *A coach must be a leader. In the absence of leadership, someone will fill the void, and there is always the danger of that person taking you in a direction you are not prepared to go.*

John Wooden once said that when coaches and players are working together, the important thing in those relationships is to find the best way—and not necessarily your way. In the 1972-73 season, our young team lost every close game they were in. Entering the 1973-74 season, we knew the team had to find confidence in order to be successful. We lost in the first round of the league holiday tournament in December, and I got word back that some of the players were starting to question our general philosophy. So we met and addressed the issues. They gave me their opinions and I was open to listening to them, and they had some good suggestions. At the end of it, though, it was critical that I exercised leadership: I reminded them that our success wouldn't come from a change in philosophy, but from simple basics. We had to get more loose balls and rebounds. We had to fully focus on each trip down the floor. We had to have more grit and determination than our opponents. And they responded— and went on to the Final Four.

I had just spent a summer weekend in 2010 at the Grand Lake of the Cherokees in northeastern Oklahoma celebrating my birthday. Celebrating with me were my beloved family—wife Michelle; first daughter Nancy Owens Wilde, her husband, Charlie, and her son, Arthur; second daughter Kelly Owens Fischer; son Teddy Owens and his wife, Ashley (their boy, Layton, hadn't been born yet); and third daughter Taylor Owens O'Connell and her husband, Nick. I wondered how 80 years could possibly have gone so fast. I was overwhelmed with the thought that I still had so much to accomplish.

I wrote this book about my life and experiences hoping that it will bring some enjoyment to those who use their valuable time to read it. I wanted to look back at events and people who have influenced my beliefs and actions, in order to understand where I came from and who I am today. I had considered writing it earlier, but until that birthday weekend and the realization of how much I had left to accomplish, I could never justify the time and effort to make the book happen.

My story is about growing up in America during a time when economic hardships surrounded us but a spirit of hope and faith prevailed. The people around me believed that if a person worked hard, developed skills and talents and gained all of the knowledge that could possibly be gained, he or she could overcome difficulties and experience success. Those who have had the good fortune I have had to be surrounded with the love and support of family, teachers, coaches and friends, will certainly maximize their chances.

> *"Ted, Teddy Lynn, Dad, Granddad, Coach. These are just a few of the names that sum up Ted Owens as an incredible friend, husband, son, father, grandfather and basketball coach. However you know him, you are unbelievably blessed. His smile is contagious, his hugs melt your heart and his passion for his family, Christ and basketball is unsurpassed. I am so proud to know Ted Owens as Dad. He is unquestionably the best man I have ever known."*
> —*Taylor Owens O'Connell, daughter*

> *"I am who I am because of my dad. Because of his passion for basketball, I am passionate about basketball. Because of his passion*

> *for his former players, I try to build lasting relationships with my players. I will do anything for the players I coached because I care about them as people first. My dad taught me that you are only as good as the people you lead."*
> —*Teddy Owens, son*

My daughter Taylor and I watched a game at Allen Fieldhouse.

Introduction

Coach's Life Lesson: *Life will present many obstacles or difficulties and our challenges sometimes appear insurmountable, but we should never lose sight of our goals and we must stay focused on our purpose.*

These types of challenges seem to happen about every day. With my teams, I would tell them to focus on doing everything in their power to be the best they could be, to focus on the little things: bringing great attitudes to practice, working diligently on fundamental skills, and concentrating on our execution as a team. If we stay focused on our purpose of being the best we can be, the rest—those wins and championships—will take care of themselves.

I often asked myself what I wanted to achieve in life. Philosopher and baseball great Yogi Berra once said, "If you don't know where you are going, you are liable to end up someplace else." Each of us has to find our purpose in life. There are some who don't believe that there is meaning in life, but I do.

At my age, I know that I have limited years ahead of me and I want to make the most of them. For many years, I played golf with Bob Taggart and brothers Odd and Skipper Williams, and as we approached the 18th tee, Odd would usually say, "It's finishes that make champions." That is what I am motivated to do: to finish strong, to finish with a purpose and to leave something of value for others.

Quite frankly, I like attempting to live my life in the service of a purpose greater than myself. One of the huge challenges in team sports is to play for something that is greater than just you—to play for the welfare and success of the total group. The same thing is true of your relationship with family, as you strive to benefit the group as a whole. The joys of giving and contributing far outweigh the rewards of receiving.

I know that there is so much I want to accomplish during my time on earth and that it will be impossible to accomplish it all. I hope that my family and friends will share some of my beliefs and pass those beliefs on to their children and others. Jesus didn't convert very many people to Christianity during his ministry, but he taught his disciples and empowered them to spread the word to the ends of the earth. We may not be able to influence very many people, but if we can impact just a few, we can have a significant effect on the future.

While I would like to influence others, I recognize that I have so many faults of my own. I need to temper my judgment of others, knowing that each of them is every bit as important in God's eyes as I am. I need to become more giving and less selfish. I need to become more patient with the differences that I have with others, remembering the wisdom of Coach John Wooden, who said, "That you can disagree without being disagreeable." I need to have the courage to speak the truth as best I understand it. I need to stand up for the principles that I believe are vital to the well-being of our families, our communities and our country.

First, I have learned that taking care of your body with the proper diet, regular exercise and adequate rest are essential to having the energy and the positive frame of mind necessary to pursue your goals and purposes.

Second, I have learned that words can be most helpful to others, to let them know they are loved, to encourage them, and to let them know that you believe in them. Spoken impulsively or out of anger, though, words can have an ill effect on the lives of others and, in some cases, can cause lifelong separation from family and friends.

Third, I often fight the temptation to say something humorous or clever before fully realizing the consequences of my words. Dr. Phog Allen had an expression, "pause for poise," which meant that a player should gather himself before acting. I often tell myself to "pause for poise" before I proceed with a statement or story.

Fourth, I have learned to accept responsibility for failures in my professional and personal life. None of us wants to admit that we are wrong, but there is something therapeutic about being accountable for your actions.

I suggest that we listen to the wisdom of my dad, Homer Owens, a cotton farmer from southwest Oklahoma with a seventh-grade education. He repeatedly told his sons to live within our means. In some ways, my dad was saying that we shouldn't try to be somebody we are not.

On many occasions, I told my players that they shouldn't try to be somebody they are not, and that they should play within their abilities. My years of playing, coaching and observing the game of basketball have taught me one thing: *bad shooters are always open*. Just because a player is open doesn't necessarily mean that he should shoot the ball. And not shooting doesn't mean that when time permits, a player can't try to improve his shooting skills.

I have learned that you need to seek the advice and counsel of others, but then you must make a firm decision. Once you have done that, you can't be swayed by the criticism. As Dr. Allen once said, "If a postman takes time to kick at every barking dog, he will never get his mail delivered."

I have learned that a person can rarely achieve success without assistance. There is no question that an individual must be motivated, willing to commit time and energy, and dedicated to acquiring the knowledge a project demands. But somewhere along the way, some caring and thoughtful person opened the doors of opportunity. Take the time to let that person know. There is nothing that touches my heart more than to hear former players and students say that I made a difference in their lives, and it makes me want to assist someone else.

I have learned how important it is to reach out to people when they are experiencing difficulty, whether it is an illness, death of a loved one or a life crisis. Your presence alone can be helpful. One weekend, during the time I was coaching at KU, I traveled with my family from Lawrence to visit Mother and Dad in their home in Hollis, Oklahoma. Dad asked me to ride downtown with him, so I climbed into his pickup and drove to town. Having just completed a fairly successful season, I was certain that Dad wanted to take me downtown and show me off to his friends. I was a little bit surprised when we pulled up in front of a nursing home. I followed him in and he proceeded to make his rounds, saying hello to each of the residents. They just beamed when he entered the rooms, and all of them said, "Homer, thank you for coming." They couldn't have cared less that a basketball team had won a few games that year. They cared that a friend was taking the time to visit and listen to them. It finally occurred to me that Dad wanted me to come along not as the focal point of the visit, but that I might learn a lesson in serving others.

I have learned that life, with all of its joys and all of its blessings, includes hardships as well. How you respond to those difficulties will determine the direction of your life. The apostle Paul, writing in his letters to the Romans, said that we should rejoice in our sufferings because we know that suffering produces perseverance, perseverance produces character and character produces hope.

Growing up in the Great Depression and witnessing an abundance of suffering—yet seeing my parents respond in such a positive way—prepared me for responding to setbacks throughout my lifetime. In some respects, the attitude reflects what my father was saying to us in the middle of the cotton fields when he trailed us in our competition to see who could gather the most cotton bolls: "It's not what you have now that matters, but what you have at the hang-up." I learned that life is full of successes and setbacks, but we must never lose sight of our ultimate goals.

I have learned that the most difficult task that we have in teaching, coaching or parenting is to train our players, students or children to make do without us. If you have ever attended a game in Allen Fieldhouse, you have heard the incredible noise level and you can imagine how difficult it is for a coach to communicate with his players. It was vital that a coach had trained his players to know what to do in every situation with limited direction from the bench. It is equally difficult to see a child leave for college, military service or a career and hope that the lessons you taught them will be enough for the challenges they will face. As Abraham Lincoln said, "The worst thing you can do for those you love is the things they could and should do themselves."

One of the problems with having reasonably good health and a long life is suffering the loss of family, friends, teammates and players. In 2011, I spoke at the funeral service of one of my college teammates, Stan Grossman. His son, Mark, talked about his dad and told the following story: A man wandering lost in the wilderness came upon an empty cabin. He found that someone had left a note with these words: "Welcome to our cabin. If you are tired, there is a bunk bed with some blankets and quilts to help you rest. If you are hungry, there is a pantry with food that you are welcome to eat, and if you are cold, there is a fireplace here in the cabin and a stack of wood out back. We ask only one thing of you and that is when you leave, please leave the woodpile a little higher than you found it."

So in the years I have ahead of me, I want to leave the woodpile a little higher than I found it. For my family, my players and my friends, I want my actions to be an example worthy of following. My fervent hope is that at the final "hang-up," I will have fulfilled some of the purpose that God had in mind for me.

Coaching Lesson: *Preparing players*

The recent 115th reunion of Kansas basketball reminded me that we, as coaches, have the responsibility first to prepare our young people for their life's work. The lessons that we teach—teamwork, individual responsibility for actions, responding to difficulties, time utilization, developing sound fundamental skills, gaining all the possible knowledge of your field and playing for a cause greater than yourself—are not a distraction from our pursuit of successful teams, but are catalysts for achieving those results.

Chapter 1

The Luxuries of Life

Coach's Life Lesson: *There is the enduring faith that comes from a mother and father who believe that there is a purpose in each of our lives and a divine providence that guides our steps.*

I saw examples of my parents' faith practically every day. I vividly remember the Dust Bowl days when those big north winds would come in and blow away our crops, and we would have to replant everything. Each and every time, Dad and Mother remained incredibly upbeat about our ability to overcome. Their faith was in the Almighty, in the promise that if we worked hard and kept our faith, we would succeed. Our luxuries were nonexistent and every day was a battle to stay afloat, but I never for one minute thought we wouldn't accomplish our goals.

Born during the Great Depression on July 16, 1929, I had few of the luxuries of life. However, I was surrounded with all the necessities. First, I had a loving mother and father who taught me the value of hard work and doing things correctly, the importance of honesty and the obligation to assist others. Second, I had plenty of beef, pork, chicken, eggs, vegetables and fruit from our farm operation.

I grew up on a farm about 3.25 miles north of Hollis, which is three miles from the Texas border in southwest Oklahoma. Hollis is in an area called the "Short Grass Country," which years ago was grazing land for the migrating herds of buffalo that roamed the central plains of America. It continued to be a grazing land as the herds of bison diminished and the cattle industry grew. That area was at one time a part of Greer County, Texas, until the U.S. Supreme Court ruled that it belonged to the U.S. So

As a baby on the farm, I was too young for chores ... but that didn't last long.

Congress assigned Greer County to the Indian Territory, then known as the Oklahoma territory. In 1907, Oklahoma was admitted as a state and a year or so after statehood, Greer County was divided into Jackson County, Greer County and my home county, Harmon.

When my dad, Homer Owens, was three years old, his family boarded a train and moved from the northern Alabama town of Haleyville to the regional railway center of St. Joseph, Texas. Leading teams of horses and wagons, my grandpa, Miles Emerson Owens, hauled freight from the railways to towns in the region. In 1907, Grandpa Owens moved his family to Greer County.

The Owens family first settled a few miles southeast of Hollis, just across from the A.J. Abernathy farm. My dad met their neighbor, Annie Ava Abernethy, and they attended school together, graduating from the seventh grade at Valley View School, which was quite an achievement in those days. They married when Mother was 16 and Dad was 19. They had been married 70 years when Dad passed away at the age of 89. Mother lived to be 95, dying in 1996.

I was one of three sons born to Homer and Annie Owens. We were delivered by Dr. Hopkins in our little farmhouse. Although some babies were being delivered in the hospital in Hollis, many were still being delivered at home in the rural communities. My brother Quentin was 10 years older than I, and my brother Fred was two years older. We grew up in a two-bedroom house with no indoor plumbing and no heat in the bedrooms, although we did have a coal-fueled stove in the living room and a cooking stove in the kitchen. Instead of refrigeration, we had an icebox that was filled with blocks of ice from the ice plant in Hollis.

Located about 100 yards from our house, the outhouse had seats for two—a "two-holer," which set it apart from the normal outhouse. I often wondered why we had two seats, as if going to the toilet was a social event.

We raised cotton, wheat and grains. We pulled the cotton by hand and filled our wagons with about 2,000 pounds of cotton bolls. The bolls contained the seed and the cotton lent. At the gin the lent would be separated, becoming a bale of about 500 hundred pounds. The seed would be used for replanting and for producing cottonseed oil. Regarded as valueless back then, the bolls were thrown away.

My brothers and I pulled cotton bolls in the fields with some of the migrant workers from the Waco, Texas, area. The migrant families were black, and during the harvest season, they would move to the house on our wheat farm, which was about a quarter-mile south of our farmhouse. Our families became close, and I particularly admired the accomplishments of the older members of the migrant families. Talking about productive days in the cotton field, my dad said that a standard for excellence was pulling 1,000 pounds in a day (and a typical day was 12 hours), and several of my black friends managed 1,000 pounds. My best ever was 750 pounds, so I greatly admired their achievement. For their work, they were paid 50 cents per 100 pounds. My pay and my brothers' pay was the privilege of having food on the table and a roof over our heads.

Pulling cotton is one of the worst experiences I have ever endured. I remember hooking the sack over my shoulder and pulling two rows at a time, one row with my right hand and one row with my left hand, gathering the bolls in my right hand before flipping them into the sack with a pronated action of my fingers and wrist. My back would be bent in such a manner that I could only manage to walk in that position for a short period of time, and then I would drop to my knees, covered by kneepads, and continue to pull the sack and harvest the cotton.

Late in the day, Dad would bring the empty wagon back from the cotton gin, get his sack out and challenge us to try to pull more than "old Dad" could pull. We were bright enough to understand that he was just trying to motivate us to work hard when we were dead tired. We first would go through a period of annoyance, thinking that we weren't going to buy into his amateur psychology. But then our competitive instincts would take over and we would take the bait.

We would be going as fast as we could and would holler at Dad that it looked like we were going to beat him. He always responded, "It's not what you have now that matters, but what you have at the hang-up," referring to the amount of cotton in our sacks when we hung them up on the scales to be weighed at the wagon. Well, we thought we had beaten him many times, but he always had us beaten at the "hang-up." His phrase stayed with me the rest of my life, whether in business, sports or life itself.

As a young boy, one of my chores was to clean the chicken droppings on the hen house floor under the roosts. It required someone smaller who could get under the roosts with a "flattened-out" hoe. I tried to see positive aspects in every experience, and the only possible value of cleaning droppings is that it strengthened my defensive stance in basketball.

With no distractions such as television or radio to keep us up at night, we went to bed early, around 8 p.m., getting up at 4 or 5 a.m. My brothers and I had to have all the chores finished—the cows milked, the chicken and hogs fed and the horse and cow manure cleaned and stacked in a fertilizer pile—before the sun came up. As soon as it was daylight, we were on our way to the fields to plant, cultivate or harvest the crops.

My brothers and I slept in one small, unheated bedroom. Mother and Dad slept in the other bedroom, also not heated, but with a feather mattress, one of the few luxury items that we owned. In the winter, my mother would stack on our beds a number of quilts, usually made at the community quilting parties, and then heat bricks on the living room coal stove, wrap them in towels and put them at the foot of our beds. The theory was that if your feet were warm, your entire body would stay warm. I believe that is true, even today.

When the weather would start to get colder in November and December, Dad would say, "Boys, it's cold enough to kill hogs today." Since we had no refrigeration, we had to wait until it was cold enough to hang the butchered meat in the smokehouse.

Not having a tractor at the time, we used horses and mules to pull the plows. Until I was mature enough to plow the fields, I was given the task of cleaning out the horse tank, which was fed by a windmill that pumped gypsum water from the well. During the week, we would take our baths in the horse tank, when the extremely cold water led to short baths. On Saturday, the entire family would take a bath in a No. 2 washtub. My mother would heat the water in the sun and we would carry the tub into the house where Dad, Mother, Quentin, Fred and I would bath, in that order. The water was pretty gritty by the time it was my turn.

Occasionally, Mother would put an ice cream freezer in the horse tank to soak and seal the cracks in the freezer. What a great feeling it was to come in from the fields and see that freezer in the tank and know that we were having ice cream that night.

My brothers and I would alternate turning the crank and sitting on the freezer until the crank wouldn't budge. Then we would pack the freezer with ice and put it the storm cellar, the coolest place on the farm, and let the ice cream harden more. If there were any leftovers after we had finished eating our share,

we would pack it and leave it overnight in the cellar. My brothers and I would get up early in the morning and slip into the cellar to finish off the ice cream, but Dad was there every time, sitting on the steps eating the last of the ice cream. We couldn't beat him at anything.

Farming meant working from dawn till dusk. Here, I worked with cousin Bobby Graves (left) and the milk cows.

Hollis, my home

With a population of 3,000 at its largest, Hollis was not an enormous town. The main street and a few side streets held a majority of the businesses. The old expression of "dragging Main" was pretty accurate. Those with a car and money for gas would drive the length of Main Street and circle back, to see their friends—but more importantly, to be seen.

Harmon County was a farming area with many consolidated country schools. Social activities revolved around schools, churches and a weekly trip to the county seat, Hollis. Farming could be a lonely experience in those Depression days, as a family eked out a living, engaged in a struggle against the land and the elements of nature. Farm wives were isolated because it was rare for a family to have more than one car and, anyway, the car was mostly used for the farm's operation. The wives were busy with household chores and cooking three meals per day for their hungry families. The meals were large, filled with meats, vegetables and fruits. The expression "eat like a farmer" has some real meaning.

Once a week, the wives would take the laundry and drive to Hollis to use the "wringer" machines in the laundry there. Few farmers had the luxury of owning such a machine, which squeezed the water from the wet, clean clothes and lessened the time that it took for clothes to dry on clotheslines.

Saturdays in Hollis provided an opportunity to see friends and to shop on Main Street. The first stops on a Saturday trip to town were to deliver the farm's produce to one of the grocery stores—Warren's, Paul Metcalf's, Doc Charleston's, Gale Hollis IGA or Wilson's M System store. The next stops might be to shop for clothing at Hills, J.C. Penney's or C.R. Anthony's. In the meantime, we visited with friends.

A highlight was to attend a movie at the LaVista Theatre; on Saturday afternoons, movies were always westerns. The early heroes were Buck Jones, Tom Mix and Ken Maynard, most of whom wore white hats. I wasn't too big on Roy Rogers and Gene Autrey because they were singers, and I didn't see how a cowboy could be tough and chase the bad guys if he was a singer. I hadn't matured enough to experience the joy of singing, which I love today.

Dad would give my brother Fred and me 15 cents each. We would spend a dime on the admission to the movie, and I would buy a sack of popcorn with my remaining nickel and Fred would buy a cherry limeade with his, and we would share the refreshments. We didn't think that life could be much better.

The only way that our Saturdays could be enhanced was when Dad would purchase a couple dozen tamales at Mr. Betchan's sidewalk stand. He would wrap them in newspapers and take them home to eat with Mother's chili. As

Dad would say, "Boys, we are walking in tall cotton."

The men would stop at one of the many barbershops—Cleveland's, Lindsay's, Sumpter's or Jelly Moore's. I didn't have my hair cut by a professional barber until I was in the 10th grade because Dad cut our hair with a manually operated hand clipper. We would turn around backwards on a chair and sit on a bucket to raise us to the necessary height and hold the handles on the chair firmly, because those old clippers didn't function too smoothly all the time.

Usually the barbershop conversations centered around two subjects: "Did you get any rain out your way?" and "How are the St. Louis Cardinals doing?" In those years, the Cardinals were the closest major league franchise; the Texas Rangers, Houston Astros and Kansas City Royals had not yet become a reality.

Hollis and Harmon County were filled with hard-working people who survived those difficult days with creativity and humor; our problems were never so great that we couldn't find something to laugh about. Consider the example of Winford Warren, who opened a grocery store with his wife, Maudie. The Warrens graded and candled the eggs that they took in from the farmers in the county. When the State of Oklahoma (in concert, no doubt, with big egg producers) enforced new regulations requiring all retailers to buy eggs from wholesalers, small farmers who depended on selling eggs for income were cut out. In support of his farming friends, Winford immediately quit selling local eggs. He put up a sign that said, "Notice: Positively no eggs for sale in this store. Purchase the containers, the eggs are free." The state took him to court but a jury exonerated him, saying the customers had the right to buy the empty containers and that Winford had the right to fill them with eggs.

Eventually, an appeals court sided with Winford, and so did the Oklahoma Supreme Court. But before the case arrived in the high court, egg-headed state agents, convinced that the Warrens were skirting the law, went into action. One day, two men in suits and ties, clearly not from Hollis, arrived at the grocery store and took a carton of eggs to the counter to buy them. "They're

Main Street in Hollis, Okla., in 1947, my senior year in high school.

Photo courtesy of the Harmon County Historical Society picture archives

26

free," said employee Arthur Kirby, but added that the men could buy a carton. They told Kirby just to hand them the eggs; they didn't want the carton. He handed them the eggs and their hands were full, so they asked if he had a sack. After filling the sack with eggs, Kirby informed them that they owed him money. They insisted that they were told that the eggs were free, and Kirby said, "They are, but the sack is the same price as the cartons." They just smiled, left the eggs on the counter and left. That is Hollis humor and creativity—and a fine example of how people looked out for one another.

Surviving the Dust Bowl

Survival in those Dust Bowl days required making use of every resource available. It also required the teamwork that a family provided. Each of us had a role to play, and we didn't complain (complaining was not an option around my dad).

Frequently, we would look to the north and see dark clouds of dust forming—"Northers," we called them—and know that the dust would hit our farm in a few hours. My dad would tell us to prepare the scratchers, the straight steel rods that came down from the farm implements where the plow points would attach. The purpose of scratching was to bring the wet soil to the top of the beds so that the sands would not cover the young cotton plants. We would cover four rows at a time and with two plows operating, we managed to lessen the damage of the storms. Even today, when the wind starts to blow, I can hear my dad telling us to get the scratchers ready. And while we worked in the fields, Mother would tack sheets of plastic over the north windows of the house to try to minimize the damage. Even with her efforts, the wind was so strong that the linoleum would rise off of the floors, and a perfectly clean house would be covered with the dust. We would tie handkerchiefs over our mouths and noses, like bank robbers, to keep from inhaling too much of dust. Dust pneumonia caused many deaths in those days.

Historians talk about how difficult the Depression was, but we didn't realize it. My friend, Tater Metcalf, said we all knew that John Steinbeck had written "The Grapes of Wrath" about those times, but we just didn't know he was writing about us. As my dad would say, we were as poor as Job's turkey... but no one else had anything either.

In the summer, the house was so hot that we moved our beds to the front porch to try to find a little breeze, even though a state highway ran within a few yards of our home. (Security was not a problem and we never locked our house, whether we were at home or away.) Many people hitchhiked through the countryside looking for employment. Frequently, hungry and thirsty travelers stopped by for a drink of water out of the cistern or for some food, and Mother would take food out to the porch for them to eat.

People looked after one another. If our neighbor was sick, we quit working in our fields and went over to provide for them. We knew that they would do the same for us. There was a trust and honesty factor that served as the rule, not the exception.

My dad and mother had taught us to follow the second-greatest commandment, to love our neighbors as ourselves; and the Golden Rule, to do unto others as we would have them do unto us. Treating others with respect and dignity is a practice that I have followed throughout my life. Growing up in the Depression, when survival was dependent on people helping their neighbors, had a lasting impression on me. My experiences taught me that there are no self-made men. None of us could have experienced success without the assistance of others, and we should never fail to express our gratitude to them.

My beloved parents

My saintly mother, Annie Owens, was the dearest, most precious person I have ever known. She lived only to love and serve her family. For the good of our family, she made every possible sacrifice. Her biscuits and gravy, banana pudding, fruit salad and vegetables have never been equaled. The only contradiction in her sweet, warm personality was when she would grab a chicken by the neck and ring its head off when she prepared fried chicken. That change in her personality remains a mystery to me.

I saw my mother and my dad have different opinions on only a few occasions, but one that I remember brings a smile to my face. For a while, we milked 15 cows and sold the milk to a Kraft Cheese plant in Hollis. After long days in the field, we would spend a couple of hours feeding the hogs and chickens and milking the cows. When Dad would purchase a cow from a neighbor, he would call the cow by the former owner's name. In this case, the cow's name was Staton.

The cows grazed in the wheat pasture near the house, which would sometimes cause their bowel movements to be runny and get on their bushy tails. Now, old Staton gave a lot of milk but was

My parents, Homer and Annie Owens, on their wedding day in 1917.

frisky. One evening, as Dad milked her, she swatted her tail at some flies and hit Dad squarely in his face. Knowing she was in trouble, Staton whirled around to get out of the stall, sending Dad flying through the wall of the stall and leaving only a silhouette of him in the wall. When Dad finally managed to struggle to his feet, he picked up a piece of fence post and chased down Staton, hitting her right between her horns and dropping her to the ground. Mother, hearing only the last part of the episode, came running out to the barn in time to see Dad land the blow. "Homer, you've killed that cow!" she said. Dad had a hard time accepting that Mother was more concerned about the cow than him, but the good news is that Staton recovered and Dad's bruises healed. Meanwhile, my brothers and I managed to keep our emotions in check until we could get far enough away from Dad to let them explode.

On a more serious note, it was not customary in those days for a man to show affection to others by hugging them. I saw my dad cry only three times: once when his mother, Sara Jane Owens, died; another when my dear brother Quentin died at the age of 42; and the last when I boarded a plane on my way to San Francisco for embarkation to Korea. He was not a hugging-and-kissing person, but a man who gave you a strong handshake. Still, he loved his family, and we knew it. One of the most secure places in the world was when I would sit in his lap as a child and he would let me look at the pocket watch that he kept in the bib of his overalls.

Many people in my hometown touched my life, and none more than my parents. Homer and Annie Owens may have had only seventh-grade educations, but they had more wisdom than all the scholars I have met.

The young convert

The Antioch Baptist Church had been founded by a group of local farmers, including my grandpa. Grandpa was one of several deacons who had the privilege of leaning back in cane-bottomed chairs along the wall. When the preacher was making a very strong point, Grandpa would say, "Amen, preacher, you tell 'em."

Due to my affiliation with the church, I did have one memorable experience: my conversion. Each summer we had a week-long revival meeting. The visiting preacher, Preacher Green, must have been paid by the number of conversions because he always kept the invitation song going until someone stepped forward. It was very hot under that brush arbor, with all the adults fanning themselves with handheld fans. One night after about the seventh verse of "Just As I Am," I could feel the pressure of all of the adults looking at the 12-year-olds. I stepped out into the aisle (or I was pushed; I'm not sure which) and went forward to the altar.

I don't remember too much of what Brother Green said. It was customary for the minister to ask the person if they believed that Jesus was the Son of God, and I suppose that is what he asked me. Anyway, I was pretty nervous as a 12-year-old going down to the altar.

Later that night, I went back to our farm and walked out into the wheat field alone. With the beautiful stars and moon shining down, I asked God to come into my life, taking the first step in a relationship that has lasted for a lifetime.

I recently visited the site of my first church, the Antioch Baptist Church in Hollis, Okla.

A Love for Sports

Coach's Life Lesson: *Leadership is best exhibited through your actions and by setting an example, as these carry much greater weight than your words.*

When I was in the Army, I noticed that the infantry officers coming out of Ft. Benning, Georgia, had patches on their shoulders that said "Follow me." I asked one of them what it meant. He said, "It's very simple. You don't tell the people serving under you to 'Go take that hill.' You tell them, 'Follow me.'" At KU, JoJo White was a great example of this leadership. He was a very quiet leader, but his actions were an inspiration to others. I can never remember him having a bad practice—he brought his work ethic every single day.

It is funny the things that we remember and cherish as we get older. I remember quite clearly when I fell in love with the game of basketball. It was the day that I made my first basket. During the Depression, we rarely received more than one present for Christmas. This particular year, when I was about five years old, we received a basketball, which was laced with strings and had a bladder inside. My dad built us a goal, placing a wooden backboard and a rim without a net onto a steel pole. The backboard was rectangular, until the rounded backboards became popular and Dad cut it for us. Under the basket, the level surface was made of dirt.

Here I am with Bill Cummins at the hoop on a barn where we often played as youngsters.

One day sometime after Christmas, while I was waiting

for Quentin and Fred to be dropped off by the school bus, I took the basketball from under our bed and went out to the goal. Using two hands, I lifted a scoop shot up from between my legs so that I could get the ball all the way to the basket. Somehow, I made it. I could hardly wait for the bus to come into view so that I could tell my big brothers what I had done. I must have waited a couple of hours, and I'm not sure they believed me. I fell in love with basketball that day, and it is a love that remains with me even now.

Quentin, Fred and my dad shared a love for sports, and it was only natural that I followed in their footsteps. My brothers played basketball and baseball, and attending their games became the major social event of our family. Most of our leisure time was spent with sports. When we arrived home from school, Dad would come in from the fields, get his baseball bat and hit us fly balls and grounders, or "skinners," as we called them. (I still have his bat, and it's one of my most cherished possessions.) I didn't have any idea how tired he must have been until I grew older and had a full-time job and would come home and my son, Teddy, would want me to pitch to him.

My dad always said that if he hadn't pitched on a cold day one time as a teenager and ruined his arm, he most likely would have pitched in the "big show." That was as close as I ever came to doubting my dad. Years later, when I was playing basketball at the University of Oklahoma, I told that story to Harold Keith, OU's legendary sports information director. When my dad came to campus for one of our games, Harold went over to where my dad was sitting and introduced himself as Tom Greenwade, the famous Yankee scout. He told my dad that because of WWII, they were running short of pitchers and wondered if he had any interest in pitching for the Yankees. My dad told that story to everyone in Hollis who would listen. I am sure that Dad figured out the joke when he saw Harold at the next game, but he never let on.

Jokes aside, Dad truly was strong. After church on Sundays, the Owens clan would assemble for a meal. As the ladies prepared dinner, the men would whittle and tell stories of the past, about the Civil War, World War I or other events. As a boy, I loved to hear those old stories, and the tales grew mightily in my mind over the years. Dr. Phog Allen once said that "We shouldn't let the truth get in the way of a good story," and he would've been pleased at the performances. Sometimes the storytelling would be replaced by feats of strength, and Dad's specialty was doing one-armed pushups. He would trim the head off of a match and place it between the thumb and index finger of his right hand. He would put his right hand on the ground and his left arm behind his back, and lower himself to the ground and pick up the match with his mouth. If you think that is easy, try it sometime.

Soon after the bombing of Pearl Harbor, my brother Quentin and other older friends were called into the service. Quentin joined the U.S. Army Air Corps and trained as a pilot, but his flying career ended when he experienced motion disorientation at higher altitudes. He finished his Army career as a military policeman and participated in the invasion of Okinawa.

Because we were too young for the service, Fred and I were left on the farm and attended our country school, Arnett High School. We both played basketball and baseball, and the big sporting event for the country schools each year was the Harmon County basketball tournament in Hollis. One year when Fred was playing, his team won the county tournament. The players on that Arnett team, and the state champions of 1941, were some of my earliest heroes, alongside Quentin and Fred.

A knock on the door

One day as WWII was progressing through its second or third year, a tall, gangly man came to our farmhouse door. "Homer and Annie," he said, "the war has taken most of the boys from the Arnett team and they don't have enough players to field a team." His name was Joe Bailey Metcalf, the Hollis basketball coach and junior high principal. He went on to explain that he had visited with the Arnett school board and superintendent Henry Vaughn, and they had agreed to let my parents transfer five acres of their land, which bordered on the Hollis district, to the town so that Fred and I could play basketball and baseball for Hollis.

There were two problems. One was that we didn't have transportation back and forth to school. Coach Metcalf solved that by letting Fred, who was to be a senior, drive a bus route to Hollis with only one stop to pick up the Curry girls. Then Jesse Meeks, a school employee, would drive the route in the afternoon while we were in practice and leave the bus at school for us to drive home.

The second problem was that Hollis was so short of athletes that they expected all males who participated in sports to go out for the football team. Neither of us had ever played football—and not only that, we had never even seen a football game. Despite the problems, we entered this new adventure in Hollis when I was a sophomore and Fred was a senior.

Hollis Tiger football was a great source of pride in the community. In 1942, Hollis was one of the few undefeated teams in the state, but since the state did not have a playoff system, the only ratings were from *The Daily Oklahoman*. The newspaper rated Enid as the No. 1 team in the state, so Dick Highfill, our local football coach, challenged Enid to a game to determine the real state champion. Enid declined the offer, so both teams claimed to be the champions. Who could argue against the Hollis claim, since the Tigers were scored on only three times the entire season?

Fred and I, the country boys, started practice in the fall of 1944 and were the subjects of all the pranks that players pull on rookies. When we asked how to put on our hip pads, the others told us how... exactly opposite of the correct way, with the support for the tail bone in front, protecting our private parts. We found it difficult to run that way, but our new teammates got a big laugh out of it.

We practiced on a field next to our stadium. Sometimes used as a parking lot, the field was filled with goat heads and sand burrs. The thought of falling on them motivated you not to lose your balance when blocking. Our coach was Guy Gardner, who had replaced Dick Highfill when Highfill took a college coaching job. In the war years, we had gas rationing—"A" stickers for normal driving, "B" stickers for farmers and "C" stickers for truckers. The father of one of our players, Forest Logsdon, had a vehicle with a "C" sticker, so we loaded onto the back of it and headed to Plainview, Texas, for our first game.

I was playing defensive end and the linebacker on my side, Don "Square John" Prock, told me to knock down the interference and he would make the tackle. I asked him, "What is the interference?" He explained that they were blockers in front of the runners. After my response, Don didn't appear to have a lot of confidence in me—and as the game progressed, what little he had vanished. Things did not go well, and we lost our first game. We followed that with losses to other Texas schools that made up much of our early schedule.

Early in the season, we had very few highlights, apart from the admiration I had for my teammates, many of whom were really dedicated players. One of them was Don Fox, a senior captain who had been starting since his freshman year. His leg was often badly swollen from osteomyelitis, which had no cure at the time. When his leg would become infected and swollen, Don would go down to see Dr. Will Husband, our team doctor and a legend in that part of the country. Don would have his leg drained and be back in the lineup the next day. That leg was painful just to look at. I never saw a greater example of courage in athletics than Don's. His example said something to all of us about the importance of Hollis football.

I played high school football in Hollis, Okla.

Fred and I finally broke into the starting lineup, which might account for some of the team's losses. Desperation to win overcame Coach Gardner, and he started to play service veterans who were home on furlough. One day he took two veterans, a big, strong lineman named J.C. Hunt and a starting center from the previous year's team, Cotton Pendergraft, to Quanah, Texas, to play. J.C. was wearing the uniform of an underclassman, Don Simmons. The Quanah team was killing us with their quarterback, so one of our service veterans rushed him, jumped in the air and hit him right in the helmet, knocking him out.

At halftime, our superintendent, J.T. Martin, was concerned about the incident and came to our circle at the end of the field to discuss it. He asked to see Don Simmons, but instead, he found J.C. in Don's uniform. When we arrived back home, we contacted Quanah to apologize, but they didn't have much to say. Later, it was rumored that the Quanah quarterback was home on leave from the service as well, doing the same thing J.C. was doing. When you traveled across the Red River, there were no rules.

We arrived home to find that Coach Gardner had been dismissed and that Joe Bailey Metcalf had been assigned to coach football as well as basketball and baseball. It was a move that dramatically changed the direction of our football program.

Holding down the farm

Many of our finest players and friends volunteered for the service at the end of that year, including my brother Fred—but not before I had the privilege of playing high school basketball with him. We had a very successful team but fell short of making the state playoffs. Now both of my brothers were gone in the service, and it caused a lot of anxiety for our family.

Given the shortage of manpower, it was difficult to plow, plant, cultivate and harvest crops. Guiding plows pulled by our mules and horses, Dad did the cultivating and I did the hoeing. There is nothing as lonely as being by yourself in a 40-acre cotton patch with a hoe in your hands. It did give me time to think and dream. Many times, I would swing the hoe and pretend that I was batting in the World Series, usually connecting for base hits in crucial spots.

At noon, we would go home for dinner. Our mules and horses had a sense of when we had made the turn at the end of row and were headed in the direction of the house. When heading any direction away from the house, they struggled to pull the plows, but when they turned at the end of the row and headed toward home, they were completely energized. Years later, I was reminded of their motivation when my players seem more enthused about running to the offensive end of the court for a possible shot at the basket but strained to run back on defense.

After a large meal at noon, my brothers and I (before they left for the service) would lie down on the linoleum floor for a nap because we were much too dirty to lie down on the bed. Dad would sit down in his rocking chair and take a 10- to 15-minute nap. Then we would go to the cistern and fill our water jugs, which were wrapped in gunnysack material and soaked so that the water would stay cooler longer. When we arrived back in the fields, we would place the jugs in the shade of a cottonwood tree. When we would hoe close to the cottonwood, we could hear the leaves rustling in the wind and know that the cool water awaited us. I still love the sound of cottonwood leaves blowing in the wind.

Finishing high school

One of the fondest memories I have of growing up in Hollis is traveling with the high school basketball team to Oklahoma City on the back of a cattle truck to see the Harlem Globetrotters, led by Reece "Goose" Tatum, play against Langston University in 1946. Langston happened to have the greatest dribbler in the history of the game, Marques Haynes, and Langston actually beat the Globetrotters. The Globetrotters tried to sign Marques after the game and take him on the bus with them, but he chose to stay. He eventually did join the Globetrotters and he thrilled thousands of fans with his gifts. The Globetrotters were such a talented team that they beat the National Basketball League champions, the Minneapolis Lakers, several times in 1948 and 1949.

The day after the Globetrotter game versus Langston, my teammates and I had the privilege of attending the All-College tournament, which was the granddaddy of all of the holiday tournaments. The teams and players were among the country's best: the University of Oklahoma and Gerald Tucker; the University of Texas and Slater Martin; Oklahoma A&M and Bob Kurland; Baylor University and Jackie Robinson; the University of Kansas and Charlie Black, Ray Evans and Otto Schnellbacher; West Texas State and J.W. Malone; and the University of Arkansas and George Kok. Bill Flynt of Arkansas was the first player I ever saw shoot a jump shot. When we returned to Hollis, we started to shoot jump shots and Coach Metcalf stopped us and said that he never wanted to see any of us shoot such a silly looking shot like that again. Oh, if Coach could see the game now....

My last two years of high school were rewarding, as our basketball team qualified for the state tournament both years. My senior year was special because we had to face Mangum, whose star was Gale McArthur, later to become an All-American at Oklahoma A&M. Also on the Mangum team was an outstanding athlete named Dick Heatley, who later became a running back at OU. We had to play them in the regional finals on their home court. Coach Metcalf, relying on his knowledge of psychology, was talking about how he didn't know what to do about stopping "ol' McArthur." He said that if we only had Fred, my brother, to guard him, we would be all right. Well, Fred hadn't played in two years and was then in the U.S. Navy. It was his way of getting me psyched to guard Gale, and I did get the assignment. It would be a better story to tell you that I shut him down, but the truth is that he had a big night. However, we outscored them in a barnburner, 26-25, to qualify for the state tournament.

> ### Coaching Lesson: *On motivation*
> *The Latin root "moti" means "move," so "motivation" means that there is something inside a person that causes them to move. You can stimulate someone, but the motivation has to come from within the person. In coaching, the stimulation can be delivered in a variety of ways. Players are different—one responds to praise, the other wants to be challenged. There's no single way. You have to have a feel for it. Coach Metcalf was incredible at pushing buttons. He knew when to shame someone, when to challenge their pride, when to encourage. He had a knack for it. I did, too, most of the time, but I also made some mistakes as a coach.*

In my senior year, our Hollis football team was even better, beating teams from some much larger towns—Lawton, Altus and Clinton—on our way to a district championship. We finally lost in the state quarterfinals to Lawton, a team that we had beaten earlier on their home field, 19-6. Still, we had a terrific team. Leon Heath was later an All-American at OU and J.W. Cole was a starting tackle for OU. Our team members felt a strong sense of responsibility toward fulfilling their roles and didn't want to disappoint their teammates or Coach Metcalf. In all the years following, I was never around a better group of guys than my high school teammates. They have remained my friends for a lifetime.

When we played in the state basketball tournament in Oklahoma City, the players and coaches of all the teams were treated to a dinner featuring legendary Oklahoma A&M coach Henry Iba as the speaker. He talked about the value of a two-handed shooter, and because that was my specialty as a basketball player, I loved every minute of his talk. He later came to our dressing room after our semi-final loss and told Coach Metcalf that he liked me as a player and that he would write to express his interest in my attending Oklahoma A&M.

Every day after that, I went to the mailbox hoping to find a letter from him, but I never did. Knowing all about recruiting today, I understand that he found someone he liked a little bit better and he didn't have a need for me. He had recruited Gale McArthur and another player from Byng, Oklahoma, Bob Seymour, both of whom were my size and played the same position.

One day, Bill Jennings, the OU football assistant and chief recruiter, came to Hollis to recruit Leon and J.W. I was invited into the room and at the conclusion of Coach Jennings' talk, Coach Metcalf said that Leon, J.W. Cole and I were inseparable and wanted to go to school together. (Truthfully, even though we were good friends, we had never talked about going to school together.) Coach also hinted that Oklahoma A&M sure did want all three of us. Well, OU really wanted Leon and J.W., so Coach Jennings said that they would take all three of us, with Leon and J.W. on full scholarships. The football program would pay for my books and tuition; provide me a place to live as a student fireman on the south naval base where most of the freshman classes were taught; and arrange employment for me at McCall's Super Market to pay for my food. Because I had worked all of my life, the job didn't sound like a problem at all. So I became an Oklahoma Sooner. At that time, though, it didn't seem possible that I would have such an opportunity.

Chapter 3

Joe Bailey Metcalf

Coach's Life Lesson: *In everything you do, you play to win and never play not to lose. Never lose your aggressiveness and always attempt to control the situation.*

When the Jayhawks played at Kentucky in 1978, both teams were undefeated. We had a six-point lead with 40 seconds left, which is a pretty good lead in the days before the three-pointer. But instead of playing with the aggressiveness that caused us to be ahead, we started to play not to lose. We didn't block out on a free throw, and on a screen-and-roll, we didn't roll back to the ball and it got intercepted. We lost in overtime, and it was heartbreaking. For 39 minutes and 20 seconds, they played as well as they could've played. I have never seen such devastated young men in a dressing room.

Photo courtesy of Marcia Phillips

Hollis coach Joe Bailey Metcalf had a profound impact on me, setting the foundation for my long career in coaching.

Coach Metcalf was the most influential man in my entire life, with the exception of my father, Homer Owens. There was something special about Joe Bailey Metcalf. He reminded me of my favorite movie star, Gary Cooper—tall and deliberate in his speech, and maybe not as handsome as the actor, but with the same quiet air of confidence. He was a great fundamental teacher and incredible motivator. His coaching vocabulary had all of the old clichés: "A team that won't be beaten can't be beaten," and another that he loved, "Boys, they put their pants on just like you do: one leg at a time." One of his former players, Don Matheson, offered this description of Coach: "He was not a handsome man, but not unattractive either. He was tall and had the slumping shoulders of an athlete. He had a ruddy complexion with a large nose and steel gray hair. On the field, he always wore khaki pants, a white T-shirt and a baseball cap with 'Hollis' written on it. He was quick to jerk that cap off and sling it to the ground if the plays weren't executed to his expectation. His eyes were steel blue and could make your blood run cold with one of his stares."

Coach Metcalf was a product of the Depression. His mother and father, Hugh and Lucinda, moved from Tennessee in 1900 to the Greer County area. They lived for awhile in a half-dugout, adding on rooms when they could afford it. Joe Bailey was born a year later, in 1901, in the Metcalf community where his dad managed a grocery store and a blacksmith shop and farmed 160 acres.

He later attended Metcalf School, a two-room schoolhouse that accommodated the first through eighth grades. He received his first "whipping" from the teacher, Jim Walker, with a willow switch. Joe Bailey had pushed down a girl who tried to cut in front of him in a baseball game of "cat," which some called "work-up." By the time he started to teach and coach, he had mastered the art of corporal punishment, as many of his students and players learned.

Coach Metcalf lost his dad when he was 16, so he stayed home to run the farm. He had previously lost his brother Charles to a flu epidemic. Joe Bailey had been working the farm for a while when, one Saturday, he went into Hollis and had an encounter that changed his life. He was walking in front of a grocery store owned by the high school football coach, Hap Briscoe, and the coach stopped him to ask if he had an interest in coming to Hollis to attend school and play football.

Since there wasn't much to do on the farm in the month of September, Joe Bailey decided to attend, and he joined 15 other boys who went out for the team. His biggest fear was not football but whether he could compete in the classroom with the town kids, but he soon found that his education in the two-room Metcalf School had prepared him well. His second fear was getting lost in the two-story Hollis School building because he had never been inside such a large building.

With the help of his younger brothers, Hugh and Ray, who managed the crops on the farm, Joe Bailey was able to finish high school. At the end of his senior year, the football coach at Southwestern College in Weatherford, Oklahoma, asked him to attend school there and go out for football. He thought that he would try it for a year because, at that time, a student could earn a teaching certificate in just two years. Though he had planned to stay just one year, Joe Bailey finished his degree in 1924, leaving with a life certificate in teaching. In order to accomplish this, however, Joe Bailey joined his brothers every weekend to keep the farm operating.

After teaching for a few years in the county, Joe Bailey was hired to be the junior high principal in Hollis, and his service in the public schools as a teacher, coach and administrator lasted for 42 years. It was a source of pride to him that in all of those years, he never had to apply for a job. Each promotion came at the district's request. Those 42 years impacted the lives of thousands of players and students.

Impacting thousands

The day that he knocked on the door of our farmhouse was one of the most eventful of my life. Had it not been for him paving the way for Fred and me to attend Hollis High School and participate in sports, it is doubtful that I would have had the opportunity to play at the University of Oklahoma and coach at the University of Kansas. Without his wisdom and example, I certainly would not have been as well prepared to play and teach the game.

Even after I left for college at OU, we stayed close. I would come home in the summer to help my dad on the farm and one year, after undergoing knee surgery, I leased the local swimming pool with Coach so that I could rehabilitate my knee. During that summer of 1948, when Coach went on a family vacation in New Mexico, we received the terrible news that his beloved wife, Ruth, had been killed in a car accident, and that he had suffered broken ribs and a punctured lung. Fortunately, their two girls, Meredith and Marcia, who were eight and three at the time, had survived.

It has been 65-plus years since I played for him, but I still vividly remember the lessons that I learned. First, he made sure that each of us knew that he cared about us as individuals—about our character development and about our future. He sometimes expressed this in tough ways, but there was never a time that he didn't have our best interests at heart. Today, I tell young coaches, including my son, Teddy, that they must not forget that they are not just teaching a sport. They are teaching young men and women, and they have an opportunity to influence lives in a most meaningful way.

During the Depression, on many occasions, the local school board couldn't meet the teacher's payroll and would issue warrants or promissory notes to the individual teachers. They would have to wait until a date in the future to cash them. Coach Metcalf owned a farm operation and would cash those warrants and notes for them so that the individual teachers could care for their families.

As a coach, Metcalf believed in simplicity: run very few plays, but run them efficiently. Whatever role each player had, Coach expected him to master the fundamental skills necessary to successfully execute the play. In basketball, he emphasized dribbling, passing and shooting technique, and he was passionate about positioning our opponents away from the backboard. It is true today that the team with the most rebounds, the least turnovers and the highest percentage from the free throw line will usually win the game.

'One more time'

In football, Metcalf wanted perfection in executing the few plays that we ran. Stan Robertson, a former player who graduated from OU with a degree in engineering physics, relates a lesson that he learned from Coach. "Several times in my career and in the Air Force Aviation Cadet program, I found myself at the extremity of my perseverance," Stan said. "I thought, 'That's it. I am going to quit.' Then my mind would go back to those August days practicing football on that hard-panned parking lot in 98-degree weather, with no water, swallowing salt tablets and surrounded by goat heads and sand burrs.

"After running the same play about 10 times—or was it 110 times?—I could hear that distinctive voice of Joe Bailey saying, 'Let's run that play one more time.' So, in pre-flight, after pulling grass for eight hours and standing at a brace for two more, I would think about quitting. Every time that I did, I reminded myself of his words and I would continue to try 'just one more time.'"

At one point, five players Joe Bailey Metcalf had coached as an assistant or head coach at Hollis—Darrell Royal, Leon Manley, Leon Heath, J.W. Cole and Bill Covin—were on Bud Wilkinson's OU football team together. In that same period of time, Bill Cummins and I were playing on the OU basketball team and Merwin McConnell, a former Hollis football player, was a conference broad jump (now called long jump) champion. Other colleges in the State of Oklahoma also benefited from the many players who were trained in the Metcalf academy of fundamentals.

I know of only one occasion when Coach Metcalf wasted anything. There wasn't anything that occurred involving his players on or off the football field that he didn't know about. One night, Willie Ray "Sprout" Seddon, a speedy wing back who was probably the best 125-pound back to ever play the game, asked Coach to tape one of his ankles. Sprout was dating a girl whose boyfriend was in the service, and Coach talked to him about it, wanting Sprout to do the right thing. He talked to him for quite a while about making correct choices. Finally, at the conclusion of the taping, he asked Sprout if he had anything that he wanted to say. He replied, "Yes, sir. You taped the wrong ankle." That day, Coach not only wasted tape but an abundance of time.

My teammate, Bill Cummins, reminded me that Coach's words before a game were instructive: "Play for respect. If after the game you have earned the respect of your opponents, your coaches and your teammates, then it makes no difference what the score is. If you have won this respect, the score will take care of itself—and I will be proud of you."

He wanted his players to be responsible for their successes and failures and to never shift the blame to someone else. About referees, he always said, "They have a job to do, and I've not seen many of them that I thought deliberately caused us to lose a game." Then he would tell us that a missed block, a blocked punt, a fumble or an intercepted pass caused us to lose the game.

The mediator

When I was a junior, we rode to Tipton to play football. Tipton's star running back of the previous year, Merwin McConnell, had transferred to Hollis because his dad, a minister, had accepted the pastor's position at the First Methodist Church in Hollis. The Tipton team was determined that Merwin would not have a good game and every time they tackled him, there was some unnecessary contact and conversation (which today we would call trash talk). In spite of this, Merwin had a good game and we won, 13-0.

As we walked off the field, some of the disgruntled Tipton players started a fight with the three worst Hollis players they could have picked—Paul Horton, J.W. Cole and Leon Heath. Tipton lost that contest, too. But when we stopped for a meal at a downtown Tipton restaurant, a mob formed and surrounded the bus. Coach, as always, was very calm and told us not to say a word, but just to follow him in. Nothing eventful occurred during the meal, but afterward, when we had boarded the bus, some members of the crowd reached through the bus windows and hit some of our players on their heads. As we drove out of town, two pickups full of troublemakers tried to drive the bus off of the road. Finally, Coach had had enough. He told the bus driver to pull over and told us to unload and take care of the matter. The pickups and their occupants immediately fled, and that was the end of the situation. That was Coach Metcalf, always calm, always making the right decisions.

A master of psychology, Coach knew what we were thinking before we said a thing. Don Matheson said that Coach knew which buttons to push. He would praise some and challenge the pride of others, and he found a way to get the best performance out of everyone.

Another colorful expression that we frequently encountered was his response to an apology for missing a block or some other assignment. When we would say, "I'm sorry, Coach," his response was always, "Sorry? Sorry's backside! [edited] Sorry doesn't win a football game." We learned not to apologize for mistakes. When one of my players in later years would say, "My bad, Coach," I would remember Coach's expression and fight the urge to use it.

For those of us who where were privileged enough to spend our high school days with Coach, Matheson summed it up the best: "Coach Metcalf, next to my parents, was the greatest influence on my life." Coach taught me to never give up, to never quit and to admit my mistakes. I learned that it is OK to be afraid, but that I can't be afraid to face my fears. He taught that sometimes things don't end up the way I wish. He taught me to take responsibility for my actions, be proud of where I came from, and to not do anything to embarrass my parents.

> *"My husband, Clifford 'John' Prock, came from a broken family and through Coach Metcalf's help, went on to a successful career as a football coach at Harding College in Searcy, Arkansas. Clifford died last year, but he would have told you that Coach Metcalf was like a father to all of us. He'd whip your tail or hug your neck when you needed it. So many of us were from poor homes or broken homes—and he was a father to all of us."*
>
> *—Charlene Prock, friend*

When I would travel home to Hollis during my playing and coaching days, my first stop was to see my beloved parents. My next stop was to visit Coach, his wife, Iris, whom he married years after Ruth's tragic death, and Meredith and Marcia while they were still at home. When Coach lost his fierce battle with cancer years later, they were all there to support him.

> *Coach Metcalf, I want to thank you, from all of us, for the great lessons in life that you shared with us. It was an enormous honor and privilege to have had you as our coach.*

Chapter

Oklahoma-Bound

Coach's Life Lesson: *Take care of yourself physically. The Greek philosophy of a sound mind and body is equally true today as when it was originally proposed.*

When Murray State came to Lawrence for a game in the 1973-74 season, I was surprised when the coach asked if there was a handball court that he could use on the day of the game. It was a great lesson for me, that an exercise routine will remove stress and a coach can go into a game with a more positive attitude. So I started doing that later in my career, and I still have a routine today.

Coach Bill Jennings, the OU freshman football coach and chief recruiter, had notified J.W. Cole, Leon Heath and me that we should report for freshmen orientation a few days before we checked out our pads for the beginning of football practice. My dad drove me to the old south naval base, which had been used by the military during the WWII, in search of the fire station where I was to make my home.

The fire trucks were stationed below our living quarters, which were comprised of lockers and bunk beds scattered throughout the upper floor. Next to our beds, we kept our fire pants tucked around our boots. When an alarm sounded, we would jump out of our beds, slide our feet into the boots, jerk our suspenders over our shoulders, zip up our pants and slide down the fire pole. Our helmets and asbestos coats were hanging on the wall next to the truck to which we had been assigned. Within seconds, we would be on our way to the fire.

Freshmen football players attended the varsity workouts, and I remember being stunned with the size of the individual players. The war had ended and OU had loaded up with veterans, many of whom had played football in the military under the direction of Jim Tatum and Charles "Bud" Wilkinson, who came to OU after the war, in 1946, as head coach and assistant coach, respectively, to run the football program. Veterans could transfer to new schools without losing eligibility, so having access to the military teams allowed the coaches to bring in some outstanding players.

I was most interested in seeing two of Hollis's hometown heroes, Darrell Royal and Leon Manley, who had been in the service before joining the varsity team. It was at my first practice in 1947 that I saw Bud Wilkinson, recently named the new head coach. If one were ordering a football coach out of the Sears Roebuck catalogue, he would have looked exactly like Coach Wilkinson—tall, athletic and handsome. We had no way of knowing that we were getting ready to witness the beginning of one of the greatest eras in the history of college sports.

One day during orientation, I stopped by the field house to see the basketball court. Under the guidance of future Hall of Fame coach Bruce Drake, the Sooners had recently played in the 1947 national Championship game. There was great interest in Sooner basketball, so much so that students could only buy tickets for alternate games. With university enrollment ballooning overnight because of the end of the war, athletic tickets were in great demand. Players' friends who couldn't get tickets usually gained entry through the varsity dressing room casement windows.

Round-ball introduction

When I entered the field house, there was a basketball on the floor. I grabbed it and started shooting two-hand set shots when assistant coach Jerome "Shocky" Needy came over to talk to me. Having seen me play in the Oklahoma state basketball tournament in Oklahoma City, he said that he and the OU coaches liked me as a player, and he asked if I was coming out for the team. I told him I would like to play basketball but the football program was paying for my books and tuition.

He told me that Coach Drake was in east Texas signing one of the first big men OU had ever recruited, 6'11" Marcus Freiberger. As soon as Coach Drake returned, Coach Needy said, they would speak to Coach Jennings, the freshman football coach, about me playing basketball. The basketball program would pay my books and tuition and I would continue to work at the fire station and grocery store to pay for my housing and food. I'd like to tell you that the football program put up a fight to keep me, but the truth is that they had the Hollis players they wanted—J.W. and Leon—so it was an uncontested transaction.

School began that Monday. Each day when I finished my classes, I would catch a bus to the main campus and walk downtown to the grocery store on Main Street. My job was to stock the shelves, drive a delivery truck and perform tasks that no one else wanted to do. There seemed to be a pattern to my job skills.

With my wages, I paid Ma Richter for my meals. Her home was on the corner of Jenkins and Boyd streets, where she fed football players and a few basketball players with family-style meals. The food was great, and it was even better to be in the company of the football players. I was so very proud that my hometown had five players on the roster.

I tried to stay as close to the OU football program as I could. As a freshman, I was a member of the chain gang, moving up and down the field as the teams made first downs. When I became an upperclassman, I was a spotter for the radio broadcasts, identifying players and situations for the broadcaster. One of the great joys of my OU days was to watch my Hollis friends become such key factors in the early success of Coach Wilkinson's career.

Our freshman basketball team, under the guidance of Coach Needy, was solid, led by Marcus, the 6'11" center; Wayne Glasgow, a red-shirt transfer from Northwestern State and one of the toughest competitors I have ever been around; Vernon "Snuffy" Turner; Jack Angel and others. The varsity team was comprised of older service veterans who had experienced the hardships of war and had played prominent roles on the team that advanced to the national title game in the previous year, such as Ken Pryor, Paul Merchant, Paul Courty, Bill Waters, Bob Jones and Harley Day. Another member of that team was Keith Miller, who later authored Christian books including *A Taste of New Wine* and *What To Do With the Rest of Your Life.*

I met some interesting people in my early days at OU. I joined the National Guard, as those in reserve service were required to do in those days. One of my fellow truck drivers was a man named James Bumgarner. James was a nice, friendly guy, but none of us dreamed that he would one day star in one of television's most popular series, *Maverick.* Better known as James Garner, he was and is one of my favorite actors.

A football powerhouse is born

In the fall of 1947, after victories at Detroit and Texas A&M, OU lost to the University of Texas, tied the University of Kansas and lost to Texas Christian University—and fans were wondering if this young coach, Bud Wilkinson, was going to get the job done. But the team followed the early losses with five straight victories to close the 1947 season, including a win over Don Faurot, the University of Missouri coach who had been the head coach at Iowa Pre-Flight and had collaborated with his assistants there, Jim Tatum and Bud Wilkinson, to develop the Split T formation.

Quarterback Jack Mitchell was perfect for the offensive schemes of the Split T. With his quick first step, he ran the option beautifully. Alongside Mitchell at OU, Darrell Royal played halfback on offense and safety on defense. For years, Royal held OU's record for interceptions. An incredible punter and kick returner, he was the most versatile player on the team. In a crucial conference game in Columbia, Missouri, Darrell punted the ball out of bounds inside the 5-yard line on three occasions. Missouri fumbled following one of those punts, leading to a crucial touchdown for the Sooners.

The 1948 football team, which won nine straight after losing the season opener to Santa Clara, was rewarded with a berth in the Sugar Bowl against North Carolina and their renowned back, Charlie "Choo Choo" Justice. There was a corny saying in North Carolina at the time: "There is no justice in this world, except Charlie." But Sooner justice prevailed; we were too much for UNC and Charlie, winning 14-6 for our 10th victory.

Learning the game

While enjoying the success of the 1947 football team, I started practicing with the freshman basketball team. The freshman coach, Jerome "Shocky" Needy, was an outstanding coach of fundamentals. He taught us how to play without the basketball and to keep our defensive man's attention so that the defender would not be able to provide weak-side support. He taught us the value of using every minute of practice to improve our fundamental skills. His footwork drills allowed me to become a more effective player, and I incorporated many of his ideas into my coaching philosophy.

Coach Drake was a uniquely talented man. As a collegian at OU, he was a quarterback, an All-American basketball player and the conference pole vault champion. In addition, he was an excellent handball player and golfer. He coached the OU golf team and tutored such standouts as Charlie Coe, a leading amateur in the Masters, and Jimmy Vickers, an NCAA champion.

Coach Drake and Coach Needy collaborated to develop an offensive continuity system called "The Shuffle." For years it was known as the Drake Shuffle, and later, with its success in the SEC under Joel Eaves, it became known as the "Auburn Shuffle." The shuffle was designed so that each player would ultimately play every position on the floor. The initial cut to the basket, off of a post man's screen, caused the defense to provide support, and then the defender was screened in a tactic known today as "screen the screener." The scheme not only forced post defenders to guard out on the perimeter, it forced the offense to play the big guys out on the perimeter.

Today, the shuffle cut is still a part of many a coach's offensive tactics. Air Force Academy coach Bob Spears and his assistant, Dean Smith, ran the shuffle as their primary offense for years, and Coach Smith continued to run the initial cut all through his coaching career at the University North Carolina.

Our varsity team was quite good, but in that era a team had to win an outright conference championship to qualify for the NCAA tournament. The champion of the Big Six (later to become the Big Eight with the admission of Colorado and Oklahoma State) usually played the Missouri Valley champion in the first round of the NCAA tournament. The winner of that game would qualify for what we know now as the Elite Eight. The coaches of that era who worked so hard to win a conference championship and an NCAA berth would not believe what happens in the modern era—that an 8th-place conference team could possibly qualify for the tournament, as happened during the 2008 and 2010 tournaments, or that a 9th-place conference team, the University of Connecticut, could not only make the tournament but win the NCAA title.

Before the basketball season got started in 1948, I enjoyed seeing my high school teammates, Leon Heath and J.W. Cole, join the varsity football team, which included three other Hollis players—Darrell Royal, Leon Manley and Bill Covin. Leon Heath had survived a tough freshman year in which the coaches told him that they were going to convert him to an end position. Leon replied that he was a running back and if he couldn't play that position, he would go somewhere else. When we were in high school, Leon never lost an argument—and he didn't lose this one. The day they decided to leave him at running back was a great day for Oklahoma football because Leon became a tremendous fullback. His exceptional running ability was complemented by a vicious stiff arm, and his incredible blocking skills made our sweeps effective. In later years, he spoke of his blocking ability, saying how proud he was that Coach Wilkinson had personally taught him the blocking technique.

Shortly after an opening loss to Santa Clara, the Sooners began to emerge as an untouchable powerhouse. It was the beginning of the era of Bud Wilkinson. Late in the 1948 season, OU hosted Missouri in a critical conference game in Norman. Legendary broadcaster Bill Stern was on hand to call the game, so Harold Keith, the OU sports information director, arranged for the construction of a special booth atop the press box. In those days, the Sooners' stadium seated only about 38,000, and it was packed. OU whipped Missouri, 41-7, in a game that proved that the Sooners could play with anyone in America.

A basketball watch

The 1948 basketball season did not get off to a great start with an early loss to the University of Texas and their talented backcourt of Slater Martin and Al Madsen. Our veterans were so accomplished that the only sophomore who was seeing any time was 6'11" Marc Freiberger. Coach Drake always called a sophomore who was playing in his first varsity season "freshman" or "rookie." Versus Texas, when Coach sent me in with about a minute to play, he said, "Freshman, go in for Merchant." With about 15 seconds to go, he sent Vernon "Snuffy" Turner into the game. Snuffy didn't have time to get his warm-up pants off, so he played with them on. We didn't have uniforms with snaps back then, so it took some maneuvering to get those pants past our shoes and off our legs.

Soon after the Texas game, we left for a road trip to Illinois, and Snuffy and I roomed together. Snuffy—who had played 15 seconds in the previous game, *in his warm-up pants*—was staring out the window and said, "Now that I have the Texas game under my belt, I am ready to play some ball." It took all the self-discipline I had to keep a straight face. After the Illinois game, we traveled to Chicago and loaded onto the Commodore Vanderbilt train bound for New York City.

In those days, City College of New York was the best team in New York, and we played them in Madison Square Garden. At the end of a great game, City College pulled ahead of us with two seconds left, and Coach Drake called a timeout. He designed a play that freed clutch shooter Kenny Pryor for a shot—but it wouldn't go down. (I ran the same play, which I called "Grand Slam," many times at the University of Kansas.)

After the big city, we departed for Kansas City and the Big Six conference tournament, which we won, thanks to our veterans playing with unbelievable skill and confidence. As a result, we tied with Nebraska for the conference championship. Because we had beaten them twice during the season—the normal tie-breaker—we figured that we were headed for the NCAA playoffs. However, we were stunned when Coach Drake told us that Big Six Commissioner Reaves Peters had gone against all previous tie-breaking precedence to rule that we had to play Nebraska in Kansas City on the coming Monday. The winner would earn the NCAA berth and the right to play the Missouri Valley champs the very next night.

Our veterans were really upset at Peters' decision, and on a first ballot, the team voted not to go. After a talk by Coach Drake, they relented and voted to go. This was on a Saturday night, so we had to catch a train for Kansas City and ride all day Sunday. Not being in a very good frame of mind, we found ourselves trailing Nebraska by one point with 15 seconds to go. Coach Drake was at his creative best and called a screen-the-screener play. One of my teammates broke free along the baseline for a lay-up, but an errant pass trickled off his hands and fell out of bounds ... and there went our NCAA berth. That defeat ranks as my biggest disappointment as a college player.

Coach Drake had told us that if we beat Nebraska and qualified for the NCAA tournament, we would receive a wristwatch for participating. I had never owned a watch, so the honor was really important to me, not to mention the honor of participating in the NCAA playoffs. Now, the errant pass thrown to our wide-open player under the basket was a knuckle ball—it had topspin on the ball rather than the desired backspin. Every player who ever played for me had to listen to that story illustrating the importance of putting backspin on passes. For effect, I would look at my naked wrist with no watch.

During the year, a highly touted freshman left OU, freeing up a full scholarship for me. So I moved into Jefferson House, where I lived and ate at the training table. I appreciated the opportunity to live at the fire station, but I was glad to begin living with my basketball and football friends. The scholarship also allowed me to leave my job at McCall's Supermarket.

I owe much to my friend O.T. McCall and his wife, Virginia. Although they're no longer with us, their generous spirit, love and support were qualities I badly needed as a freshman away from home for the first time.

A banner year

My junior year, 1949, meant more playing time for me in basketball and a banner year for the Hollis players on the OU football team. Darrell Royal had become the quarterback, Leon Heath was having a great year, J.W. Cole was getting more time, and Leon Manley was playing well.

Undefeated after 10 games, the OU team was picked for the Sugar Bowl in New Orleans, set to play against the local favorite, Louisiana State University. The Sooners demolished LSU, 35-0. Darrell played a great game, and Leon was named the MVP thanks in part to an 86-yard run that was until recently a Sugar Bowl record. The 1949 unit was one of OU's greatest football teams of all time. Had it not been for national championships being awarded prior to bowl games in that era, there is little doubt that OU, in view of their dominating performance in the Sugar Bowl, would have had considerable support for the title.

In the 1949 basketball season, OU failed to repeat as champions—but we did notch a notable victory over Oklahoma A&M in Norman. Two OU football players from Chickasha, Sam Allen and Merrill Green, had told my teammate Wayne Speegle about A&M's Don Johnson, a Chickasha friend of theirs who happened to be a handsome guy and a very good basketball player. Sam and Merrill told Wayne that if he guarded Don, he would want to know that Don hated to be called "Pretty Boy." So, when Wayne called Don "Pretty Boy," Don took a swing at Wayne, who then took a dive. The referee, seeing only part of the action, kicked Johnson out of the game. We went on to win—and I would like to say that we would have won the game anyway, but it's hard to say how the game would've played out with "Pretty Boy" on the court.

A Sooner senior

My senior year, the 1950-51 year, was very rewarding. OU won national championships in football, wrestling and baseball. Leon Heath was named an All-American, J.W. Cole was a starting tackle, and the rest of us, as fans, witnessed two spectacular games in Norman. One game was the ninth of the season, a contest versus the University of Nebraska and Bobby Reynolds, who was sensational. But Reynolds' performance was matched by Leon and Billy Vessels, a sophomore from Cleveland, Oklahoma, and OU prevailed, 49-35.

The other outstanding game was early in the season, when Texas A&M brought a talented team to Norman and led by seven, 28-21, late in the game. Claude Arnold, the OU quarterback who had been recruited to the team from intramural football, then led us to a touchdown, and we thought we would soon tie the game. However, big Jim Weatherall missed the extra point. His shoulders slumped, and you might think the hopes of Sooner fans did the same. Yet in spite of the miss, the fans rose to their feet with a thunderous ovation for Jim. On A&M's next possession, we stopped them and forced a punt with only three minutes left.

What followed was one of the most magnificent drives in OU history, completed when Leon Heath crossed the goal line carrying half of the Aggie line with him. The Sooners prevailed, 34-28. I really believe that if Jim had made the extra point to tie the game at 28-28, we might have been satisfied to hold the Aggies to a tie game. But the swelling of support for Jim was inspiring, and it capped the most thrilling football game that I have ever witnessed.

At the University of Oklahoma, I played for Hall of Fame Coach Bruce Drake. This picture was taken my senior year.

When the Sooners were declared the national champions in the last poll, we realized that a loss or tie in the A&M game would have cost us the national title.

In just a short period of time, OU football was elevated to incredible heights, with four conference championships, two Sugar Bowl victories and, in 1950, a national championship. On account of all of the service veterans and outstanding high school recruits, the program had unusual depth at most positions. Coach Wilkinson could replace the starters with substitutes and still have a very good team on the field.

During the 1950-51 basketball season, we were scheduled to play Oklahoma A&M in Norman on a Saturday night. The Aggies were undefeated and ranked No. 1 in the country. On the Friday night before the basketball game, the wrestlers of both schools were slated to compete in the OU field house. A perennial power in wrestling, A&M brought a long duel-match streak to Norman, while OU, under Port Robertson, had started a program only a few years before. To create interest in wrestling, Port scheduled the matches after basketball games in hopes that some of the fans would stay over to watch. In a short period of time, he had built the program into a national contender.

On that Friday night in the field house, OU's Billy Borders started our wrestling team off with a win. Tommy Evans, soon to be one of the nation's best wrestlers, had just been released from the infirmary with an illness, so he couldn't cut weight and was forced to wrestle at a higher weight than usual. Even so, Tommy defeated Byron Todd, an Aggie wrestler who was a defending NCAA champ and his former Tulsa high school teammate, in the key match. Tommy was so overcome with the moment that he cried—and so did we.

The next evening, we hosted Henry Iba's Aggie team. Undefeated and top-ranked in the nation, A&M was led by Gale McArthur, my high school archrival from Mangum, Oklahoma. We managed to win a hard-fought battle, 44-41; Marc Freiburger led with 15 points and I added 12. The victory capped the greatest weekend of my college career.

While we weren't a league championship contender that year, we had some impressive wins, beating CCNY and Minnesota, handing Kansas State, the conference champions, their only conference defeat; winning against the nation's top-rated team, Oklahoma A&M; and notching a comeback against a powerful Kansas team in Hoch Auditorium, where victories were rare. That KU team went on to win the NCAA championship the very next year in 1952.

The Kansas victory was special because the Jayhawks were so difficult to beat in Hoch Auditorium. They were a strong team, led by big Clyde Lovellette in the post and a great supporting cast of Bill Lienhard, Bob Kenney, Bill Hoaglund, Dean Kelley, Charlie Hoag, Bert Born and Dean Smith. All of them became my close friends in later years.

We tried to sag on Clyde, but he was still getting his baskets. Their perimeter shooting was hurting us, too, and we trailed by 10 at halftime. Coach Drake told us to full-court press on defense in the second half, although we were not normally a pressing team. But the press lengthened the passing lanes into Clyde, and we gradually closed the gap with the help of superb play by our big man, Marc. Late in the game, we gained the lead and tried to hold the ball, but Charlie Hoag ripped the ball out of my hands at half-court and scored a lay-up, putting KU up by one. Coach Drake called a timeout and set up a last-second shot for me. When I was doubled, though, I flipped the ball to my roommate, Johnny Rogers, who nailed a two-handed set shot (my specialty) at the gun, winning the game and stunning the crowd. (I was stunned, too, when a woman came running out on the court directly toward me. I was relieved to discover that it was my cousin, Paulene Calloway Sherriff, who had moved to Kansas with her husband, Joe.) The win over KU was a game that I will always remember. Even today, many KU fans think that it was me who hit the shot—and I have done nothing to discourage that story.

The threat of gambling

During the summer that preceded my senior year, several members of our team had been invited to play at summer resorts in the Catskill Mountains. They worked as bellhops or bus boys during the day and then played against teams from other resorts at night as entertainment for the hotel guests. Some of the country's best players assembled there.

Unfortunately, the players were not the only people who assembled there. At the resort where they played, three of my teammates, Jim Terrell, Doug Lynn and Marc, met a jeweler named Salvatore Salazzo. While OU was playing in New York City during the Christmas holiday, the Salazzos invited Jim, Marc and Doug over for dinner, but only Jim went.

Salazzo told Jim that it was too bad that Marc wasn't with him because Marc could have made some Christmas money. Nobody on our team had a clue what all of that meant until later that year when the news broke that Salazzo was a key figure in a gambling scandal that rocked the world of college basketball. He and others had paid prominent college players to either throw games or to hold the margin of victory under the point spread. They did this mostly with players but also with some officials.

Some of the top programs in college basketball—Kentucky, Bradley, CCNY and Long Island University—were involved. Dr. Forrest C. "Phog" Allen of Kansas had warned the basketball world that gambling was a real threat to college basketball. He refused to take his team back to New York and Madison Square Garden because of this perceived threat, and the Eastern press blasted Dr. Allen for his allegations. When they realized the accuracy of his predictions, it was too late. College basketball had suffered a blow to its integrity.

Because of the threat of gambling, I have tried for years to convince the NCAA Basketball Rules Committee to pass a rule that a player cannot be eliminated from a game after the fifth foul. With the exception of being carded in soccer, basketball is the only sport in which a rules infraction eliminates a player from the game. Instead of elimination, punish the player and the team more severely, should he foul again. Why? A gambler's best chance at altering a game is to eliminate the best players from the game.

Unfortunately, most coaches and rules committee members do not share my anxiety over gambling, and there seems to be no sense of urgency to move in the direction of a rule change. I genuinely hope that my concerns will never come to pass and that gambling will never again tarnish basketball, because it is a beautiful game.

An eyewitness to segregation

I have so many fond memories of my years at OU. My relationships and experiences provided opportunities for me that I never could have imagined. However, there was one negative experience that I will never forget.

When I arrived at OU in 1947, there were no black undergraduates on campus, as the State of Oklahoma was then operating under the U.S. Supreme Court's "separate but equal" ruling. However, there was a great deal of publicity about Ada Lois Sipuel, who had graduated from Langston University in 1945, at that time an all-black state school. Denied admission to OU's law school, Ada Lois sued for the right to attend, prompting a legal battle that led all the way to the U.S. Supreme Court with Ada Lois being admitted to the OU law school in 1949.

Out of curiosity, I walked over to the law school one day and looked in to see if I might catch a glimpse of this lady who was headlining the newspapers. What I saw was Ada Lois separated by a rope barrier from the rest of the students. That was the first example of segregation that I had visually witnessed.

I knew that in my hometown I could not go to school with my black friends, with whom I worked in the fields, and I suppose I had just accepted it as the way that it was. But seeing with my own eyes—a fellow human being, separated from other students by a barrier—left a lasting impression on me. A few days later, I went back to the law school and looked in another classroom and saw Ada Lois separated from her classmates by a tri-fold dressing screen. I had never felt such compassion for anyone in my life. The rest of the story is that Ada Lois graduated from the law school, had a distinguished career as an attorney, and later served on the University of Oklahoma Board of Regents.

The starter

The season of 1950-51 was a rewarding year for me personally, as I was finally successful in winning a starting position. It made all the hours that I spent worthwhile—hours in the field house at OU, in the gym at Hollis during the summer and at the outdoor goal that my dad had built. In a win over Nebraska in Norman, I finally had a great shooting night, scoring 26 points. At the time, my total was the fourth-most points scored by a Sooner in a single game. Only three of Oklahoma's greatest players, Gerald Tucker, Jimmy McNatt and Bud Browning, had scored more in a single game.

When I went onto the court the night of the Nebraska game, Coach Drake had said to me, "You've got the 'go' sign, lad. Let it go." Although I missed my first four shots, I kept shooting because of his encouragement, and at one point I had hit seven shots in a row. In my future years in coaching, I remembered the importance of that encouragement and tried to pass it onto my players. One of my most cherished memories is when Coach Drake said after the game that it was the greatest shooting exhibition that he had ever seen.

> *"I was one of the last of the two-hand shooters. I was the only one at OU—they'd all gone to one-hand shooting by then. In southwest Oklahoma, the wind blows a lot. If you can make baskets in the wind there, it builds confidence. Indoor shooting was almost a lay-down."*
> —*Ted Owens*

My 26-point night was especially rewarding because my mother and dad were in the stands. Homer and Annie Owens were good luck charms for us that year, as we never lost a game that they attended. Before games, my teammates always asked if my parents would be there.

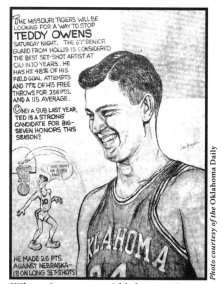

Photo courtesy of the Oklahoma Daily

The greatest honor that I received at OU was when Coach Drake asked our team, "Who would you want in a fox hole with you if you were at war?" Along those lines, before the A&M game, he asked us to vote on whom we wanted to see in the starting line-up. Years later, I found out I was the only player selected by a unanimous vote. I still cherish the feeling of confidence that my teammates had in me.

The night that I played my last game in an Oklahoma uniform was a sad night. And to think, none of it would have happened if Leon Heath and J.W. Cole had not been such outstanding

When I was an Oklahoma Sooner in 1951, an artist wondered how the Missouri Tigers would manage to stop me, a player "considered the best set-shot artist at OU in 10 years."

football players and attracted the attention of Bill Jennings and the OU staff, and if I hadn't had a high school coach, Joe Bailey Metcalf, who cared so much for his players and their futures.

My experiences at OU were terrific. My coaches were very helpful, not only on the court but with our personal and academic lives as well. Shocky and his wife, Helen, were the proctors at Jefferson House and lived there with their son, Jerry, and I got to know them. I also grew close to Coach Drake's family, and they remain my dear friends today. Donna, the younger of the two Drake daughters, would stop by practice on her way home from school, sit in the stands and watch. Donna's daughter Paige and her family remain some of my closest friends. Deonne, the older of the two girls, dated and later married Monte Moore, my good friend and high school teammate from Hollis. Monte became a famous telecaster with the Oakland Athletics when the A's were dominating Major League Baseball.

Driving from Norman to Hollis at the completion of my college days proved to be one of the saddest days of my life. I had made the trip many times as a student, often hitchhiking with Leon, J.W., and Merwin, but the last trip took on a new meaning. The trip gave me an opportunity to reflect on four of the greatest years of my life—the difficulty of leaving the farm and my parents, the blessings of a high school coach and teammates who opened the doors of opportunity for me, working at the fire station and the grocery store, taking classes from talented instructors, playing basketball for such outstanding coaches and alongside great teammates, and fulfilling the dreams that I first had while hoeing or pulling cotton on the Harmon County farm.

Chapter

Coaching, Korea and Houston

Coach's Life Lesson: *Avoid a lot of rules with established consequences. You lose the ability to judge each situation on its own merits. Try to discipline in a way that punishes the individual without bringing harm to the team.*

In my first year as a head coach at KU, Al Lopes missed curfew by three minutes, so I didn't play him against Iowa State—and we sustained a damaging loss. I was too caught up in my own rules and couldn't judge the situation on its own merits. Instead of Al paying for his tardiness by running stadium steps at 5 a.m. on Sunday morning, his teammates, coaches, and fans paid for it. I'm not suggesting that a coach shouldn't have discipline, but leave yourself the flexibility to deal with issues in a way that punishes the individual without punishing everyone else.

OU assistant coach Shocky Needy, also a reserve officer, was called into the Korean Conflict in 1951. Although I had finished my playing career and graduated with a degree in history and social studies, I still had a couple of ROTC courses to complete before receiving my commission in the U.S. Army. I was thrilled when Coach Drake asked me to fill in for Shocky until the coach returned from his service commitment. I knew it was a fantastic opportunity for me to learn from a Hall of Fame coach while I started my master's degree program in education administration.

Offensively, we were committed to the Drake Shuffle, and I had the responsibility of teaching the system to freshman players. The Drake Shuffle was a continuity offense—interchangeable positions with no designated post players. It was similar to the more recent "flex" offense but, in my opinion, the angle of the cut in the shuffle was much more difficult to defend. The night we played Stanford, the guest team in the Big Seven conference Christmas tournament in Kansas City, OU's Sherman Norton scored 39 points, mostly shooting lay-ups off of the initial shuffle cut.

Working close to Coach Drake, one of the most creative offensive coaches I ever knew, was an invaluable experience. He was quite busy that year serving as the president of the National Association of Basketball Coaches. In addition to his many accomplishments as a coach, he was a member of the basketball rules committee that eliminated defensive goaltending, which I believe to be the most important rule change in the game's history.

Blocking vs. goaltending

In the early 1940s, Coach Henry Iba at Oklahoma A&M had recruited Bob Kurland, a 7-foot-tall Missourian who was one of the country's first true big men. When basketball historians discuss some of the best rivalries in sports history, they usually mention the battles between Kurland and George Mikan of DePaul. In the early stages of Kurland's days at A&M, he was stationed around the basket, knocking away any shots that opponents took. Coach Drake felt that allowing a player to bat the ball away from the basket after the ball had started its downward arc was a tactic that was harmful to the sport. Coach Iba himself did not like the practice of goaltending and hoped that Kurland's effectiveness would lead to the change, but until the rule did change, he was going to take advantage of his size.

One night when OU and A&M played in Norman, Coach Drake invited Jimmy St. Clair, the chairman of the rules committee, to attend the game. Coach Drake had a perch built for St. Clair, which was high enough for the chairman to clearly see the shots that were batted away after starting their downward arc. Coach Drake decided to shorten the game to just a few shots by instructing his players to hold the ball for long stretches of time, making the number of shots that were deflected by Kurland even more significant. The game ended with an A&M victory, 14-11, and the number of deflected shots definitely factored into the victory. Coach Drake and OU sports information director Harold Keith wrote an article in the *Saturday Evening Post* entitled "Seven-foot Trouble," in support of banning defensive goaltending, and the article led to the rule change.

The experiences afforded me as Coach Drake's assistant opened future doors for me. The University of Kansas, which would win the conference championship in 1951-52, was coached by the legendary Forrest C. "Phog" Allen, who was ably assisted by Dick Harp, one of his former players. Before KU and St. Louis played in the NCAA tournament, the KU coaches contacted Coach Drake about scouting St. Louis, so Coach sent me to Tulsa to scout them. I suppose that Kansas was satisfied with my scouting report, because the Jayhawks defeated St. Louis and went on to win the NCAA championship.

A military man

I received my ROTC commission late in the school year and was called immediately into the service, assigned to a field artillery unit at Fort Sill in Lawton, Oklahoma. Since I had been an athlete, I did not participate in many of the military drills at OU, and I knew little about how to dress properly or to march with precision. When I reported to my unit at Fort Sill as a fresh second lieutenant, I didn't have my uniform starched and my cross cannons on my collar where pointing into the ground. The first sergeant grabbed me and quickly corrected my faulty dress before Capt. Hankins, the battery commander, could see me. When we moved the troops, I asked the first sergeant to march them. What would young second lieutenants do without experienced first sergeants?

In spite of my poor beginning, I soon acclimated to army life. Since my military record reflected that I had been an assistant coach at OU, I was selected to become the head basketball coach of the Fort Sill Post team. I had some talented players on my team, including Gene Wilson of Kansas State, one of the first black players in the Big Seven conference; Jack Brown of Southern Methodist University (SMU), Charlie Shoptaw of Lamar University and George Macuga of Bradley University. I was the fifth starter—and, of course, my position was pretty secure. Seriously, though, being a player-coach is a position of incredible pressure—pressure to play well and to be unselfish as the coach. We scrimmaged against the junior college team in Lawton, Cameron College, under the leadership of Harvey Pate. I became good friends with Pate and the Cameron athletic director, LeRoy Montgomery, who in later years hired me as the Cameron coach.

One of my fondest memories of playing basketball in the military service was winning the Fourth Army Championship in 1953. We beat the Sandia Air Base team, which had two All-Americans, Ernie Barrett of Kansas State, an old nemesis and friend of mine, and LaDell Anderson of Utah State. The Sandia team had beaten us in the tournament's opening game and we had to work our way through the loser's bracket and beat them twice to win and advance to the All Army Championships in Fort Meade, Maryland. We beat Sandia in the game that would have eliminated us, and then we rested for only an hour before playing Sandia again. Late in the second game, we were dead tired, yet I remember filling a lane on a fast break when every bone in my body resisted, and I hit a crucial lay-up. The play was one of the proudest moments of my playing career because I forced my body to do something despite being completely exhausted. We made a good showing in the All-Army tourney, but we were eliminated.

Shortly after basketball season, I attended the Basic Battery Officers

School at Fort Sill and waited for my next assignment. Usually, a few officers were assigned to Europe, but most were shipped to Korea. Receiving my orders to Korea, I drove home to Hollis to tell my mother and dad that I was headed overseas.

Shipping out

I had witnessed the strain on my parents when my brothers Fred and Quentin served in the Pacific arena in World War II, and I could see that look again in their eyes. In 1953, they took me to the airport in Amarillo, Texas, and I will never forget those moments. Mother stayed in the car because she couldn't bear to see me flying away to the Far East. After boarding the plane, I looked back to see my dad—and he was leaning over the fence weeping. Up until that point, I had handled the situation pretty well. It made me realize how important a child is to a parent.

I first flew to San Francisco and assembled with others at a base nearby. After receiving some of our gear, officers from Fort Sill, West Point and the National Guard were allowed a weekend in beautiful San Francisco. We crammed in a stop at Joe DiMaggio's restaurant to view the ball that he hit in his 56-game-hitting streak, heard Nat King Cole at the Venetian Room and watched a Browns-49ers game featuring two of the game's greatest quarterbacks, Otto Graham and Y.A. Tittle, at Kezar Stadium. After seeing the sights, we boarded the troop ship, passed under the Golden Gate Bridge and sailed for the Far East. I was happy that I had taken the time to stop by the Hollis Drug Store so that my cousin, Earl Groves, could give me Mother Sill's seasick pills.

After two weeks at sea, we landed at Yokohama, Japan, and the officers were allowed to leave the ship for the night. When we caught a cab to take us into the city, I was terrified—first, because we were driving on the wrong side of the road and second, I looked at the speedometer and we were going at what I thought was 140 miles per hour. Of course, in Hollis, we didn't know about kilometers per hour.

We boarded the ship again and later landed in Sasebo, Japan, to pick up supplies and weapons. As an officer, I received an M1 rifle and a .45 pistol. Trained on the rifle, I was a pretty good shot, but any enemy would be perfectly safe if I had to shoot that .45. My Fort Sill friends who had already been to Korea had given me a list of items that were difficult to find in Korea, so I loaded up on those items in Sasebo.

Several days later, we landed at Inchon Harbor. With the tide out, we had to carry our bags and weapons a long distance on the improvised docks, making me regret purchasing all of the supplies that my buddies had suggested.

Reaching land, we were loaded on trucks and driven to a distribution center to await assignment. I was assigned to the 2nd Division Artillery and the 37th Field Artillery Battalion. Upon arrival, the commanding officer Gen. Beringer spoke to the new, young officers and gave us some advice that I have remembered and used ever since. "Gentlemen," he said, "while you are in Korea, be guided by this principle: Assume nothing, anticipate everything."

My first assignment was as a forward observer with the French infantry. The U.N. had sent many units to the conflict, but no complete divisions apart from a U.S. division. Because the French sent an infantry battalion, the U.S. had to furnish artillery support. For those who aren't familiar with the lingo, an artillery battalion is made up of three components. First, forward observers stationed with the infantry on the front lines locate and direct fire toward targets. Second, a fire direction center converts information received from the observers into commands for the third element—the firing battery of howitzers, which fire on the targets using the adjustments that the forward observer sends.

The French had a lot of fun with me, particularly at suppertime. The forward observation bunker was overlooking the Han Tan River Valley, and there were three American soldiers—me, the reconnaissance sergeant and the liaison corporal who doubled as the jeep driver and radio and telephone operator. The French would send up French bread and omelets in the morning, and at noon, we would eat C-rations. At night, we would travel down the mountainside, the jeep's lights blacked out, on winding roads that U.S. engineers had built. There, the French would have a five-course meal with wine every night. (Those officers sure did know how to fight a war.)

As for me, they wouldn't let me eat until I read the menu in French, and they would roar with laughter when I tried to pronounce the words with my Oklahoman nasal twang.

A few months after South and North Korea signed a ceasefire agreement, the French infantry battalion I served with was sent to Vietnam, another trouble-spot for France. The Viet Cong surrounded Dien Bien Phu, the fort to which my French friends had been assigned, and cut off their supply routes, and many of my friends met with their deaths there. Back in Korea, after

I served as a field artillery officer in Korea in 1953.

the French left for Vietnam, I returned to my unit and was assigned the responsibility of teaching reconnaissance sergeants and new officers how to adjust artillery fire.

I met a couple of people in Korea, Guy Strong and Arkie Vaughan, who became lifetime friends. When we were short-timers with only a month or so to go before shipping out for home, Arkie, a tank officer, and I were assigned to division headquarters. He and I became friends in Lawrence, where he was in business and I was coaching at KU, and he is the godfather of my youngest daughter, Taylor.

We came home from Korea on a troop ship that took the northern route in order to deliver Canadian troops to Seattle. As a result of my time in Korea, I only had two problems: I was around the firing batteries of howitzers enough to have developed some hearing problems, and my toes were often numb because of the cold winter. We wore thermal boots called "Mickey Mouse" boots, which kept our feet warm if we continued to move them. But because some soldiers had used frostbite to get out of duty in Korea, frostbitten feet became an offense punishable by court martial. So even though mine were a little numb, I never reported it. Both of these conditions have bothered me ever since.

I arrived in Seattle and flew to Camp Carson, Colorado, to get my discharge. Those of us who had been together in Korea celebrated, staying up all night and barely making it in time for our final physicals. When the nurses took blood from the soldier next to me, he fainted, and we laughed and pointed at the guy. However, shortly after they had drawn blood from me, I walked over to the hearing table and the person whispered to me, "Can you hear me?" As I leaned over to try to hear him, I fell to the floor in a dead faint. That's what I get for laughing at the poor guy at the blood-testing table.

Renewing a player career

Shortly after I returned, it was time to plan my future. I knew that I wanted to finish my master's degree at OU, but I also thought that I might have some basketball-playing left in me. There were only eight teams in the NBA at that time and without television airing the games, the pay wasn't much better than playing in the National Industrial Basketball League. The advantage of playing industrial basketball was that at the conclusion of an athlete's playing days, there was a job opportunity waiting.

The most powerful team in the league was the Phillips 66ers, based in Bartlesville, Oklahoma. I had interviewed with them after my college days, but they found out that I had a service commitment in front of me. Apart from the 66ers, I was excited to learn that my college freshman coach, Shocky Needy, was now coaching the Houston ADA Oilers, owned by Bud

Adams—who, later, was more well-known as the owner of the Houston Oilers (now the Tennessee Titans).

I also interviewed with the Goodyear team in Akron, Ohio. The team president, Vic Holt, was a friend and former teammate of Coach Drake's. My Goodyear host took me to see my first major league game—the Cleveland Indians versus the New York Yankees—and, wow, what a thrill that was to see Larry Doby, the first black player in the American League: the great Indians' third-base slugger Al Rosen; and fellow Oklahoman Allie Reynolds pitch for the Yankees. Although I had a wonderful weekend, I didn't want to miss the opportunity to play for Coach Needy again, so I decided to join a solid team in Houston.

The highlight of the year was beating Phillips on their home court, which didn't happen often. The victory was especially thrilling to our owner, Bud Adams, because his dad was Boots Adams, the chairman of Phillips and a former player himself. As for me, I didn't get off to a good start. I had gained too much weight in the service, making me a step slower than I already was. I was an effective college player because of my footwork, but now I had some conditioning to do.

One of the most memorable moments occurred in Peoria, Illinois, where we played against the Peoria Caterpillars. We had arrived on our private plane, dressed in Stetson hats, custom-made boots and camelhair topcoats adorned by a big oil derrick and the ADA Oil Company logo on the lapels. The day before the game, we had a good workout at the arena, which had an elevated court. That night, all but two team members ate dinner at the Pierre Marquette—and everyone who ate there grew ill that night with food poisoning. The vomiting and diarrhea continued into the next day.

In the middle of a closely contested game, Johnny Stanich found himself at the point of a three-lane fast break. One of our forwards, Elton Cotton, was filling one of the lanes ... until he felt the immediate need to get to the bathroom. So he simply leaped off the elevated court and sprinted to the dressing room. Knowing what had happened, Johnny stopped, dropped to a knee in the middle of the court and started laughing. People asked our bench what was going on and in a few minutes, word had spread throughout the arena and the whole place was in an uproar. I have never witnessed anything funnier in my entire life.

I improved my conditioning, lost some weight and positioned myself for a good finish to the season when, late in the season, Bob Carney, our starting guard, joined the NBA's Minneapolis Lakers and left an opening for me. I had one solid night against Milwaukee, scoring in the twenties and holding their star to zero points, but it was pretty obvious that my playing days needed to come to an end. Having always admired and respected my high school and college coaches, I was convinced that I wanted to pursue coaching as my profession.

The honorable profession

In those days, in Homer and Annie's view there were three honorable professions: doctor, preacher or teacher/coach. If we ever criticized a teacher/coach my dad would get the razor strap out. I was brought up in an environment in which teaching and coaching were regarded as one of the best things you could do. My decision to coach was probably based on the way my parents felt and the deep affection that I had for Coach Metcalf. And I also had two great coaches at OU, coaches Drake and Needy.

When I returned to OU in the summer of 1956 to finish my master's degree, one member of my degree committee was James "Sleepy" Taylor, who later served as the dean of instruction at Cameron College. Another committee member, Charles Grady, the principal at Southeast High School in Oklahoma City, offered me a job as the head basketball coach. I accepted and drove to Hollis to pick up my clothes and see my parents. But a stop in Lawton, Oklahoma, changed my plans and my future.

I stopped there to see Ron Blue, an Oilers teammate I had coached under Coach Drake in my first year out of college. Ron had a service commitment and was stationed at Fort Sill. When I arrived, Ron mentioned that *The Lawton Constitution*, the local paper, had a story that day about Harvey Pate, the Cameron coach, accepting a job with Guy Lewis at the University of Houston. He asked if I would be interested in the Cameron position. Since I had gotten to know LeRoy Montgomery, the Cameron athletic director and football coach, during my stay at Fort Sill, I decided to stop by and see him.

I found LeRoy on campus and told him that I had read the paper and I wondered if the job was open. LeRoy said that it was—and asked me if I wanted it. He told me that if I took the job, in addition to coaching basketball, my duties would also include coaching football, starting a baseball program and teaching four classes of U.S. history. He said the salary would be $4,200. With that kind of money, I had no choice but to take the job.

When I called Charles Grady at Southeast High, I was concerned that he would not release me from my contract. Apparently, though, the decision to release me was simplified because the previous coach was suing the school to get his job back. I was relieved to hear the news and I headed for Cameron College.

Chapter 6

Cameron College

Coach's Life Lesson: *Always let your players know that you care about them, their families, academics and campus relationships. A player will accept discipline, strenuous conditioning and other responsibilities if he knows that you genuinely care about his welfare.*

Darrel Royal, my Hollis High School teammate and later the University of Texas football coach, put it this way: "A lot of coaches feel that a boy doesn't have to like you if they respect you. But if I had all the respect and discipline and a boy left school without a personal feeling for me, it would be a pretty empty profession." Players see through phoniness. I was always interested in them, their families, their schoolwork, and their lives. My parents taught me to care for my neighbors and that we were dependent on each other, and that's just the way I am.

Even though my primary responsibility was becoming the head basketball coach, my other duties at Cameron College were to be the defensive secondary coach, start a baseball program and teach four classes of early U.S. history. I felt confident in all of those activities ... except for teaching college-level history. Although I was an adequate history student, teaching the subject was a whole different ball game.

Much to my good fortune, I was saved by my fellow instructors, who were willing to have breakfast or lunch with me every day in order to review my notes and prevent me from making a colossal mistake. I learned to mix in stories of my experiences in sports and the Army with readings from a book called *Laughing Historically* and other anecdotes. My history class became known as "Uncle Ted's Story Hour" and I usually had a full class enrollment.

To this day, I'm a big believer in remembering names. To a class of approximately 30 students on the first day, I said, "If you can tell me every individual's name in the class when you come in for the final exam, I will give you an 'A' on the final." It never occurred to me that anyone would take me up on my offer. But several months later, the final exam day came, and one student, Burl Richardson, said that he was ready to identify all of his classmates. He named them correctly, so I gave him an A—and prayed that the dean of instruction wouldn't find out what I had done. Fifty years later, after a distinguished career in teaching at Texas A&M University, Richardson credited part of his success to remembering names.

We started preseason football practice in August, several days before the beginning of school. Coach LeRoy Montgomery and his able assistant, Charlie Dean, were putting the veterans and new recruits through some challenging drills. Anyone from southwestern Oklahoma knows how brutal the days of August can be, with temperatures easily climbing into the 100-degree range.

Cameron's biggest in-state rival in football was Northeastern A&M of Miami, Oklahoma, coached by Red Robertson. Both he and LeRoy were very competitive, as were the games, which were nearly always won by the home team. The visitors had to be considerably better because the officiating crews were on a first-name basis with the local players. Recently, I saw a former Northeastern football coach Chuck Bowman, a personal friend, and I asked him what happened to the local barber and the other Miami guys who officiated the games. He replied, tongue in cheek, that they all had been inducted into the Northeastern A&M Hall of Fame.

The Huddle Play

LeRoy was quite a recruiter, later serving as the recruiting coordinator for Kansas State and Arkansas. He was also quite creative. He invented a play called the "Huddle Play," to be run after receiving a punt or a kick-off. As the officials were spotting the ball, the team would quickly huddle up on the line of scrimmage on the opposite hash mark, as though the players were uncertain where the ball would be spotted and where to line up. Then the center would break out of the huddle and go over to the ball, across from where the defensive players were lined up and waiting for the offensive players. The quarterback would then step into the center's vacated position so that there were enough players on the line of scrimmage. After the center was set over the ball, he would pitch the ball across the field to the running back (the rules at that time did not require a center to snap the ball between his legs, although the snap had to be in one motion) and the runner would simply follow the mass of blocking down the sideline for a touchdown. The Huddle Play won a game for us against Compton College.

At one point, LeRoy sent me to Norman to talk to Bud Wilkinson's talented assistants at OU, Gomer Jones and Eddie Crowder, about the rules of their popular 5-4-2 defense. The Sooners were in the middle of a long winning streak, so coaches around the state and nation were trying to copy their methods. Gomer and Eddie had befriended me while I was at OU and they were gracious enough to spend time with me explaining the Sooners' defensive principles.

At the conclusion of the meeting, I thanked them for their patience and offered to show them a play that might win them a game. Describing the Huddle Play, they hollered at Coach Wilkinson saying, "Bud, you have to come in and see this play that Teddy is showing us!"

A few months later, after Notre Dame had ended OU's winning streak at 47, Coach Wilkinson called, wanting to know more about the play. I asked LeRoy to join me on the phone and we explained the play again. I could hardly wait to listen to the OU-Nebraska game in Lincoln on the radio the following Saturday. After the kick-off, the announcer said that OU was lined up in an unusual formation—and then he began screaming, "Bob Harrison flipped the ball to Clendon Thomas, who is on the 40, the 50, the 40, the 30 ..." Oklahoma opened with a 7-0 lead and went on to win the game.

On his coaching show on Sunday, Coach Wilkinson was asked about the play and he acknowledged that he had gotten it from a former OU basketball player, Teddy Owens. Now, it wasn't a state law that everyone had to listen to Bud's show, but most did, so I started getting congratulatory calls from friends across the state. I handled the compliments with my usual modesty: "You may not remember this," I would explain, "but my first year as a student at OU in 1947 was Coach Wilkinson's first year as head coach, and I have secretly been giving him plays for all of these years."

A new coach

While I was assisting with coaching the Cameron football team, I peeked into the gym where my basketball players were working out. Although I couldn't join them until October 15, I wanted to get a feel for the quality of players that I was inheriting from Harvey Pate. I was particularly fascinated with two Native American players from the Kiowa nation, freshman Bud Sahmaunt and sophomore Fred Yeahquo. They were very athletic, but both violated what I considered to be the proper way to shoot a basketball. The ball came off their hands with side spin rather than the traditional back spin. However, the strangest part of their unorthodox shot was that the ball still went through the rim on a consistent basis.

At first, I thought that I would soon show them how to shoot properly. Fortunately, I had enough common sense to leave their shots alone. Fred even employed a jump shot at the free throw line, a first—and a last—for a player I coached.

By the time October 15 came around, I was ready to embark on my first college coaching experience. Although my history instruction was becoming less painful, I still had daily meetings with my colleagues. They might've resented my casual use of the word "colleagues," as if I meant to imply certain equality, which was not the case. At the very least, the dean was not receiving any calls about my classroom performance.

I inherited a solid group of players and, more importantly, a set of terrific young men. Most of the players—Fred Yeahquo, Bud Sahmaunt, Gerald Hertzler, Jackie Martin, Ronnie Feger, Fat Sinclair and Bill Flurry—were from Oklahoma high schools. One exception was a transfer from Kansas State, Gene Miller. Jackie Martin, later to become a starter, was still playing football.

> *"Frankly, most of us were not too impressed at first with this new coach, Ted Owens. Owens wasn't much older than we were and was also from a small farming community in southwest Oklahoma. What were his credentials? Could he coach? Would we like him? Would we win games? To make matters worse, we found out he had no coaching experience ... Then we learned he had played big-time basketball as a starting guard at the University of Oklahoma, and as team meetings and practices began, it soon became obvious that this guy knew a thing or two about basketball. Our respect grew each day.*
> *— Gerald Hertzler, Cameron College, forward, 1956-58*

We had an active group of alumni and supporters, one of whom was Dr. Ernie Winter, brother of Kansas State coach Tex Winter. Other supporters included Smokey Torbert, a former Cameron football player; Lew Johnson, *The Constitution* sports editor and a former player; Tuffy Roberts, the head of the Lawton Jaycees, who was largely responsible for attracting the NJCAA regional tournament to Cameron's soon-to-be completed gymnasium; the Waid boys, Cuffie and Brian; Judge Luther Eubanks; Ralph and Mary Wolverton; the Wigingtons and more.

> *"Coach Owens had come to the Cameron job after a tour in the U.S. Army and undoubtedly applied some leadership skills acquired from his Army time to managing a basketball team. He praised good work openly and disciplined privately. He often used something of a 'horse whisperer' technique. During practice he might stop and call a player over. He would stare at the floor and then make eye contact. In a calm voice, he would say something like, 'Remember, you play in a game like you play in practice.'"*
> *— Gerald Hertzler, Cameron College, forward, 1956-58*

While we awaited the completion of the new arena, games were played at the old college gym. I introduced the team to Coach Drake's single-post offense, which we had run at OU, and I used many of the same OU fast-break principles that Drake had taught. We played a pressing half-court man-to-man defense and later lengthened the pressure to full court. These offensive and defensive sets became the basis of a system that I employed for the next four years at Cameron.

At halftime of one of our early games, I checked with the scorer about our foul situation before going to the dressing room. When I walked into the dressing room, Ernie Winters was in there, chewing out some players for not blocking out on rebounds. I called him aside and told him that I didn't allow anyone in the dressing room except the players and me.

I called Ernie's brother, Tex, and said that I had asked Ernie to leave and that I didn't want it to hurt our relationship. He laughed and told me that when I came to Norman or Stillwater to see Kansas State play, I had to promise to keep Ernie away from Tex's team, or Ernie would also invade the Kansas State dressing room. After that occurrence, Ernie stayed away from the dressing room, and he became one of my dearest friends.

Stiff competition

The Cameron basketball season got off to a good start with a tournament championship in Arkansas City, Kansas. Competing in the Oklahoma Junior College conference, we made an early-season trip to Eastern Oklahoma State College, in Wilburton. The game was hotly contested and the public address announcer must have thought he was a combination play-by-play announcer and official. He wouldn't shut up, and late in the game I looked over to see our athletic director, LeRoy, leaning over the railing trying to hit the guy with his Stetson hat. It's probably best that LeRoy couldn't reach him, because we might've had a riot. Unfortunately, we lost in overtime.

Though we mostly played against junior college competition, we played several games against freshman teams from major colleges. On one occasion, we were playing the Oklahoma City University (OCU) freshmen and trailing late in the game, 62-61. Ronnie Feger, a Cameron starter from Enid, dribbled into the corner along the baseline, picked up his dribble, and frantically looked for a teammate because time was running out. OCU's defenders backed off of him and looked to shut off passing lanes to our other players. When Ronnie couldn't find anyone open, and with the time running out, he dribbled a second time, going directly to the basket for a lay-up and a 63-62 victory as time expired.

Paul Hansen, the able assistant of OCU coach Abe Lemons, chased the referee, Mel Ross, to the dressing room, complaining that Ronnie had double-dribbled and the basket should not have counted. Admitting he had forgotten that Ronnie had already dribbled, Mel said he was going through some personal problems and he had simply lost his focus. Paul thought he was going to have a heart attack over that explanation. In later years, Paul and I never had a conversation without that double-dribble coming up.

Our old gymnasium had minimal seating, so with great anticipation, we looked forward to the opening of the new gym and its auditorium-style seating, which was quite a luxury when the auditorium opened in 1957. Through the efforts of Tuffy Roberts and the Lawton Jaycees, we hosted the NJCAA regional tournament in the auditorium.

Favored to win the tourney, we opened against a Murray State College team that we had beaten by 24 points just a few days earlier. We played in a daze, losing to Murray, 53-52, and bringing my first season, otherwise successful, to a disappointing close. That disappointment became a motivating factor for the following season.

> *"Our long winning streak began in our second year when we joined the Pioneer Conference. There was little or no scouting information about the teams we were to play the first time, but Coach was a great tactician. He could size up an opposing team early in the game, making the appropriate personnel adjustments, and apply the most effective offensive and defensive strategies. During one closely contested game, Coach called a timeout. For the first time, though, he seemed to be at a loss for words. He said nothing. As the buzzer sounded to resume play he looked at us and said, 'Okay, you know what to do.' It was the ultimate vote of confidence and we finished off the opponent doing what Coach had taught us to do. "*
> — *Gerald Hertzler, Cameron College, forward, 1956-58*

Catching the rabbit

Guy Strong, who I served with in Korea, had played at Kentucky for Adolph Rupp. Guy and I would sit on those Korean mountains and talk basketball for hours. He told me of a game in which the opponent changed their defense and Kentucky called time-out. When the players came over to the huddle, one of the players asked, "Coach Rupp, they have changed to a match-up zone. What do we do?" After much thought, Coach Rupp said, "You know what to do; do it." I can't tell you how many times that I wanted to give that answer to my players in future years.

A Kansas native, Coach Rupp had played for Dr. Allen and taught many of the same skills that he learned at KU. He told me of the time Rupp was asked about the importance of teaching fundamental skills, to which he said, "If you look in a recipe book for rabbit stew, what is the first thing that it tells you that you must do? It says to first catch the rabbit." When I started my coaching career, I always reminded myself of the importance of catching the rabbit.

Integration in Oklahoma basketball

When the 1957-58 school year started, we held great hope for a successful basketball season. In January of 1957, I took a phone call from Norman Lamb, a Cameron graduate who was involved with the OU basketball program. It seems that the Sooners had recruited a player from LaOverture High School, an all-black school in McAlester, Oklahoma. His name was Homer Watkins, a superb athlete who stood 6'7" and was perfectly built, with good strength and mobility. He was the first black basketball player ever recruited by OU.

Because freshmen were not eligible for competition in the Big Eight Conference, Homer did not participate that year. Experiencing difficulty in his academic work, he decided to benefit from academic and basketball development at the junior college level. I drove to Norman to visit with him, and I was immediately taken with his great smile and good attitude. I told Homer that we would help him to become a complete player and that we would make sure he was academically prepared to be successful at a four-year institution. Homer transferred to Cameron, becoming the first black player to participate in junior college basketball in the state of Oklahoma. Some time after leaving Cameron, Homer called me at 2 a.m. to say that he had graduated from Idaho State University, and he knew how important that was to me.

The same year, Coach Wilkinson had recruited Prentice Gautt, OU's first black football player, from Oklahoma City. Gautt was an outstanding running back for the Sooners and ultimately became the Big Eight assistant commissioner.

The timing of our athletic teams' integration corresponded to Cameron's entrance into the Pioneer Conference, which was made up of Texas schools. The integration caused some travel problems with housing, dining and attending movies together, and only one serious in-game confrontation. I tried to work with opposing schools to find hotels and restaurants that would accommodate all of our players. As a coach, I was always hopeful that I made the right decisions to protect my players from occurrences that may embarrass them, but I am certain that I could have done more.

One night we were on the road in Decatur, Texas (near the Dallas-Fort Worth area), and arrived at the playing site the day before the game. After dinner, I suggested that we go to a movie. When we arrived at the theater, we were told that Homer could not sit with his white teammates in the lower section of the theater, so I asked if the white players could sit with Homer in the section designated for blacks, and the theater had no objections. Try figuring that one out.

"[On the Decatur, Texas, road trip], we went to the motel where we were to stay. In the days when TVs were not a common item in each room, one room that was reserved for us had a TV. Coach Owens handed a set of keys to Gene Miller, who was to be my roommate for the stay, and we went to our room. When we saw the TV, we immediately knew that something might be wrong because we never had a room with a TV. Gene sensed that we may have been assigned the room by mistake and we decided we should lock ourselves in and not give up the room. In a matter of minutes, Coach Owens knocked on the door and told us we needed to change rooms. Our holdout was successful and we were the only ones to enjoy television during that stay."
— Dr. Bud Sahmaunt, Cameron College, guard, 1956-58

Crowd-pleasers

At the conclusion of the football season, quarterback Jackie Martin joined the basketball team. We had three starters from the previous year, Jackie, Bud Sahmaunt and Gene Miller. We had added Homer to play the center position, and the starting lineup was completed by Gerald Hertzler, a reserve the prior year who had made considerable progress. The team also had excellent depth, thanks to Ron Howard, an OCU transfer; returning lettermen Bill Flurry and Jimmy Marr; and freshmen Dexter Rolette, Donnie "Fat" Sinclair, Tommy Self and LeEster "Grasshopper" Alexander. We may have had lofty expectations, but the season that followed went beyond even our wildest dreams.

After two competitive and close games against the OCU freshmen and a team from Bethany, Minnesota, we rattled off 24 consecutive wins, entering the National Junior College Athletic Association tournament undefeated and ranked No. 1 in the national polls. We were the first team to ever enter the tourney with an undefeated record.

While the team was a quality offensive team, its greatest strength was tough man-to-man defense. (Nearly all of the quality teams I've been associated with over my career were characterized by solid defense and rebounding.) The guards, Bud Sahmaunt and Jackie Martin, applied tenacious defensive and offensive pressure up front, while Homer Watkins, the leading scorer, added scoring punch inside. Forwards Gene Miller and

Gerald Hertzler were complete players, contributing in scoring, defending and rebounding. Reserves Bill Flurry and Ron Howard played prominent roles. In the regional tournament when Homer ran into early foul trouble, Bill came off the bench with a sensational performance to lead us to a berth in the NJCAA tournament in Hutchinson, Kansas.

Playing in their new arena, this exciting team attracted quite a following in Lawton. Attending our games became an important social event and we played to packed houses. The games were usually followed by a dinner at a supporter's house. Those potluck events were some of the most enjoyable occasions of my life. The Cameron basketball program had truly become a family affair.

Our fans followed us to Hutchinson in large numbers, staying in the same hotel and, in some cases, on the same floor. We entered the tournament with great anticipation of winning a national championship.

After defeating the team from Joliet, Illinois, by 30 points, we faced Coffeyville Junior College in the quarterfinals. Their team was coached by Jack Hartman, who became my friend and coaching adversary. We defeated them, 63-53, but no victory over Jack was ever easy.

In the end, though, our run at a national championship ended with a defeat to Weber College of Utah. A magical year had come to an end.

My 1958 team at Cameron College finished the regular season undefeated and ranked No. 1 in the country, earning the NJCAA regional trophy. (Left to right) Ron Howard, Bill Flurry, Jimmy Marr, Dexter Rolette, Fat Sinclair, Gerald Hertzler, Gene Miller, Jackie Martin, Homer Watkins, me, Bud Sahmaunt and athletic director Leroy Montgomery.

Returning to Lawton, I faced the challenge of replacing some outstanding players. Little did I realize it at the time, but some of the Pioneer conference schools would conspire to deprive Homer of his last year of eligibility. Everyone knew that Homer had not participated in games at OU because freshmen were ineligible. But the conference concluded that if freshmen had been eligible, he would have played in games. Being the lone Oklahoma school in a conference full of Texas schools deprived us of support among other conference members. If it were up to me, I would have pulled out of the league, but the Cameron football team was tied into the league with future scheduling.

Already suffering the loss of starters Gerald Hertzler, Gene Miller, All-American Bud Sahmaunt and Cameron's most complete player, Jackie Martin, due to graduation, the loss of Homer compounded the problem. I was even more eager to hit the recruiting road for prospects. The year's success had energized the community, and I didn't want to lose that momentum.

"As I have observed the coaching profession over the years, I have come to realize how talented Coach Owens was at that relatively young age. Wins and losses accumulate into a record and, unfortunately, the record is most often used as the measure of a coach's success with little regard for the impact made in other areas, especially the impact on players' lives, attitudes, scholastics and preparation for future success in the real world. He taught 'integrity in all things' before those became buzzwords. He taught respect for others and hard work, not just in basketball but in all endeavors. For most of us on that first team, these were building blocks for our own future successes, on and off the court."
— *Gerald Hertzler, Cameron College, forward, 1956-58*

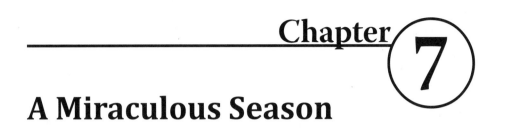

A Miraculous Season

Coach's Life Lesson: *Make certain that everyone in your program understands what their roles are and how each role is important. Reunion meetings today prove to me that being part of the team is what was important.*

In my first year out of the University of Oklahoma, I stayed on as an assistant coach under Bruce Drake, and we had an excellent scorer named Lester Lane, who later played for the Wichita Vickers in the National Industrial Basketball League. In 1960, he was named to the Olympic team with Jerry West, Oscar Robertson, and more—a team regarded as the finest until the 1992 Dream Team. The coach, Pete Newell, knew that the team wasn't functioning well, and told Lester that they didn't need more scorers; they needed someone to distribute the ball and handle pressure. So Lester assumed this new role and started for the Olympic team. It reminds me of when Jesus told his disciples that those who are servants become the greatest.

It had been years since Cameron had fielded a baseball team; no record of a team between 1929 and 1957 existed. Athletic director LeRoy Montgomery had felt that baseball would help Cameron recruit football, basketball and baseball players who wanted to continue playing baseball beyond high school. But when Cameron joined the Pioneer Conference, we learned that the conference didn't have baseball as a competitive conference sport, so Cameron administrators leaned toward not having a baseball program—even though I had been hired to start the program.

Many of the baseball players, some of whom were on the basketball and football rosters, expressed their desire to play baseball that spring. I felt an obligation to them because the athletes were told that Cameron would have a baseball program, and I thought honoring that commitment was the right thing to do.

I was also ready to coach baseball. I had played the game most of my life, including summertime semi-pro baseball for the Wellington Dukes, Texas, (Get it? The "Dukes of Wellington"?) during my college days at OU. I also played freshman baseball at OU and took theory courses taught by OU's coach, Jack Baer.

So the baseball program was born. We practiced on the military drill field, fielding a team without scholarships and on a severely limited budget. Because we didn't have a backstop, a pitcher's mound or uniforms, we limited our opponents to various Fort Sill units, giving us an opportunity to hit and field on a regular diamond. After we played several games at the military base, several players came by my office to say they had read that the National Junior College Athletic Association (NJCAA) was going to sponsor the inaugural national baseball championship on the diamond of our archrival, Northeastern Oklahoma College in Miami, Oklahoma.

To pacify my players, I called the regional NJCAA director in Amarillo and asked him how Cameron could qualify. He asked about our record and I told him that we hadn't lost to a college team all season ... even though I failed to mention that we hadn't played a college team all season. Two days later, I received a telegram stating that we would need to play Sayre Junior College in a best-of-three series. If we won the series, we could host Bacone College, runners-up in the Oklahoma Collegiate Conference, in Lawton, with the winner qualifying for the national tournament. So my next step was to figure out where to find uniforms, since we had no money in the budget.

I drove out to Fort Sill to talk to the 5th Field Artillery Battalion coach, who had told me that they were getting new uniforms. They were kind enough to give us their old ones, so I took the uniforms to an embroiderer in Lawton. She stripped the lettering off of the jerseys and embroidered "Aggies" across the chests. Anyone who looked closely, though, might have thought that we were the 5th Field Artillery Battalion Aggies.

Unfortunately, there weren't enough uniforms for me to wear one, so I dressed in basketball sneakers, sweat pants and a black Cameron T-shirt with gold letters. I didn't have a cap either, so when I went out to coach first base, I borrowed a substitute's cap so that I could call signals. The signals were pretty basic: a hand on the face or skin on skin was the signal for a steal and a hand on the bill of the cap was a signal to bunt. Coaches with a series of sophisticated signals would have been embarrassed for me with my limited repertoire of choices.

The team was comprised of athletes from other sports plus some students who hailed from areas of Oklahoma where high school baseball was serious business. On the team, we had basketball players Homer Watkins (the 6'7" pivot man), Jackie Martin (also the Cameron quarterback), Dexter Rolette, Donnie "Fat" Sinclair and Jimmy Marr. Earl Tankersley, a military veteran and a quarterback at Fort Sill, had also pitched against service competition, and he shared Cameron's quarterbacking duties with Jackie. Wayne Tedder was also on the baseball team. He had come to Cameron on a boxing scholarship, but when the sport was dropped he joined the football team as a running back and return specialist. (He continued to box independently, winning the Oklahoma featherweight championship in Golden Gloves competition.) Terry Byrd, Pat Odell, Sid Griffin, James Ray and Tony Owings joined the team from solid high school programs.

Play-in games

With Sayre College coming to Lawton for the first games of the series, I had to locate an adequate baseball facility. I finally secured Memorial Park, which at one time was the home of a Class D League team. Without free agency in those days, teams had to build strong farms systems with D leagues throughout the country. Although Lawton hadn't had a team for several years, the old ballpark was still there.

In the opening game of the Sayre series, Earl Tankersley took the mound and pitched a five-hitter. Earl, who had pitched a year earlier for the 52nd at Fort Sill, had a great knuckleball as his primary pitch. If the ball was jumping, he was difficult to hit and catch. Fortunately, we had two quality catchers, Terry Byrd and Fat Sinclair, who handled his pitches well. (Fat, at 5'8" and 140 pounds, had a twin brother named Pee Wee. If Donnie was nicknamed Fat, we had to wonder how much smaller Pee Wee was.)

In the game, Dexter, the third-baseman, made some outstanding defensive plays, including a rally-killing double play in the third inning. Wayne made six terrific catches in the outfield. Dexter, Byrd and shortstop James Ray led the offense with two hits apiece. We scored six runs in the second inning to put the game on ice, especially thanks to Earl's effective pitching.

The second game was rained out when we were leading 4-0, so the games were moved to Sayre for the second game and the third, if needed. On the Aggies' mound was Homer, who wore glasses off the field but didn't wear them during athletic contests. At 6'7", his towering presence and muscular build were intimidating enough—but add in his squinting to read the catcher's signs and his perceived vision problems, and it took a lot of courage for a batter to dig in at the plate.

Sayre managed only four hits in the contest and didn't score. For us, an 11-run fourth inning put the game away early. Wayne and Jackie accomplished the unusual feat of recording two hits each in the same inning. Homer added to his cause with a monster home run that plated two, and James added another run by hitting a triple. We returned home to prepare for the regional championship series with Bacone and their coach, Claudell Overton.

Making every hit count

Earl was rested and ready to pitch the opening game of the best-of-three series. This Aggie team had two characteristics that were evident even in a relatively short season: They scored early and they made every hit count. With consecutive singles by Dexter, Wayne and Terry, we jumped ahead with a run in the bottom of the second inning. The team followed that with five runs and we took what appeared to be a comfortable lead of 6-0 after three innings.

Unfortunately, no lead is comfortable in sports and Bacone battled back with a rally of their own. For one of the few times in the season, Earl's knuckler wasn't jumping anywhere except off the Bacone bats, and the Indians collected four hits, two bases on balls and a hit batter. Just like that, the game was tied, 6-6.

Scheduled to be a seven-inning game, the game was tied going into the bottom of the sixth when Jackie led off with a single and stole second and Jimmy followed with a walk. The runners advanced to second and third on a ground ball by Earl, and then Pat drove in the two runners with a single in the gap, and we led 8-6. That was all that Earl needed, as he didn't allow another runner after the Bacone rally in the fourth inning. He finished with a four-hitter, and we found ourselves one game away from participating in the very first national junior college tournament.

Homer took the mound again in an attempt to nail down the series. He struggled in the first inning and gave up two singles but did not allow a run. True to form, the Aggies came out swinging in the first inning and scored two runs. We followed with another run in the second when Jimmy and Pat doubled to the right-field wall. We didn't know it at the time, but that was all that Homer would need. He didn't allow another hit and finished with a two-hitter. In the fourth, Jimmy walked and Fat doubled, and both scored when James tripled off the left-field wall and later scored on Dexter's second hit of the game. That was more cushion than needed, and we had qualified for the national tournament in Miami, Oklahoma.

The underdogs

The next weekend, we loaded into two college vans and drove across the state to Miami and the host school, Northeastern A&M College. It was the general feeling of the press and the other coaches that we were the decided underdogs; few gave the Aggies any chance of winning. In the eight-team, single-elimination tournament, we were the lowest seed, as expected. We were paired against Phoenix, the No. 1 team in the nation that entered the tourney with 50 or 60 wins and only a few losses ... compared to our 5-0 record. Even though our players knew of the low expectations, they were a group of guys who enjoyed playing the game and had confidence in their abilities.

I had decided to start Homer and use Earl to bail us out when we ran into trouble. When Homer took the mound, Phoenix proceeded to hit line drives all over the field—fortunately, though, the balls were aimed right at our fielders. Outfielders Wayne, Jackie and Jimmy must have caught a dozen or so of those liners. A double and a single fell in, though, and Phoenix grabbed an early lead, 1-0.

Phoenix was so confident of their superiority over the unheralded Cameron team that they didn't start their ace pitcher, Don Herrick, who had won 13 straight games. Their second-best pitcher breezed through the first two innings, but in the third, he made the mistake of walking the first two batters, Jimmy and Homer. Pat sacrificed to advance Jimmy and Homer to second and third, and James then drove them both in with a single into left field, giving us a 2-1 lead. That was the continuing story of the underdog team—making use of every hit—as we scored two runs on one hit.

Strong defensive play kept us in front until Phoenix managed a run in the eighth inning off of Homer, who was starting to tire. He hit a batter and then followed with a throwing error, leaving runners on first and third. Phoenix squeezed their man home with a bunt down the first-base line. We held them to the single run and entered the bottom of the eighth tied at 2-2.

Entering our half of the ninth, we had managed only four hits off of Carlson, but James came through again and lined a single into centerfield. Sid laid down a bunt and Phoenix tried to throw James out at second, but he beat the throw and we then had two men on base. Our next batter, Dexter, was hit by a pitch. The bases loaded, Phoenix brought in their ace closer, Bonham, who walked Wayne to force in the go-ahead run. Jackie then hit a grounder, but Phoenix threw the ball away trying to get him at first base, so Dexter scored, giving us a 4-2 lead.

Then it was Tankersley time. He came in to pitch the ninth, and hopefully the last, inning. Earl struck out the first two batters with his knuckleball and we were ever so close to defeating the nation's top-ranked team, but it was not going to be easy. After giving up a single, Earl walked the next two batters to load the bases. With everything on the line, he settled down to strike out the last batter and earned Cameron the right to play Navarro College of Texas in a semifinal game later in the day. It was a typical win for the team: being out-hit 10 to five but making every hit count.

For the afternoon game, I had a decision to make: pitch Earl, who had pitched a lone inning in the morning, or try to get a few innings out of Dexter, regularly the third baseman, who had pitched well against Midwestern in his only outing of the year. Homer was not an option, having pitched eight innings that day.

I decided to give Dexter a shot, and he responded with a three-up, three-down first inning. In the second, Sid grounded out, but Jackie, who had filled in for Dexter at third base, lined a single and Fat followed with another. With runners on first and second, Wayne forced Fat at second while Jackie took third base. Then Jimmy reached base on an error and Martin scored. Right fielder Tony Owings singled to load the bases and Pat delivered another clutch hit, plating two runs. James, too, was up to the challenge, driving in two additional runs with a single, and we led, 5-0, against Navarro's ace pitcher. We had five hits and five runs, but managed only one more hit the rest of the game.

There's no time to relax and enjoy an athletic contest until the final result is in, and what happened in the bottom of the second was a perfect example. Dexter walked a batter to start the inning, but forced the runner at second on a ground-out. After that, the plate started to jump around on Dexter, and he walked the next two batters to load the bases. He wasn't that wild, but was just missing the strike zone.

Navarro scored their first run on an error, making it a 5-1 game with the bases loaded. I was hoping for two or three more innings out of Dexter, but he walked two more batters and the score was 5-3. I couldn't wait any longer and went to the mound to talk to Dexter. What followed was not what I expected. I told Dexter that I had to take him out of the game. "Coach, you can't take me out," he said. "I have a no-hitter going." As I said before, this was a pretty loose group.

Nevertheless, Earl came in, and he was at his best, scattering four hits over the last seven-and-two-thirds innings, and we survived, 5-3. Unbelievably, this team that we had put together only a few weeks before, with a group of players assembled from the ranks of the football and basketball teams and the student body, would be playing the next night for the national championship.

A rag-tag bunch in the finals

Archrival Northeastern A&M earned the other berth in the finals. Homa Thomas coached the Norsemen, who were regarded as tourney co-favorites alongside the Phoenix team. The northeastern Oklahoma region featured a number of committed high school baseball programs, and Homa managed to land more than his fair share of recruits. After we defeated Navarro, the smile on his face didn't conceal his pleasure at the good fortune of catching this rag-tag bunch from southwestern Oklahoma in the championship finals.

With only a day's rest, Homer took the mound for the game. I figured that we might get a few innings out of him, possibly a few out of Dexter, and finish with Earl, although he had pitched more than eight innings in two games the previous day.

We were the first to score, as we had throughout our abbreviated season. Pat led off the third with a walk and James reached base on an error. Jackie was hit with a pitch to load the bases for Homer, who drilled a liner right past the shortstop to score the first two runs of the game. When Terry Byrd hit a deep fly ball to right field, Jackie tagged and scored to put us on top, 3-0. The team's trademark efficiency gave us three runs without a hit. In the fourth, we added to the lead, capitalizing on a Norsemen error on a ball hit by Wayne. With two out, Dexter doubled to right center to score Wayne, and Homer drove Dexter in with a single for a 5-0 lead.

The Norsemen, champions of the Oklahoma Junior College league, were too talented to hold down. They fought back with a run in the fourth and three more in the fifth before Earl came in to stop their rally, but our lead was cut to 5-4 and the momentum had shifted to the host team.

'Brilliant' strategy

In the seventh, I made a decision that had a serious impact on the game. I had only utilized two signals—a hand on my cap bill to signal a bunt, or a hand on my face for a steal. From the third or fourth inning on in our games, it was no surprise that when I gave signals, the opponents would holler "bunt" or "steal" almost in unison.

Between innings, I called the team together and told them the obvious, that the Norsemen had picked up on our signs. In an effort to confuse the opponents, I switched the signs; a hand on the cap was now a steal and a hand to the face was now a bunt. With two outs and runners on first and second base, Sid was at the plate with a 3-2 count. I wanted to start the runners, so I gave what I thought was the steal sign ... but I forgot that I had changed the signs, so my signal meant "bunt." When I flashed it to Sid, he stepped out of the batter's box and just shook his head, but he stepped back in and laid down a perfect bunt toward third. The third baseman was playing back, as any sane person would do with two strikes on the batter, so the catcher had to field it. When he threw the ball away, we scored two runs. Terry followed with a single to move Sid to third, and Sid scored when the Norsemen relief pitcher committed a costly balk. Our lead widened to 8-4.

We tallied another run in the eighth when Pat scored on Dexter's grounder, taking a 9-4 lead. Northeastern made one more attempt to salvage the game with three singles in the eighth, but Earl bore down to hold them. In the ninth, with two outs, Jackie's sure hands gathered in a fly ball to end of the hopes of the home team. It was an incredible moment to see this group of young men achieve something so special. More than 50 years later, the victory still brings smiles to the faces of those of us who shared that miracle season.

After the game, I was approached by several major-college coaches who spoke of the brilliance of my strategy of bunting with two out and the fielders playing back. One even said that it was the most brilliant bit of strategy that he had ever seen. No one ever knew that when Sid laid down that bunt, I was as surprised as everyone else in the stands.

On the drive back to Lawton, I reflected on the season and the young men who wanted to field a team, who wanted to play at the highest level in the country, and who had confidence that they would succeed when few others believed. I was reminded of the last verse of a poem I learned long ago:

> *Life's battles don't always go*
> *to the stronger or faster man,*
> *But sooner or later, the man who wins*
> *is the man who thinks that he can.*

The 1957-58 school year was a remarkable one for Cameron, considering a top-rated basketball team undefeated in the regular season and, now, a national-champion baseball team. The athletes combined their obvious skills and talent with love for the game, and I am grateful that I had the opportunity to coach them.

Chapter

Maintaining Momentum

Coach's Life Lesson: *It is important to hold your best players accountable to the highest standards. If you do this, the others will most often follow their lead.*

I rarely ever disciplined or chewed out a substitute. I focused my discipline on my best players and held them accountable for their actions and responsibilities. Look at Kevin Durant. He's set out to become a better passer and shoot a higher percentage, and become a more complete player and defender, and he's impacted his entire team in a positive way.

The summer of 1958 featured two events of note. First, *The Lawton Constitution* sports editor, Lew Johnson, gave me the nickname "Tactful Ted." Second, in June of 1958, I married Nancy Amis. I met her when she was a student at Cameron. At the time, I was not sure how the administration would view a teacher and former student dating, but the college president was very supportive of the marriage.

There was no time to celebrate Cameron's 1957-58 baseball national title and an undefeated basketball regular season, because our basketball talent and experience had been depleted. Fortunately, Oklahoma produced tremendous high school players, and I was able to recruit Bobby Pollan, George "Whistle" Davidson, Carl Cabbiness, Jim Southard, Jim Martin (Jackie's younger brother) and Alvin Thurman. Reserves Dexter Rolette, Fat Sinclair and Tommie Stinnett returned. In addition, I turned to other recruiting sources and managed to land three college transfers: John Bryant, Tom King and Oscar McGuire. Even with the loss of some terrific players, the future seemed bright.

The 1958-59 basketball season was quite challenging, with the mixture of newly graduated high school players, three transfers from different colleges and a few inexperienced reserves. Most junior college coaches face this dilemma on an annual basis because every year means starting over. This problem was compounded by a schedule that opened with four consecutive road games because, in my youthfulness, I had not mastered the art of scheduling "dogs" at home in the early season.

After losing two of the first four games on the road, we came home to large crowds, a testament to the interest that had developed because of the previous year's team. But after two more losses at home, we were still struggling to find the right combination. Then the team started to become a solid unit, led by freshman guards Whistle and Bobby and transfers Johnny, Oscar and Tom. As the younger players meshed with the veterans, they managed to win 14 of the next 17 games prior to entering the NJCAA regional tournament, which we hosted at our arena. Highlights of that stretch of games included the great guard play of Bobby and Whistle, John's shooting and Tom's rebounding, and Oscar maturing into a fairly effective post man.

For the first time in the state's history, we were starting a line-up with a majority of black players (Tom, John and Oscar). We didn't encounter any problems at home, but we got into a brawl in Wharton, Texas. We had beaten the all-white team from southern Texas in an earlier game and their coach had left the court very agitated. At halftime of our game at Wharton, we noticed that the Wharton football team had moved over to the seats behind our bench. When an altercation between Tom and one of their players started, we were mauled from behind by the footballers. Luckily, we survived.

We had developed a serious rivalry with San Angelo during our two years in the Pioneer Conference. Their coach, Phil "Legs" George, led a solid program. When we played at San Angelo, he reminded our players and me that most teams who played there contacted Concho Valley fever and had trouble moving on the court. I am not certain that it was true, but we did lose at their place. However, we finished the regular season by thumping San Angelo in our last home game.

By the time the All-States Jaycee Classic, featuring some of the nation's best junior college teams, rolled around, we were merging into a solid unit. Tom was the tournament's most valuable player with an astounding 46 rebounds in the two-day event. John had a sensational shooting night with 36 points in the finals against Lon Morris' team, which had defeated us twice earlier in the season.

The NJCAA regional opened on our court. After wins over Connors and Bacone, we faced the Murray Aggies and Gerald Stockton, the former Oklahoma A&M standout. We managed to beat their fine team in overtime, 69-65, and qualified for the national tournament in Hutchinson, Kansas, for the second consecutive year.

After an opening victory over the LaSalle, Illinois, team, we found ourselves face to face with a familiar foe: Legs George and his San Angelo team. Coach George was a big kidder and there was a lot of trash talk when we encountered him and his team during the practice sessions. What followed was a classic that measured up to all the talk. We prevailed, 83-79, in a battle that proved to be worthy of a championship game. In the national semifinals, we went up against Bruce Larson and his team from Weber, Utah, the same school we had faced in the previous year. Unfortunately, the outcome was the same, as they beat us, 55-51, and won the title the next night.

Considering the team's inexperience and the season's slow start, we considered the year a success.

The summer of 1959 brought us great joy. Nancy Lynn was born on July 8, 1959. Nancy is her mother's and grandmother's name and Lynn is my middle name.

Three straight national semifinals

Although I didn't realize it at the time, the 1959-60 school year would be my last at Cameron. Guards Bobby Pollan and Whistle Davidson returned, along with reserves Carl Cabbiness, Jim Southard, Cotton Davis and Jim Martin. Through my national contacts, I found transfers Mike Surface from Kentucky and Richard Hall, who had been tutored in Ralph Tasker's famous pressing defensive system in Hobbs, New Mexico. We also added three freshman: LaDon Radford, who had played in Tulsa for one of Oklahoma's greatest high school coaches, Bill Allen; Bobby Joe Parrish, an exciting, lightning-quick guard from Kentucky; and Gene Mullins.

Mike Surface represented our only size, so we made a commitment to pressing full court to take advantage of our quickness, speed and depth. When Surface, who was married, decided to return home to Kentucky, we were left without height in the post. However, Cotton and LaDon did a magnificent job filling in.

Winning 13 of our first 15 games, we got off to a strong start. Good guard play will always give a team a chance to win, and Bobby, Whistle and Bobby Joe provided just that. However, a lengthy road trip and an injury to Whistle led to five losses in seven games. One of those games was at San Angelo, where we caught that Concho Valley fever and fell to them, 61-49.

When Whistle cracked a bone in his hand, the local doctors recommended that he not play for the rest of the season. I decided to seek another opinion— one that would agree with me, of course—and I knew the right man for the job, Kenny Rawlinson. Previously, Kenny had been a trainer with Bud Wilkinson and the OU football staff, but at that time, he was the varsity basketball trainer. On the way to Norman to see Kenny, I convinced Whistle (and myself) that Kenny was the last word in orthopedics and that we were fortunate to get an audience with him. Kenny, an old-school trainer and a coach's dream, said that Whistle certainly could play and told us how to tape the hand. Whistle played the rest of the year, and played very effectively.

The quality of officiating in the junior college ranks in Oklahoma had made major strides, and three of the best officials—Elton Davis, Babe Eubanks and Bill Estep, all athletes from OU—happened to be friends of mine. Unfortunately, one night Bill called a foul at the end of one of my games and the two free throws beat us, costing Bill his lodging privileges at my home. Elton, meanwhile, will tell you today that he deserves credit for any success that I had in coaching.

The regional tournament in Lawton was marked by the usual presence of the top Oklahoma junior colleges and the best of northern Texas. After defeating Bacone and Connors, we once again met Gerald Stockton and the Murray Aggies in the finals. Earlier in the year, we had lost to them on the road and eked by them at home, 64-61. Late in the game, we were able to pull ahead by two or three points, and I decided to employ a strategy of Henry Iba's delay game. The basic spread game at OU, under Bruce Drake, was similar, but Coach Iba was more closely associated to the strategy because he would use it at any time in the second half (and the tactic was accompanied by those nerve-racking cow bells in Gallagher Hall).

The tactic worked perfectly, with Carl playing the high post and feeding our cutters beautifully. We pulled out a 59-48 victory and won our way to Hutchinson for a third straight year. This time, we were not considered a threat to win because of our lack of size.

Once again, our fans followed us en masse, staying on the same floor of the hotel as the team did. We rewarded our followers with a 77-73 victory in the first game. In the quarterfinals, in a late-night game, we were trailing Arkansas State by 15 or 20 points in the first half. Our local host excused himself at halftime because he had to work the next day. He said goodnight, and I am sure he thought that it was a goodbye. But to start the second half, we changed from a man press to a zone press, completely rattling our opponents. We stunned the crowd (the few that were still there) with a marvelous comeback, winning 69-62.

With the victory over Arkansas State, we reached the national semifinals for the third straight year, an accomplishment that few teams have achieved. We then faced the tournament favorite, Labette Junior College, from Parsons, Kansas. It was a classic battle worthy of a Final Four game, and Parsons beat us, 85-80, and won the national championship the next night. Unfortunately, we had to play a dreaded third-place game against Sam Butterfield's Hutchinson team on their home court, against their great crowd.

We played a great game, winning 97-85, and I went to put in the reserves late in the game. When I looked down the bench, there were two of our fans, Smokey Torbert and Tuffy Roberts, with a concession vendor, buying snow cones for the Cameron players while the game was still in progress. Nothing surprised me with our fans.

A few weeks later, in Lawton, the team and I were honored at a banquet. At the conclusion, I was presented with a brand-new Chevrolet Impala, and I thought that it was the most beautiful car I had ever seen. If I recall correctly, my pay had increased from $4,200 to $5,500, but they increased my rent in faculty housing, so that car represented quite a raise.

The Jayhawks come calling

Several weeks later, I drove the baseball team to Muskogee to play in a tournament sponsored by Bacone College. During a 0-0 game against Bacone, Ken Hayes, the opposing coach, told me that I had an emergency phone call at his house, which was close to campus. I hurried to his house, expecting that there was a problem at home, only to find that the call was from Monte Moore, my high school friend and teammate. (Monte had joined me at OU, and while I worked hard to earn playing time from Coach Drake, Monte chose a better alternative and married the coach's daughter, Deonne. He had studied broadcasting and had become the radio voice of the Kansas Jayhawks.) On the phone, Monte told me that Jerry Waugh, a KU assistant coach, was leaving to take a job in the business world and that Monte had recommended that Coach Dick Harp and Dutch Lonborg, the KU athletic director, consider me as an assistant. Monte said that they wanted me on campus in two days.

I had known Dr. Forrest C. "Phog" Allen and Coach Harp through my playing time at OU and later as the assistant under Coach Drake, but we were not close friends. I called Tex Winter for advice and he told me that I "should take the job if it was offered, because it was a great situation." So my problem with Cameron now became, "What am I going to do if we advance in the baseball tournament?" I returned to the baseball game to find that we were still tied and we had a runner on third base. I forgot for a moment how important it was

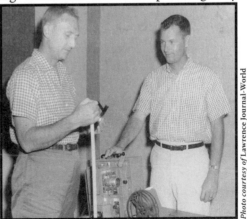

University of Kansas head basketball Coach Dick Harp and me, splicing film in 1960.

Photo courtesy of Lawrence Journal-World

for me to get the team back to Lawton so that I could get to Lawrence for the interview in two days. My competitive instincts kicked in and I did every thing I could to get that runner across home plate. The team fought hard to score in the final inning, and we won, 1-0.

Although I was happy for our players, I had mixed emotions about the win, knowing that if we won the next game, there was no way that I would reach Lawrence in time for the proposed interview. My worst nightmare became a reality when we jumped out to a 12-0 lead in the first two innings. There I was, standing there thinking that for the first time in my life, I desperately wanted to lose an athletic contest. Now, it's quite difficult to lose a baseball game when you're up 12-0. Fortunately, the opposing team was really good. With the combination of some poor playing and some very questionable coaching decisions (it could be that I used our worst pitcher), we managed to lose the game, 13-12, and headed home to Lawton. I was quite relieved that we had lost.

A Lawrence visit

Two days later, Nana, Nancy Lynn and I drove to Lawrence, where we were met by Martha Sue Harp, Coach Harp's wife. She drove us around the beautiful campus, down Jayhawk Boulevard and around the Campanile drive. I had never imagined how spectacular the campus was because, as a visiting OU player in the dead of winter, we would simply ride a bus from the Eldridge Hotel to Hoch Auditorium for games and we didn't see much of campus.

My visit with Coach Harp went well. He was a family man, a man of faith, and wanted to know more about me. We talked about my coaching experiences and my success at Cameron. I knew he was satisfied with the interview because he wanted me to speak with Dutch Lonborg. When they asked me what kind of money I would need to make the move, I considered my $5,500 Cameron salary plus housing and suggested a figure of $7,000. They agreed to that figure, and I decided to join the rich tradition of basketball at the University of Kansas. It all happened in one day, and a part of it was Monte doing a good job selling them on me.

Kansas basketball has a special place in the hearts of Kansans, both for students and alumni of the university and for those who witnessed and enjoyed the growth of the game of basketball under the leadership of the inventor of the game, James Naismith; Dr. Phog Allen, considered the father of basketball coaching; William Hamilton and Dick Harp. Even then, I was not totally aware of the importance that basketball played in the lives of the Jayhawk family—although I would learn shortly.

Telling my friends at Cameron and in Lawton that we were leaving was very difficult. The school gave me my first real coaching opportunity, and I am eternally grateful for that community's love and friendship. The fans were like family to us and the players were of the highest quality.

In November 2006, my Cameron players raised money to endow a lectureship in my name at the school, now called Cameron University. The university inducted me into their Athletic Hall of Fame in the inaugural class of 2008, along with two of my players, Dr. Bud Sahmaunt and Jackie Martin, the guards from the undefeated 1958 regular season. I will always have a warm spot in my heart for the people of Cameron, which thrives today under the leadership of Dr. Cindy Ross.

Gerald Hertzler (left) and Bud Sahmaunt (right), two of the starters from the first team that I coached at Cameron College, recently reunited with me.

Chapter

Learning the Kansas Tradition

Coach's Life Lesson: *Live your life for a greater purpose than just yourself. When you are exhausted or discouraged and are tempted to quit, it is easy to succumb to those feelings, but if you are responsible for the welfare of others, it provides the motivation to hang in there.*

When I went to Ft. Sill for artillery officer training, they noticed on my record that I had been Bruce Drake's assistant at the University of Oklahoma. So I ended up playing for the base team—and also coaching. I had to set a good example for the team. Competing in the double-elimination Fourth Army Championship, we had to come from the loser's bracket and beat Sandia twice, in two games that were 30 minutes apart, to advance to the All-Army Championship. Late in the second game, we were dead tired. I was exhausted. But we rebounded the ball and I saw an opportunity for a fast break, and I was overwhelmed with the knowledge that I had to set an example for our team. I filled the lane on the break, even though every bone in my body said "Don't do it." I pushed myself and hit a critical basket, and we won the game. If you're responsible for only yourself, there's less of a tendency to sacrifice. But if you're responsible for the welfare of others, if you're playing for a cause greater than yourself, you're a lot more apt to make that sacrifice.

Our family arrived in Lawrence and settled into a brick duplex just up the hill from the university's Memorial Stadium, in the Sunflower apartments, one of the only affordable places available to us. The apartments were a community of married students and part-time faculty members. Our next-door neighbors were from India, and it took a while for us to adjust to their music drifting through the thin walls. I can only imagine that their adjustment to this family from southwestern Oklahoma was just as great.

Head coach Dick Harp wanted me to meet those who were closely associated with the program, so I drove to Kansas City to visit with Roy Edwards, whose offices were in the stockyard area. With his friendliness and love for the university, he made a great impression on me. Roy was a huge help to me in recruiting the Kansas City area, back in the days when the rules allowed a coach to take an alumnus to visit a prospective player. Another stop in Kansas City was to see banker Ray Evans, one of KU's greatest athletes. Ray was an All-American in both football and basketball.

On my visits to prospects in the area, I would talk to the player and his parents about the basketball program and Roy would talk about the importance of being a KU graduate and living in the Kansas City area. I was always impressed with his presentation. However, one year we were meeting with Warren Armstrong, a player from across the state line in Missouri. Because it was Easter time, there was a big basket of candy Easter eggs on the table in front of the fireplace. Mesmerized by Roy's heartfelt speech, I was ready to commit to the university but I thought that I'd better glance to see the impression Roy's speech was making on Warren. What I saw was Warren leaning against the fireplace, looking off in the distance and eating candy Easter eggs, apparently not listening to one word that Roy was saying. Warren ended up at Wichita State and had an outstanding career.

At Coach Harp's direction, another stop was in downtown Lawrence to meet brothers Odd and Skipper Williams, who managed wheat acreage in western Kansas for the KU Endowment Association. (When KU alumni would pass away, some would endow their land to the university, and the association managed huge amounts of land in western Kansas.)

Little did I know at the time, but these two men would soon become my close friends and play important roles in my coaching and family life. Odd and Skipper and their dad, Dick Williams, were instrumental in starting the Williams Fund, which raised money for scholarships for the university. In the beginning a contribution of $100 was necessary to join the Century Club, which gave the donors certain parking and ticket privileges. I remember when, many years later, the Victory Club was built at the stadium for donors of more than the $100. There were some ill feelings about that decision, just as there were toward former athletic director Lew Perkins when he made decisions that led to a modernized, more competitive KU athletic department. Change is never easy.

I began my education in the tradition of KU basketball by viewing highlights of the 1952 national championship team, the 1953 national finalists and the 1957 national finalists. In the next few years, I viewed those films hundreds of times with KU players and prospects. I can still visualize Clyde Lovellette and his teammates riding across the Kansas River bridge on a fire truck after arriving home from Seattle with the national championship trophy.

In my time at Kansas and the years that followed, members of 1952 championship team became my friends, including Bill Lienhard, Bill Hoaglund, Charlie Hoag, Dean Smith, the Kelly boys, Bob Kenney, B.H. Born, Clyde Lovellette and many others. When some of them were juniors, I had played against them at Hoch Auditorium in a game that OU won with a last-second shot.

I had not fully realized that Dr. James Naismith, the inventor of basketball, was the first coach at KU and, incidentally, the only losing coach in KU history. He has been quoted many times as having said to Dr. Allen that "basketball is a game to be played, not coached." There is some truth to that statement, in that a coach's job is to prepare the players so well that once the game starts, they can play the game without the coach. Coaching is much like parenting—preparing children for the rigors of life so that they can function without parents.

In that era of basketball, there was only one full-time assistant coach. The assistant was responsible for coaching the freshmen (who were ineligible for varsity competition), assisting with varsity practice, breaking down the films (which required the coach to learn to splice film), running the academic study hall, scouting the opponents and, in his spare time, recruiting anywhere in the nation where the coaches felt there were connections that would offer an edge over competitors. Although the job was difficult and time-consuming, it was great preparation for becoming a head coach because an assistant comes to understand perfectly the importance of each of those areas.

The recruiting trail

One of my first duties at KU was to work with Coach Harp to recruit in the state of Kansas. Although KU had achieved great success in basketball from the time of James Naismith through the 38-year tenure of Phog Allen, Kansas State University was winning some of the critical recruiting battles. KSU had not come into national prominence until after World War II, but Jack Gardner and his

Photo courtesy of Lawrence Journal-World

I always took time to visit with Tex Winter, my friend and rival from Kansas State.

assistant, Tex Winters, had done a fine job recruiting veterans and high school stars, and the Manhattan, Kansas, team soon became a conference power.

Wichita State University, under the direction of Ralph Miller, a former KU athlete, was a power in the Missouri Valley and another factor in in-state recruiting. In addition, KU was in a league whose members circled the state. The original Big Six Conference consisted of KU, OU, KSU, Iowa State University, the University of Nebraska and the University of Missouri. The league expanded to the Big Seven with the addition of the University of Colorado and the Big Eight with the addition of Oklahoma State University (formerly Oklahoma A&M).

Kansas is a sparsely populated state surrounded by other thinly populated states, so we knew we weren't going to find an abundance of blue-chip players in Kansas or the surrounding states. (The exception was Missouri, with Kansas City on its western border and St. Louis on its eastern border.) That is why it became critical to not lose any of the solid prospects in KU's immediate area. Coach Harp felt strongly that if there was a good player in the state, we wanted to give him every opportunity to attend KU if he wished to do so.

Taking stock

The year before I arrived, the KU varsity team had been very successful. In my first year, the team returned several leading players, including center Bill Bridges, who had played for the legendary Ralph Tasker in Hobbs, New Mexico. Despite his lack of height at 6'6", Bridges was one of the best rebounders I had ever seen. He taught me the value of moving to the ball before jumping, and then securing the ball in front of his face. I was not a great jumper, and my high school coach, Joe Bailey Metcalf, was adamant that we would fight for inside position on rebounds and block out opponents. Bill would never hold out his opponent very long, but would release quickly to move toward the ball before he jumped. Likewise, many great rebounders don't hold a block-out long before moving to the ball. It's the guys like me, who couldn't jump very high, who had to block out an opponent until the very last second as the ball comes off the glass.

Alongside Bill, our 1960-61 front line included three fine athletes from Philadelphia: Wayne Hightower, Ralph Hayward and Allen Correll—whose interest in KU was undoubtedly whetted by the success of Philly native Wilt Chamberlain, who played at KU. The backcourt was also excellent, led by sophomore Nolen Ellison, one the best competitors I've known; shooter Jerry Gardner; and Dee Ketchum, a Native American from the Delaware tribe in Bartlesville, Oklahoma.

Bartlesville, the home of Phillips Petroleum, had produced an outstanding guard for KU a few years earlier, Dallas Dobbs. It was a strong KU town because Phillips chairmen were often KU graduates, including Paul Endicott, an All-American KU guard on the Helms Foundation's national championship teams of 1922 and 1923. (In the days before the NCAA established a national championship play-off, the Helms Foundation selected a national champion in basketball and named the college All-American team.)

The Jayhawk storytellers

Since KU was located in the center of the conference, it was practical to ride a bus to the most of the road games, with the exception of Colorado. The long rides provided time for me to learn more about the university's tremendous history and tradition. Most conversations involved Dr. Allen as the central character. The storytellers varied, from Coach Harp, who had played for and coached with Dr. Allen, to Dean "Deaner" Nesmith, a KU football player who served for more than 40 years as the head trainer for basketball and football, to Don Pierce, the sports promotion director (later called the sports information director). Each was a storytelling legend in his own right, and their tales were simply captivating.

Members of the media often entered into the bus-ride conversations, and one of them was Max Falkenstien, the radio voice of the Jayhawks. At that time, Max was working exclusively with WIBW radio in Topeka, and his voice had narrated all of the highlight films that I had studied since arriving in Lawrence. (The KU voice was Tom Hedrick, the "Parrot," who was a broadcasting prodigy of my friend Monte Moore.) These media personalities added greatly to the marginally accurate historical accounts or fables. As Dr. Allen said, "You should never let the truth get in the way of a good story."

The entire group of speakers referred to Coach Allen as "Doc," for the osteopathic doctor was famous for the treatment of injuries, particularly those relating to the sacroiliac joint. Athletes came from across the country to see Dr. Allen for treatment. I once heard a story about KU's Jim Ryun, the world-class runner who was the first high schooler to run a mile under four minutes. Ryun had complained that his back was bothering him. Now, Doc had a way of pulling a person's legs so that one leg appeared to be longer than the other, so he did just that to his patient, saying, "Look, Jim, this leg is longer than the other." Doc manipulated the sacroiliac joint and checked Jim's perfectly aligned legs. Free of pain, Jim hopped up and headed for practice.

The respect that people had for Dr. Allen was awesome. I never heard anyone say a negative word about him. Similarly, each member of that storytelling group was a fascinating character who commanded respect.

Coach Harp had played on Dr. Allen's 1940 team of national finalists, and then Harp served as Allen's assistant for many years, including the 1952 national title year and the 1953 national finalist year. Any player who participated in those years will testify to the contribution that Dick made to those teams.

In 1956, the university decided to retire Dr. Allen and a couple of deans at the mandatory retirement age of 70, and the decision did not sit well with certain fans. As a result, Dick was placed into a difficult situation when he became the head coach in the season of 1956-57, which was also Wilt Chamberlain's first year as a varsity player. In spite of an incredible year that ended with a three-overtime loss in the national finals to an undefeated North Carolina team, some critics judged the year to be disappointing. And although some tried to cause friction between Doc and Dick, I never heard Coach Harp utter anything but complimentary statements about Doc, whom he admired and respected fully.

Coach Harp was a spiritual person, as was his wife, Martha Sue, and one of the best legacies that he extended to me was contact with the Fellowship of Christian Athletes (FCA), an organization that has affected the lives of so many youngsters in such a positive way. When Coach Harp retired, he joined the FCA as deputy director and served in that capacity for many years. He was an honest man, one whom I could trust. Before I was hired as an assistant, he said he wanted me to know that if he retired in the next year, he planned to recommend that KU hire Dean Smith, a former Jayhawks player, to become the head coach. Fortunately, after I served for four years on his staff, Dick had gained enough confidence in me to support me for the head job when he left in 1964. Meanwhile, Dean Smith had become the head coach at UNC, beginning one of the most remarkable careers in coaching.

My Kansas golfing buddies and good friends while in Lawrence—(from left) Bob Taggart, Odd Williams and Arkie Vaughn—joined me in celebrating the life of Skipper Williams by playing in a tournament in Skipper's name.

Like the connection from Dr. Allen to Dick Harp to Dean Smith, the KU program's incredible tradition reaches across the basketball world. Dean Nesmith was the trainer for the 1960 U.S. Olympic team that featured Oscar

Robertson, Jerry West, Jerry Lucas, Terry Dishinger and Lester Lane, a friend of mine who was a freshman at OU when I played varsity basketball. The team was coached by one of the game's greatest teachers, Pete Newell, whose offensive footwork is incorporated into most coaches' philosophies, including mine. The team was regarded as the greatest Olympic basketball team until the 1992 Dream Team of Magic Johnson, Larry Bird and the rest.

There is no end to the stories about Don Pierce, one of the most unique men I have ever met. One day in Topeka, I asked him to play golf with me, and when he opened the trunk, I saw his bag. I am confident that you would see similar clubs in the historical Royal and Ancient Club at St. Andrews. This is no exaggeration: The woods said "mashie" and "brassie" and he even had a "niblick" club. When he opened the section of the bag that held his golf balls, several rolled out, and they could've passed for Brussels sprouts.

When I think of the history of basketball at KU, I think of the players and coaches, but I also immediately think of Doc, Dick, Deaner, Don, Max, Tom, Roy, Ray, Odd and Skipper, all of whom were my mentors. The love that they shared for the university and its basketball program was contagious, and they greatly influenced my feelings for the university and its basketball tradition.

The KU-MU rivalry

During football season, Coach Harp added color analysis to the KU football team's radio broadcasts. Late in the 1960 season, my first year at KU, he invited me to ride to Columbia, Missouri. At the time, KU had maybe the best backfield in the country, with John Hadl, later a star with the NFL's San Diego Chargers; Curtis McClinton, who scored the first touchdown in the first Super Bowl as a member of the Kansas City Chiefs; Bert Coan, a tall and swift running back from Texas; and Doyle Schick, an outstanding fullback.

Missouri was ranked No. 1 in the country and, with a victory over Kansas, had a chance to go undefeated and win the conference championship. On a beautiful fall day, the stands were packed and KU faced a hostile Missouri crowd. KU defensive coordinator George Bernhardt had designed a great game plan, and at the end of three quarters, Missouri had yet to gain a first down. Coach Harp and I were in a press-box booth with paper-thin walls and early in the fourth quarter we heard Mahlon Aldridge, the long-time Tiger announcer, call out, "It is a Missouri first down! Thank you, Tigers, thank you." But the damage had already been done, and KU came away with a 23-7 win.

I was not familiar with the deep hatred that the two states felt for each other, but I could feel it that day. The conflict's roots were deep. Missouri had entered the union in 1821 as a slave state. In the years approaching the Civil War, residents of Kansas, which was still a territory and not yet admitted to the union, were being intimidated by pro-slavery Missourians who hoped that Kansas would enter the union as a slave state. Lawrence, settled by colonists from Massachusetts and other northern states, was the headquarters of the Free State movement.

There were constant border raids, with Kansans crossing into Missouri and Missourians crossing into Kansas. One of the Kansas participants, an Irishman named Pat Devlin, was asked what he had been doing in the raids across the border into Missouri. In reply, he said, "You might say that we have been jayhawking."

> *"The term 'Jayhawk' was probably coined about 1848. Accounts of its use appeared from Illinois to Texas. The name combines two birds—the blue jay, a noisy, quarrelsome thing known to rob other nests, and the sparrow hawk, a stealthy hunter. The message here: Don't turn your back on this bird. During the 1850s, the Kansas Territory was filled with such Jayhawks. The area was a battleground. ... The factions looted, sacked, rustled cattle, stole horses and otherwise attacked each other's settlements. For a time, ruffians on both sides were called Jayhawkers. But the name stuck to the free-staters."*
>
> — *"History of Jayhawk traced to 1840s,"*
> Lawrence Journal-World, *May 28, 2004*

After Kansas was admitted to the union as a free state in 1861, the animosity between the two states remained. In 1863, William Quantrill and a band of raiders from Missouri ransacked and burned the town of Lawrence, pulling 183 male citizens out of their homes and killing them.

The NCAA forced the Kansas football team to forfeit that Missouri victory when it was determined that Bert Coan, who had transferred from Texas Christian University, had traveled to an earlier bowl game on a plane along with Bud Adams, a KU alumnus and longtime owner of the Houston Oilers and Tennessee Titans. Even having been stripped of the conference championship, KU head football coach Jack Mitchell, the first of a long line of great OU split-T quarterbacks, issued rings to his players that carried an inscription: "KU, Disputed Big Seven Champions."

Let the games begin

At the conclusion of football season, my first basketball season as a KU staff member got under way. Practices under Coach Harp were well-planned, which was a good lesson for me. At OU, Coach Bruce Drake was a creative offensive coach—and now I could learn from Coach Harp, a master of teaching half-court pressure defense. The varsity practices were intense, and we felt that we were positioned to make a run at the conference championship and an NCAA bid.

One day, Coach Harp asked me to assemble the team for an important meeting. He didn't tell me the nature of the meeting, so I was as stunned as all the players when he announced that KU was being placed on probation for violations that allegedly occurred during the Wilt Chamberlain years. Our team was stunned. Even today, I think that the news took the heart out of a team that had a chance to make a long run into the NCAA playoffs.

Late in the year, we traveled to Columbia to take on a talented Missouri team on national television in old Brewer Fieldhouse. Missouri fielded an all-white team while we started four black players. You could feel the hostility in the crowd. At halftime, Bill Bridges said to Coach Harp, "I have been called the n-word all of my life and I can handle that, but if their players keep spitting on me, something is going to happen." Late in the game, Wayne Hightower and Missouri's Charlie Henke were involved in an altercation and several hundred Missouri fans flooded the court and started punching KU players. (Search *YouTube* for "1961 MU-KU basketball brawl" to view a two-minute clip of the fight.) Fortunately, Bill Bridges cleared half of the court himself, for no one wanted any part of him, and order was finally restored. I left Columbia that day with a clearer understanding of the deep hatred that exists between the two states.

Looking ahead

Although we finished second in the league, the 1960-61 basketball season was a bit of a disappointment because the expectations were so high after reaching the NCAA regional finals the previous year. Knowing that the team was barred from the NCAA tournament, the players' spirits had evaporated.

Even so, our in-state recruiting began to improve. For the 1961-62 season, we added four solid players: Kerry Bolton, David Schichtle, Jim Gough and David Brill. We added a guard from Illinois, Dick Ruggles, and a player from Louisville, George Unseld, who became an all-conference player in his junior year.

At the time, a team had to win the conference championship to qualify for the NCAA tournament, so Coach Harp felt that the team should play as difficult of a schedule as possible in order to prepare a team for the conference race. This season was no exception. With the loss of senior Bill Bridges and junior Wayne Hightower, however, Kansas entered the 1961-62 season without the previous year's two top scorers and rebounders, and even with outstanding play from perimeter players Jerry Gardner, Nolen Ellison and Allen Correll, we could not overcome the lack of inside play and rebounding, registering a 7-18 record for the season. While the record was not acceptable by Kansas standards, the quality of young men was exceptional and each of them, including Harry Gibson, Jim Dumas and others, went on to highly successful careers in medicine, business and education. In reply to someone who asked him to name his greatest team, Dr. Allen once said, "Wait 25 years and see what they have done with their lives and I will tell you." By those standards, Doc would have been very proud of the 1961-62 team.

Integrated recruiting

Recruiting in-state and out-of-state players who were capable of playing championship basketball was critical, and prior to the 1962-63 season we were successful in landing Delvy Lewis and Riney Lochmann. Meanwhile, Coach Harp sent me to Tennessee A&I University (now Tennessee State University) in Nashville to see what, in those days, was called the National Negro High School Tournament. At the time, there were 16 states that still segregated black and white schools, and the tournament featured the best black players in the South. Most of the country's major schools didn't send coaches to scout the tournament; only George Ireland of Loyola (Chicago) and I attended. However, many of the predominantly black schools of the South sent representatives.

Famous A&I Coach John McClendon was hosting the tournament. Regarded as the "Father of Black Coaching," John was a KU alumnus, and he treated me with warm hospitality. During John's time at KU, black students could not participate in varsity athletics, but he learned the game of basketball by working with Naismith and Allen, with whom he was close.

Black students also weren't allowed to use the swimming pool, so John asked Naismith and Allen about integrating the pool. John was told that if they allowed it, there might be trouble at the pool. He returned later to suggest that the university should give it a try—open the pool, and if there were no disturbances, the pool could be permanently opened to all students. Allen and Naismith agreed and announced that for one week, the pool would be open to all students. John quickly assembled the black students and told them not to go anywhere near the pool during the announced week. After the week had passed, John went by to see Allen and Naismith, asking if there had been any disturbances during the week. They smiled, knowing that they had been outfoxed, but they honored their promise—and that's how John McClendon integrated the KU swimming pool.

At the Nashville tournament, sitting in the crowd next to a nice black gentleman, I introduced myself as the assistant basketball coach at the University of Kansas. The gentleman was Wilts Alexander, executive director of the Florida Negro High School Athletic Association, so I asked him if there were any good players in the state. Alexander told me about a 6'11" center from Dunbar High School in Ft. Myers. The young man's talent was raw. He had little experience and averaged only nine points per game, but he ran the court well and had good hands. His name was Walter Wesley.

After talking to the Dunbar basketball coach, James Stephens, I flew to Ft. Myers to meet Walter and his family. Walter's dad, LeRoy "Flash" Wesley, a former running back at Florida A&M, and his mother were divorced, but both parents were present. Walter's mother, Josie, was about 5'11", and LeRoy was only 5'10", but Walter was just as advertised—a strong 6'11." After we visited for a while at the Wesley home, I asked if I could take the family to lunch. They smiled and said that there wasn't a place in Ft. Myers that we would serve us together.

Then LeRoy said he had heard that the Howard Johnson motel and restaurant chain had announced that starting on that very day, its facilities would be opened to people of all races. They asked if I wanted to give it a try and I, of course, boldly said that I would, all the while trying to hide my apprehension. We walked into the restaurant and immediately gained the attention of everyone in attendance. As we sat down, I watched a Florida trooper glaring in our direction with an angry look on his face, unbutton the latch of his sidearm and pat the gun, in an obvious attempt to intimidate us.

> *"When Coach Owens came to visit my family and was giving his recruiting talk, he mentioned he wanted to take the family out to dinner. At the time, things were very segregated and I was attending a segregated school district; there was no integration at all. When Coach insisted on taking the family out to eat, I was thinking to myself, 'Does this guy even know where he is?' Black people did not eat in restaurants at that time. I was sitting there wondering what we were going to do when my father said that he had read in the paper that Howard Johnson's was serving everyone and we should go there. It was still funny to me, but if my father said OK, then we did it. I don't know if Coach Owens even noticed that there was a state trooper in Howard Johnson's and he held his hand on his firearm and scowled at us the entire time. The trooper did not bother us, but thinking back on it now, I think, 'Wow, it could have gone either way.'"*
> — *Walter Wesley, University of Kansas, center, 1963-66*

During our meal, we arranged for Walter to visit the KU campus. (Bradley University was one of the only schools to contact Walter. Can you imagine the recruiting competition for him in today's Southeastern Conference?)

"Bradley was recruiting me and I also talked to Illinois and Oklahoma. As a matter of fact, I had made a visit to Bradley and I was practically enrolled at Bradley. But when I visited Kansas, I had a better visit and there was a lot more contact with Kansas after my visit. I had a better feeling about the players at Kansas from the conversations I had with Coach Owens and meeting Dick Harp."
— *Walter Wesley, University of Kansas, center, 1963-66*

Walter left with his mother, and Coach Stephens asked me to join him at LeRoy Wesley's house. When we arrived, he asked if I would like a drink of bourbon. Although I had developed a peptic ulcer in Korea that had never healed, I didn't want to offend either one of my hosts, so I agreed. After a few hours of visiting and drinking bourbon, I arrived back at my hotel with the worst gut ache I could remember, and I started eating Gelusil tablets as fast as I could. Finally, I was able to go to sleep. But Walter Wesley was worth all the discomfort that I felt.

The 1962-63 season

The summer of 1962 was an eventful time for my family, as our daughter, Kelly Ann Owens, was born on July 17. The name Ann came from my precious mother, Annie. Our first-born, Nancy Lynn, had been named after her mother and grandmother, both of whom were named Nancy, and my middle name, Lynn. Kelly and Nancy are such great sources of joy for my family.

On the court, the Jayhawks' inside game improved in the 1962-63 season with sophomore George Unseld averaging more than 17 points per game and seniors Nolen Ellison, Allen Correll, Jim "Slated" Dumas and junior Harry Gibson providing stable perimeter play. However, we couldn't manage a winning record, finishing 12-13. The highlight of the season was the conference tournament finals in December in Kansas City. In a battle against heavily favored Kansas State, Nolen delivered the most courageous effort I witnessed in all of my years at the University of Kansas. At the end of regulation and each of the first three overtimes, Nolen hit the tying basket or free throw. We finally won the championship on a lay-up from Jay Roberts, a football player from Iowa. Nolen, who played the full 60 minutes, was exhausted when the game finally ended near midnight. I had begun to think that the game still might be going the next day, when Nolen was scheduled to be married.

The freshmen 1962-63 team had an amazing year, going undefeated and recording victories over archrival K-State. The Sunflower State rivalry was of great interest to fans of both universities; even the freshmen games drew crowds as big as 8,000 and were televised. When we faced K-State in Manhattan, Delvy Lewis had an incredible night and surpassed the efforts of his old high school teammate from Washburn Rural High School, Ron Paradis. Ron was such a good shooter that when he played in Allen Fieldhouse, the KU fans would chant "shoot, shoot" every time he touched the ball, even when he was dribbling in the backcourt. That freshman team, featuring Delvy, Riney Lochmann, Walter Wesley, Fred Chana, Larry Norris, Sherman Stimley and Steve Renko, showed much promise for the future.

> *"Coach Owens started recruiting me when I was a junior in high school. The first time was enough to convince me I wanted to go to KU. His enthusiasm and positive attitude about making Kansas great again was a key selling point."*
> — *Riney Lochmann, University of Kansas, forward, 1963-66*

Persistence pays off

In the spring of 1963, we were pursuing an outstanding recruit, Ron Franz from Bishop Ward High School in Kansas City. At 6'7," Ron was exceptionally mobile and played well facing the basket. He and his mother had visited the Lawrence campus and we had conducted an in-home visit, where Roy Edwards offered his Kansas City and KU story. On the day I prepared to go for a second in-home visit, I picked up the *Topeka Capital-Journal* and read a column quoting Kansas State's Tex Winter, who said he was confident that Ron would commit to the Wildcats. Obviously, I felt a real sense of urgency in my visit.

After taking Ron and his mother to dinner, we returned to their house, where we discussed the merits of Ron playing for KU. As it grew late, I asked Ron if he was ready to commit to KU and he said that he needed more time to think about it. In response, I asked them where my bedroom was, saying that I wasn't leaving until I had a decision. His mother, who I knew favored KU, went back to her bedroom to retrieve a pen, which she had saved for his graduation, and she told him how pleased she would be if he signed with KU. Ron signed with us right there and I knew that we were starting to put together the nucleus of a team that would restore the pride and tradition of Jayhawk basketball. Dr. Allen always said that in recruiting, the most important person was the mother—and the theory certainly held true in the case of Mrs. Franz.

On the court and at home, I was looking forward to the 1963-64 school year. Nana and I had purchased our first home, right next door to Coach Harp and Martha Sue on Clifton Court. The Harps' neighbor, Mr. Woestemeyer, had died, and we purchased the home from his widow for $19,000. Another neighbor, Tom Triplett, was an assistant coach and advance scout for football coach Jack Mitchell. Jack had quite a staff at KU, with Don Fambrough, George Bernhardt, Bill Pace and Bobby Goad, who had been a star end on Bud Wilkinson's earliest OU teams. I enjoyed going to Coach Triplett's house on Sunday nights to listen to the football coaches form a game plan for the following Saturday.

One of the greatest pleasures of assistant-coaching at KU was being a member of the coaches' bridge club, which was comprised of the assistant football coaches, the assistant (and later head) track coach Bob Timmons, baseball coach Floyd Temple and the coaches' wives. Once a month, the bridge club would meet at a member's house for a potluck dinner and bridge. The arrangement led to wonderful friendships that have lasted for years.

Expectations

We entered the 1963-64 basketball season with expectations of an improved record. Returning for his junior year, George Unseld did not disappoint with an all-conference performance and an 18.4-point scoring average. Upperclassmen Harry Gibson and Allen Correll joined the promising sophomore crop to give KU its strongest potential team since 1960-61. In particular, Walter Wesley was starting to show promise. He had great size at 6'11" and ran the court well, but he had two of the worst habits a basketball player could have—he didn't bend his knees and didn't carry his arms above his waist. We spent many hours with Walter working on a basic basketball stance. He also released his jump shot on the way down, resulting in a lot of blocked shots.

With Walter's jump shot in mind, I recalled seeing an apparatus in a catalogue that was described as the "Iron Defender." The device was on rollers and had a panel that could be adjusted for height. I asked Skinny Replogle, the head of maintenance, if he would make such a device so that Walter would have to shoot at the top of his extension in order to get over the deterrent. Each day, when everyone else had left the court, I would keep Walter after practice and require him to make 150 jump shots before he could leave the court. Although Walter generally had a good attitude, he would sometimes grumble about his teammates getting to leave. I would remind him that he told me when he came to KU that he wanted to become an All-American, and that it was going to take real commitment to accomplish his goal. He delivered, becoming deadly with his shot—deadly enough that he later scored 50 points in one game for the Cleveland Cavaliers, a franchise record that held until a guy by the name of LeBron James broke it.

After a fantastic performance from Walter against Kansas State, on February 1 of the 1963-64 season, we learned that he was ineligible, having flunked an activity course in wrestling. He felt awful, but no one felt as bad as I did, because I was in charge of academics and knew nothing about any difficulty in the class. Wesley adds, "I played freshman ball for Coach Owens because freshman could not play varsity. I played one semester for Dick Harp, then I became ineligible; I could not play second semester ... it was an eye-opening turn-around for me."

To compound the problem, we had lost Allen Correll to graduation at the end of the fall semester. We ended the season at 13-12, and Coach Harp resigned shortly afterward to become deputy director of the Fellowship of Christian Athletes.

An opening—and an offer

Coach Harp called me into his office to tell me that he was resigning. He said that he would support me for the head-coaching position but reminded me that outgoing coaches usually have little impact on a university's decision to hire a new coach. As I left town to recruit at high school tournaments, I knew nothing about what was transpiring in the search—and I wanted the job badly. However, I did hear that some KU alumni favored Ralph Miller, the coach at Wichita State, and the alumni pushed the new KU athletic director, Wade Stinson, a former KU football player, to hire Miller.

Meanwhile, I was in Louisville, Kentucky, watching Wesley Unseld, George's brother, lead his team to the state championship. Wes was the finest rebounder and outlet passer I had ever seen in high school, and maybe the best at any level. Wes had spent the summer working in Lawrence and living with George and Walter Wesley. And while the world of recruiting never offers a cinch or a sure thing, I felt like KU had a good chance to land Wes, even though the Louisville newspapers carried accounts that he was to become the first black player to play at the University of Kentucky.

I returned to Lawrence and heard some speculation about the head-coaching job, but nothing solid. I learned that the KU players had signed a petition asking the chancellor, Dr. Clark Wescoe, to consider me for the head job. (I had befriended Dr.

When KU Coach Dick Harp resigned, the KU players signed a petition asking the administration to hire me as the head coach.

Wescoe and his son, David, because the boy was a huge basketball fan and his father would accompany him to the fieldhouse to greet the team after road victories.)

> *"When Coach Harp left the team, I was hoping that Coach Owens would get the job because he had recruited all of us and we had played for him as freshmen. There would be some stability, and we thought that we would all get to play."*
> — *Walter Wesley, University of Kansas, center, 1963-66*

Early in the week, Wade Stinson asked me to go to lunch with him at the Lawrence Country Club. After lunch, Wade questioned me about the direction of the program. Finally, he said, "I am offering you the head basketball position." He said that Dr. Wescoe had confidence in me, which was a big factor in his decision. So at the age of 34, this farm boy from southwestern Oklahoma became the head coach at the tradition-rich University of Kansas. The feelings were indescribable. It was an absolute dream come true. I couldn't wait to call Homer and Annie Owens in Hollis, Oklahoma, to tell them that their youngest son had another new job. My childhood dreams of playing and coaching college basketball were coming true, and I wanted my parents, who had sacrificed during the Depression so that their sons could participate in sports and other school activities, to be the first to know. I dialed 8532F21 and asked "central" (the operator) to dial two longs and a short.

> *The dreams that began on a cotton farm, when I made that first basket on a goal that my dad had built, had become a reality.*

Coaching Lesson: *On being an assistant*
Being an assistant is a tough job. An assistant will have his own ideas, and while it is important to convey those to the head coach, the assistant cannot be sensitive if some of the ideas are rejected. If they are rejected, it should not deter the assistant from making suggestions over and over again. The most important thing is that if there is a disagreement in meetings, coaches must still take a unified approach to the court and to the team. Nothing is more confusing to a player than to receive mixed messages from the coaches.

Chapter

Rebuilding the Tradition

Coach's Life Lesson: *If you are in a high-profile position, you will receive criticism from others. Accept the criticism, analyze the merits and then decide if your present course is the correct one. Once that determination is made, do not be influenced by what others are saying.*

One of the challenges about coaching at KU is that the outcomes of games mean so much to so many people. If things aren't going well, you're going to get criticism and suggestions, and some of the feedback might have merit. Some of it will come from players and coaches. You need to be open, but once you decide on a course of action, you can't be swayed. As Phog Allen once said, "If a postman takes time to kick at every barking dog, he will never get his mail delivered."

Following all the press conferences and the excitement of being named KU's head basketball coach, a reality started to soak in: There was a lot of work to do to restore the program to the level of success it had seen in the 1952 national championship and the 1953 and 1957 national finalists. My contract—a one-year contract with a $10,000 salary—wasn't exactly a huge vote of confidence, but I was grateful for the opportunity.

I had a variety of feelings: joy at becoming the head coach at such a great university, an awareness of the huge responsibility that went with the position and confidence that we could live up to the tradition established by so many wonderful coaches and players. I attended the University of Oklahoma as Bud Wilkinson began to established OU's dominant football tradition and I knew how much that tradition had meant to the institution's reputation and how much it meant to the students, faculty and alumni—and the entire state of Oklahoma, for that matter. Now I knew that basketball meant the same thing for the University of Kansas. Dr. Naismith, Dr. Allen, Coach Harp and so many others had labored to build a tradition unmatched by any school in the country.

The challenges were awesome, but not overwhelming. I felt that we could restore KU basketball to its past prominence. Coach Harp and I had recruited a nucleus of good players—George Unseld, Delvy Lewis, Riney Lochmann, Fred Chana, Walter Wesley and Ron Franz—who were, just as importantly, good people. I knew that we simply had to add several more quality players to the team to achieve success, and we were able to do just that.

I took a phone call from Sam Miranda, an assistant coach at the University of New Mexico. He had played under Branch McCracken at Indiana University, where he was known as the "human delay game" for his dribbling expertise. Sam told me that he was interested in moving closer to his roots in Illinois, where he had played at Collinsville and where his family and his wife's family lived. I flew to New Mexico to see him and I was immediately impressed with his basketball knowledge, his recruiting base and his confidence. I hired Sam, and he rewarded me with 13 years of helping me bring quality basketball to KU.

The 1952, 1953 and 1957 teams were loaded with Kansas natives, but those teams had to add difference-makers from other states—Clyde Lovellette, Wilt Chamberlain, Gil Reich and Charlie Hoag—in order to compete for national honors. I felt that Sam, with his roots in Illinois and the Big 10 area, would help KU land those difference makers. In addition, I was able to hire a second assistant coach, bringing in Bob Mulcahy, George Unseld's high school coach from Louisville, Kentucky, in order to establish a recruiting base further to the east.

The recruitment of Wes Unseld was growing more intense and I was worried that Kentucky would sign Wes. When I asked Wes and George's mother what Kentucky was doing, I was relieved to learn that the Kentucky coaching staff had missed two appointments with family and that she was convinced that Kentucky was not truly serious about breaking the color barrier. Unfortunately, Louisville had made a strong pitch and when Charles, Wes's father, became ill with heart problems, Wes decided to stay close to home. It was a serious blow to our hopes because we felt that we had a distinct edge in recruiting him.

Photo courtesy of Lawrence Journal-World

Coaching in Allen Fieldhouse, I'm seen here with assistant coach Sam Miranda and player Jim Gough.

As in all cases, whether in recruiting or life, when you have disappointments, you have to lick your wounds and then set your sights on alternatives. For us, the alternative was Al Lopes, a player at Coffeyville Junior

College who hailed from Providence, Rhode Island. Coach Harp had visited Al's family in Rhode Island, making a favorable impression, and we were able to sign an active, versatile, 6'5" wing player who made an immediate impact.

Sam knew of a high school player from his hometown of Collinsville, Illinois, Rodger Bohnenstiehl, a 6'7" shooter with one of the quickest jump shots I've ever seen. Although he didn't have great speed getting up and down the court, Rodger could stick that shot of his. Tom Hedrick, the KU radio voice, described the shot as "quick as a hiccup." After signing Rodger, Sam told me about a senior at McKinley High School in St. Louis, Missouri (right near Collinsville), whose name was Joseph Henry "JoJo" White. Sam had never seen him play, but a friend whose assessment he trusted said that we should sign JoJo if we could.

Signing JoJo—without seeing him play

We immediately scheduled a visit in St. Louis with Jo, his parents and his coach, Jodie Bailey. We had a favorable visit with the Whites and were impressed with the positive guidance that Jo was getting from his parents. Jo's father was a minister and his mother was a saintly woman, and we enjoyed getting to know them in the years to come.

We planned a campus visit for JoJo that included the KU vs. OU football game in October. Jo was going to graduate at mid-term, which occurred quite frequently in large cities as a way to stagger enrollment, and not many schools knew that he was finishing at the end of the semester.

He came to visit on a beautiful October day and joined a large crowd at the stadium to witness a rare occasion when KU beat the Sooners. In celebration, students rushed the field and picked up some of the players. Jo was impressed, and so was I. We agreed with Jo that if he decided to attend KU, he would come immediately following his graduation.

> *"I was headed to Cincinnati. Oscar Robertson was a big hero of mine, but they had big issues at Cincinnati, so I got a chance to visit Kansas. I was from St. Louis and I was still around and Coach came around and gave me and my parents a chance to consider Kansas. I also held Gale Sayers as a role model and he was from KU. Coach wanted me to come to KU in January and not wait. I had already heard from the Selective Service, and I needed to enroll in college or the military."*
> — *JoJo White, University of Kansas, guard, 1966-69*

We scheduled a flight to St. Louis for one of his games, but the flight was cancelled due to a snowstorm. Jo decided to attend KU and enrolled shortly after his graduation, and we were growing anxious to see him play.

He worked out for just one or two days before the big freshmen rivalry game against Kansas State. It wasn't very far into the game before we knew we had a tremendous player on our hands. JoJo was 6'3" and 190 pounds, and if a coach were going to order a point guard off the Internet (it would've been a mail order catalogue back then), the point guard would have looked like JoJo. He was such a complete player with great court vision, a calm and confident court presence and the ability to put pressure on the opposition's point guard—oh, yeah, and he could shoot it, too. Our St. Louis source knew what he was talking about.

Coaching Lesson: *Evaluating Players*

When evaluating players, I looked at mental toughness as much as anything. You hope that you see them in competitive games, in situations where things aren't going well, to see how they respond to adversity. You look for the interaction they have with their coaches and teammates. Sit close behind the bench to see how they interact. If he's a star who comes to the huddle and is receptive to his coach and relates to his teammates, you'll be pretty confident that he's a good teammate. But if he's aloof and reluctant to stick his head into the huddle and listen, if he places blame on someone else, then he probably won't change—he probably won't relate well to you.

In addition to Jo, we gained 6'7" Bob Wilson, a talented transfer from St. Louis University. Adding Rodger, Al, Jo and Bob to the nucleus of KU players already in school gave us the depth and talent to build toward a championship team.

A running start

Now, allow me to backtrack to the start of school and the preparations for my inaugural year as head coach. When we assembled for preseason practice, we challenged the players to become the conference's best-conditioned team. Workouts began with a jog from Allen Fieldhouse, climbing the hill and heading over to Memorial Stadium. After laps around the stadium, players went inside the stadium for a sprint to the top steps, where a manager was stationed to distribute place cards; those who didn't finish in the top three had to run Campanile Hill sprints. Players would dive for the first-, second- and third-place cards, trying to avoid the dreaded Campanile sprints.

I recently called Riney Lochmann, one of the 1965-66 conference championship team captains. He had undergone a hip replacement, so I asked about his surgery and recovery. Riney said that he would still have a workable hip if it hadn't of been for me "and those d---ed Campanile sprints." Well, a team has to make sacrifices to win championships.

"When Coach became head coach my junior year, our preseason training was grueling. They made us run up several large hills while holding medicine balls over our heads. They were going to make sure we were the best-conditioned team that KU had ever had. To this day, a lot of us from that team blame this conditioning regimen for all of our knee and hip replacements."
— *Riney Lochmann, University of Kansas, forward, 1963-66*

"It definitely creates a sense of worth. Running steps and hills put us in excellent shape. One of our downfalls was not conditioning— we were always in great shape. But I will say that all the steps did not help the knees later in life."
— *Walter Wesley, University of Kansas, center, 1963-66*

"Running up Campanile Hill wasn't the hard part. That was one of the easiest. The hardest was in practice. If we screwed up, we'd have to run suicides at a full sprint up and down the court, touching the lines, and if you came in last or if everyone did not appear to be giving maximum effort, you had to run it again."
— *Bud Stallworth, University of Kansas, guard, 1969-72*

The beautiful fieldhouse

Just in time for the start of practice on October 15, the wooden floor was installed in Allen Fieldhouse. Before that date, the players had to play in the old Robinson gymnasium on Jayhawk Boulevard in the main part of campus. The fieldhouse had been opened in 1955 with a dirt floor, which was the most economical solution, so the arena without its wooden court was pretty barren from the end of March to October, even if it was a beautiful sight on game nights.

In the 1950s, the university had wanted to build an arena that was larger than the Ahearn building, the home of Kansas State basketball in Manhattan. In order to acquire the materials for the building, which was to be constructed during the Korean Conflict, several compromises were made, such as

Photo courtesy of Lawrence Journal-World

Wade Stinson (left) was the KU athletic director who hired me as head coach in 1964.

making the fieldhouse available to the track team, to the football team in inclement weather and to ROTC as a drill field. To secure funding, Dr. Allen sent two players, Claude Houchin and Jerry Waugh, to the state capitol in Topeka to convince the legislature that the Robinson gym, with its wooden surface laid on concrete, was damaging their legs. Apparently, Claude and Jerry did a great job.

The fieldhouse court was surrounded with netting and canvas and had practice baskets placed around the sides. It was necessary to sweep the floor several times during practice because of the dust flying off of the track, even though the track was watered during practice. Occasionally on winter or rainy days, the football team would use the arena. So when Skinny Replogle and his crew started installing the new floor, it was quite an exciting time for the basketball program. The players were superbly conditioned, and now we were ready to teach the skills and team play that we thought it would take to become a championship team in the Big Eight conference.

> *"Coach's practices were really hard. During those times, there wasn't an NCAA limit on the amount of practice time. If we practiced today like we did then, without water and without trainers, wow. No guidelines. Just the coaches, the players and the basketballs. It was really hard work, those sprints. NCAA guidelines would not allow that today."*
> — *Bud Stallworth, University of Kansas, guard, 1969-72*

> *"Coach Owens was kind enough to introduce me to the wonders of Allen Fieldhouse—I became acquainted with every step in the place. My idea of practice and Ted's often did not coincide, hence my utterance of a quote long before Allen Iverson ever made it famous: 'Practice? We're talking about practice?'"*
> — *Ron Franz, University of Kansas, forward, 1964-67*

Our system was to run a pressure, man-to-man defense at half court with an emphasis on low-post play on the offensive end of the court. We believed that if a team established a strong inside game, the perimeter players would be open to shoot higher-percentage shots. Our post players were senior George Unseld, an all-conference player the previous year, and junior Walter Wesley.

Practice was going well until one day during a scrimmage when George Unseld became disturbed by my criticism of his play and walked off the court. I had a rule that if a player was sent off the court, he had to stay after practice to talk to me, but George left the building without talking to me.

About two days later, George walked into my office and told me that he talked to his family and they wanted him to come back out for the team. In my first year as head coach, I knew that I had to establish a code of discipline and conduct. I told George, "When you quit, you quit—there is no coming back." Had I been an established coach, I probably would have handled the situation differently because I liked George and he was a good person. To his credit, though, he stayed in school and finished his degree.

The rookie coach

I inherited a difficult schedule from Coach Harp, who firmly believed in playing tough teams in December in preparation for conference play. As I noted earlier, a team had to win the conference to qualify for the NCAA tournament, so a loss in December wasn't a factor in making the playoffs. We were to open the 1964-65 season in Fayetteville, Arkansas, against the Razorbacks and their veteran coach, Glen Rose. On a Sunday morning just before our flight to Fayetteville, I called the Rose residence and talked to Mrs. Rose, telling her that we wanted to workout at Barnhill Arena as soon as we landed. She said, "Why, Coach Owens, Glen has gone fishing and won't be back until dark." When I hung up the phone, I thought I'd heard what was practically an act of heresy, for a coach not to practice his team the day before a game. But his ability to occasionally relax might explain why he lasted for so many years as the Arkansas coach.

When the team took the court for my first game as the Jayhawks' head coach, I was elated to see that Kenny Pryor, my college teammate and friend from OU, was officiating the game. That elation faded when Kenny called a technical on our bench early in the game. It seemed that Kenny was not aware that KU trainer Dean Nesmith had served as a voluntary advisor to the officials for many years. One of the most difficult assignments I faced at KU was to ask Deaner to be quiet while he was on the bench. He was as much a fixture at Kansas as Dr. Allen and Coach Harp were.

On the court, things were not going so well. Perhaps the players were as tight as their rookie coach. Playing against Arkansas's 1-3-1 half-court trap, my players looked like they had never seen one before when, I promise you, they had. Finally, after falling behind by 17 points, we recovered our poise and went on to win by a score of 65-60.

We returned home to face the prior year's NIT finalists, New Mexico, led by center Mel Daniels. My assistant coach, Sam, had been New Mexico's assistant in the previous year and he knew how they keyed their plays. We were well-prepared to defend them and came away with a 59-40 win in my first game as coach in Allen Fieldhouse. After a loss to Northwestern at home and then to John Egli's Penn State team and their tough 2-3 zone in the Sunflower Doubleheader in Manhattan, we returned home to play Loyola of Chicago.

I had met Loyola's coach, George Ireland, at the National Negro High School Tournament a few years earlier when I had made the initial contact that led Walter Wesley to Lawrence. (George had recruited two players at the tournament, Hunter and Rouse, who helped him win the NCAA championship with an overtime win over two-time defending champion Cincinnati.) Now, in Lawrence, the game versus Loyola became Walter's coming-out party.

> *"I had a big scoring night—more than 40, I think—and they caught me for a little interview outside before I got into the locker room. The entire team was waiting for me and stood up and clapped for me. I had never experienced that before and it was surprising to me. It was a very heart-warming experience."*
> — *Walter Wesley, University of Kansas, center, 1963-66*

I have always had an eye for potential in big players—if they are mobile with good hands and positive work habits, they can develop into great players if a coach has the patience to endure some failure. As I described earlier, Walter had the two worst habits that a player can have: he'd carry his arms below his waist and wouldn't bend his knees. With big guys, a coach will ask himself time and time again "Are they ever going to get it?" Well, this was the night Walter "got it." He scored 42 points, leading to an 80-60 victory over Loyola.

> *"The season was great. We were winning and had a great attitude. The fans were filling the stands again and they were talking to us, and about us, again."*
> — *Walter Wesley, University of Kansas, center, 1963-66*

After that, it was time to hit the road, and we traveled to play three of the great Eastern powers—Cincinnati, the University of Maryland and St. Johns University. Although we played a great game against Cincinnati, we lost, 72-76, evening our record at 3-3. But the next game in College Park turned our season around. Maryland had two solid, young players: Jay McMillan and Gary Williams (who later coached the Terrapins to an NCAA championship). Toward the end of a fierce game, we trailed by two points with a few seconds left. Jim Gough, a reserve from Chanute, Kansas, converted two free throws to send the game into overtime. Tom Hedrick, the KU radio voice, described the action: "And Jimmy Gough hits the second free throw to send the game into overtime, and they are dancing in the streets of Chanute tonight!"

After Maryland, we traveled to New York, where a tough opponent, St. John's, awaited us. I had sent assistant coach Bob Mulcahy to the St. John's vs. St. Joseph game to scout our opponent. He reported that St. John's had good guards and a versatile big man in Sonny Dove, and that they played a two-man game on offense and often ran the Eastern give-and-go. As a defender, Walter hadn't really covered anyone out on the court and we doubted that he could guard Dove effectively. Also, Coach Mulcahy had noticed that St. Joseph's 1-3-1 zone caused problems for St. John's, even though St. John's still won the game.

Planning our attack, we decided to play some zone to keep Walt in the game as long as we could. So in practice on the Sunday before the game, we worked on a basic 1-3-1 half-court zone. In the game, we started in the zone, hoping to milk 10 or 15 minutes of time for Walter. He played quite well on the offensive end, and with the zone bothering St. John's more than we could have possibly imagined, we stayed in it for the rest of the game. The end result was that we beat a tremendous St. John's team, 71-56. The highlight of the night for me was having Joe Lapchick, a legendary coach, walk down the sidelines and sit with me on the bench to congratulate me during the last 30 seconds of the game. What a thrill for this rookie coach!

The Phog legacy

When we reached the dressing room, the players stood and cheered for Walter, who had scored 36 points. One of New York City sportswriters filling the dressing room asked, "Tell us about that zone you played. Wasn't that one of Phog Allen's defenses?" (Every writer wanted to tie Dr. Allen into any story on KU basketball.) I explained to them several times that it was just a basic 1-3-1 zone, but they would have no part of it. Finally, to get them off the subject, I said, "Well, you are right. That was Dr. Allen's stratified, transitional man-for-man defense with zone principles." They hurriedly wrote down every detail, and Dr. Allen's zone became the headline the next day—and the articles carried the thought that Walt might be Kansas' greatest center since Wilt Chamberlain.

> *"I was asked about [being the next Wilt] all the time. My response was that there was only one Wilt—never be another. He stands alone in his greatness. I met him the first time when the team was in California and he came to the team hotel. It was great ... and I met him many times when I was playing in the NBA, but those meetings were not as much fun."*
> — *Walter Wesley, University of Kansas, center, 1963-66*

We returned to Lawrence to prepare for the Big Eight's annual holiday conference tournament in Kansas City. The tourney was held each year following Christmas, and fans from all over the Midwest planned their holidays around the event. All the teams stayed at the Muehlebach Hotel, just across from the Municipal Auditorium, which had been the site of the NCAA finals the previous year. We opened the tournament with a 72-55 win over Iowa State, leading us to a match-up with Kansas State.

K-State had been the league's dominant power and a Final Four participant the previous year. Tex Winter, the Wildcats' respected coach, was a close friend of mine through my association with his brother, Ernest, while I coached at Cameron College. In the biggest challenge of my inaugural season, our team responded well and we won a huge game against K-State, 54-52.

Earning respect

In the finals, we faced the Colorado Buffaloes and Coach Sox Walseth. Sox was never given enough credit for his work there, and the Buffaloes haven't reached the same level of success since he retired. With the score tied at 51 and time running out, Riney Lochmann and Fred Chana simultaneously tipped in a missed shot to give our team a victory—and the first of eight conference holiday tournament titles during my tenure, a record for that event. And while the Jayhawks hadn't been considered a championship contender at the beginning of the season, our tournament victory gained us some respect.

Facilities in the Big Eight, with the exception of KU's and Kansas State's, were not known for their quality. Our first 1964-65 conference loss was at Colorado, which had an elevated court and poor lighting—about 10 candlepower—on one end of the court. In Columbia, Missouri, Brewer Fieldhouse was another uninviting venue, with an elevated court and chicken-wire supports attached to steel poles on each end of the court.

The Armory at Iowa State was so cold that one year, on the bench, I wore my topcoat during the game. In Lincoln, Nebraska, we called the Coliseum the "bowling alley," because fans were seated so close to court that the arena appeared to be narrower than it was. I also remember well the beloved fieldhouse in Norman and Stillwater's famed Gallagher Hall, later renamed Gallagher-Iba Arena in honor of Henry Iba.

In the middle of the conference season, I learned an important lesson. We were preparing to play a televised game against the Cyclones in Lawrence on a Saturday afternoon. As a coach, I adhered to a strict curfew on nights before games. Al Lopes showed up three minutes late because he had been at the library and couldn't get a ride home (at least that was his story). We didn't play him and his absence gave Iowa State a chance to get off to a good start.

As they gained confidence, we were not able to overcome their lead and we lost a damaging home game. The lesson I learned was this: *If at all possible, punish the players without punishing the entire team.*

On the nights before road games, it was not unusual to have dinner with the host coach. I loved playing in Boulder because Coach Walseth would come over for coffee on the morning of the game while we were eating breakfast. I didn't allow the players to listen to him because he was a master of telling us how bad his team was and how he expected a rout that day. His pitch was the same every year, and he was so convincing that we were always tempted to take the bait. Of course, when the game started, the Buffaloes would play all-world.

After one Saturday afternoon game in Lawrence, I wanted to scout the Cowboys in their Saturday night game against Kansas State in Manhattan because we were headed down to Oklahoma State for a Monday night game. When I called Coach Iba and asked if he knew of any members of the media with whom I could catch a ride, he insisted that I ride to Stillwater on his team's bus after the game, and it was a ride that I will never forget.

The bus was unusually quiet. The players either slept or studied, and there was absolutely no horseplay. Coach Iba was a big fan of Western novels, so former player and loyal assistant coach Sam Aubrey read to him during the trip to Stillwater, from either a Zane Grey or Lash LaRue novel. I had this vision that someday I would be successful enough and so respected by my staff that one of them would read a novel to me. Apparently, I never reached that level.

In the hunt

Road wins were hard to come by, but we managed to win four, and with five games left, we found ourselves very much in the championship race. With a victory against OSU in Stillwater, we could move one game ahead of the Cowboys with four games remaining. Unfortunately, we lost the game in four overtimes, even with the last shot to win in regulation and in each of the first three overtimes.

Returning to Lawrence, we won three straight games against Kansas State, Nebraska and Colorado before facing the Cowboys once more with a chance to forge a tie for the conference title. Henry Iba was respected by players, coaches, administrators and officials—so much so that conference administrators had voted to admit OSU into the Big Eight Conference because of their respect. Now, at the end of the conference season, members of the media were writing about how wonderful it would be for Coach Iba to win his first-ever conference championship, and the referees, coaches and fans were caught up in the idea that Coach Iba would achieve one of his goals. Not everyone was caught up in the idea, though; I was coaching on a one-year contract and I had yet to hear anything about a renewal.

As the game started, I harbored this built-in expectation that the officials were allowing their positive sentiments toward Coach Iba to affect their judgment and, unfortunately, I started letting the thought affect me and my emotions. The Cowboys played well and led us at halftime, and then in the second half, the Cowboys delivered a classic demonstration of ball-control basketball. Without a shot clock, they attempted only 13 shots in the half, making 12 of them. We lost a heartbreaker, 64-58.

Despite finishing the season with a 17-8 record and a second-place conference finish—much higher than the preseason predictions—I walked off the Allen Fieldhouse court very disappointed that we had lost a chance to tie for the conference title. After I spoke to my players, KU athletic director Wade Stinson came into the dressing room. He told me he was proud of my work with the team and rewarded me with another one-year contract. The contract was written on a single sheet of paper, as all of my KU contracts were.

Although I was confident that we had made improvements and I had received nothing but encouragement from Wade and the chancellor, the new contract was a relief. Now I could get to work for the next season with renewed confidence that our approach was working on and off the court.

"We were a great unit. We respected each other and we had a certain harmony about us."
— *Walter Wesley, University of Kansas, center, 1963-66*

Missing out on the conference title and a berth in the NCAA tournament ranked as huge disappointments for me in my first season at the helm. However, I was convinced that our philosophy of a tough half-court defense and an offense oriented around the low post was a sound one. I also believed that our teaching methods and conditioning programs were successful in preparing the players for major competition. Looking ahead to the 1965-66 season, most of our key players were returning, while JoJo, Rodger and Bob Wilson would join the varsity team. All in all, we knew that we were close to restoring Kansas basketball to its prominence on the national stage.

"When we won, you bet he'd be wearing the same suit, blazer or jacket for the next game. Well, we won often, and yes, those suits repetitively appeared as he paced back and forth along the sideline like a caged lion."
— *Nancy Owens Wilde, daughter*

Chapter 11

1966: A Historic Year

Coach's Life Lesson: *There is small difference between "doing your best" and "doing what it takes." This small difference separates champions from others who achieve moderate success. As a coach once said to me, "Son, you are trying, but you are trying too easy."*

I once asked Jim King, who played for Bulls and Lakers and later coached at the University of Tulsa, to speak to my players. He gave this example: If your children were in the next room and that caught fire, would you try your best to get them out, or would you do whatever it takes to get them out? We have to find that extra effort inside of ourselves that makes us do whatever it takes. The real winners know the difference. You can see it in some players. They'll bring up something from within themselves, and it makes the difference. Too often, we're trying, but we're trying too easy.

On KU's campus in the fall season, one of the best views was from the football stadium looking up Campanile Hill toward the academic buildings along Jayhawk Boulevard. Of course, from a basketball player's viewpoint, the vantage point from the bottom of the hill might not have been ideal—for it was there on the stadium track, the stadium steps and Campanile Hill that preparation for the 1965-66 season began.

The Campanile runs were brutal, but the conditioning helped the team enter the season in superb condition. Weight training was a fairly new concept, too, and we didn't have a facility or a staff member to oversee such a program. (Even at the end of my KU career in 1983, the program had just two full-time assistants who were responsible for every aspect of the program: academics, conditioning, scheduling, filming, scouting and recruiting.) It's safe to say that the players didn't universally like the conditioning. Walt Wesley had some difficulty with what he called the "cross-country training." The 6'11" center wasn't a cross-country runner, and when the players would circle the stadium and then enter the track inside the stadium, sometimes we couldn't account for him. He took vanishing tablets.

"I didn't sneak out of running, but I occasionally took a different route. I didn't realize that the coaches were watching us all the time and I would sometimes take a short cut. They changed my thinking very quickly because the extra work I had to do was worse than the running we were doing."
— *Walter Wesley, University of Kansas, center, 1963-66*

As usual, we were faced with a challenging non-conference schedule, opening against Arkansas, Texas Tech and New Mexico State before tackling two Eastern powers, St. John's and Maryland, in the Sunflower Doubleheader, which was played at Manhattan one night and then at Allen Fieldhouse the next night.

To open the season, we defeated Arkansas at home with Walt, Al and Bob leading the way. Next, we played in Texas Tech's new arena, which would host the Midwest NCAA regional later in the year. We edged the Red Raiders in Lubbock, with my brother Fred and his family, who resided on the west Texas plains, in attendance. Walt's season was off to a great start with a 34-point output against Texas Tech, while Al scored 18. Against New Mexico State, seven players—Walt, Al, Ron Franz, Riney Lochmann, Fred Chana, Del Lewis and Robert Wilson—reached double figures as we broke the century mark with a 102-51 win.

We won the two Sunflower games, but not without a great deal of resistance from St. John's and Maryland. In Manhattan against St. John's, our team played a solid game with balanced scoring from Walt, Del, Riney and Ron, and we won, 61-55.

After the Sunflower games, we flew to the West Coast to take on the defending national champions, the UCLA Bruins, and the legend himself, John Wooden. Coach Wooden's teams had been very successful in pressing opponents with a full-court, 2-2-1 zone press. His players didn't try to double-team the ball, only attempted to get opponents to play at an accelerated pace—a pace that the Bruins could play much better than most. We drilled our players to be patient, emphasizing that the 10 seconds they had to get the ball across the centerline was a long time, and that we would still have plenty of time to explore every option in our press offense.

Unfortunately, the officials whistled us for several 10-second violations, causing our players to hurry. We committed several turnovers, with the pace of the game favoring UCLA, which thrived on a faster pace. At halftime, I told Ernie Filiburti, a well-respected West Coast official, that I thought my team wasn't getting a full 10-second count.

When we returned to the floor, Ernie called me aside and acknowledged that the young official working with him had erroneously started the count as soon as we took the ball out of bounds rather than when the ball touched a player in bounds. We had only been getting from seven to nine seconds, depending on how quickly we threw in the ball.

We couldn't overcome the Bruins' lead, losing our first game of the year to a fine and well-coached team. Even worse, we let the disappointment of that defeat influence our performance the next night against USC, and we lost to a strong Trojan team lead by center John Block, who years later served as my assistant.

While disappointing, the West Coast trip was a valuable teaching and learning experience. One thing we learned is that KU alumni truly love the university and its basketball program. KU alumnus Mike North, a talent agent for actors in the "Bonanza" television show, arranged for us to visit the set where we met Lorne Greene, Michael Landon, Dan Blocker and Pernell Roberts, all members of the show's "Cartwright" family.

> *"I still have the Bonanza photo on my wall at home. Hoss and Joe and all of them. It was a very exciting time, meeting them."*
> — *Walter Wesley, University of Kansas, center, 1963-66*

Dan Blocker, who played Hoss Cartwright, was extremely friendly and had us laughing with an incident that happened during the shooting of a scene. A villain was mounting his horse when Ben Cartwright (Lorne Greene) drew his gun and shot the bad guy. Then the villain (replaced with a stand-in) fell from his horse, and as the animal trotted away from the scene, it left a large bowel movement behind.

A worker rushed in to scoop up the droppings in a shovel. Hollering at him, Dan said, "Why don't you quit and get a real job?" In reply, the worker said, "What, and give up show biz?" Well, our team nearly fell over laughing.

Correcting mistakes

We returned home to correct the mistakes we had made on the road trip. One of the defensive weapons we were developing was a half-court, 1-3-1 trap deployed after made field goals, a system made more effective by our team's athletic ability. The trap had not been introduced to Midwest teams, and many were not prepared to attack it. We first tried it in our next game at Ohio State against the Bill Hosket-led Buckeyes. Our team played well, coming away with an 81-68 victory.

Now we were ready to head for Kansas City and the Big Eight holiday tournament. JoJo was to become eligible at the beginning of the semester, so he accompanied our team and practiced but didn't dress for games. The media bombarded me with questions about whether we would play him at the start of the spring semester, meaning that his career would conclude at mid-term three years into the future, or wait until the following season, giving him three full seasons. At that point, I had yet to make up my mind.

We opened a competitive tournament with victories over K-State and Iowa State. In the finals, we faced Nebraska and their energetic coach, Joe Cipriano. Joe had been a member of the 1953 Washington Huskies team that lost to the Jayhawks' famous "Mongoose" press team, 79-53, in the NCAA semifinal game, and Joe wanted to beat Kansas more than any other team. But our players had other ideas. We won, and Riney Lochmann, our co-captain, was named tournament MVP.

> **Coaching Lesson:** *Defensive anticipation*
> *Phog Allen's defensive press was called the "Mongoose" because of a film that Coach Allen would show his teams before most seasons. The film depicted a battle between the mongoose and the cobra. The cobra would coil and strike at the mongoose, but the mongoose would anticipate the strikes and move quickly to avoid them. Doc's lesson was that a team should play defense as the mongoose does against the snake: anticipate an opponent's movements and react to avoid them and constantly look for your opportunities to strike.*

The conference gauntlet

Since the only way to qualify for the NCAA tournament was to win the Big Eight regular-season championship, our season truly began with the first road game. Beating Colorado, 69-55, was a tremendous start to the conference race.

We followed the road win at Colorado with blowout wins at home against Iowa State and Oklahoma. Walt was becoming a highly effective low-post scorer and led the way with 39- and 27-point performances. We then journeyed to Ames, Iowa, to play the dangerous Cyclones in an Armory packed with 7,000 fans. Because there was no shot clock, the Cyclones possessed the ball for long periods of time and held a 30-26 lead at halftime. They collapsed around Walt, who had burned them in previous games, and the tactic was even more effective because we couldn't throw it into the ocean from the perimeter. In the second half, though, our team responded. An Al Lopes-led surge caught the Cyclones at the end and we won a thriller, 49-47.

Next up was a visit to Lincoln and the Coliseum for a game that we knew had great significance in the outcome of the conference race. Just before the half, in an emotional and competitive game, Ron and Al picked up their third fouls. While they were on the bench, Nebraska's pressure suddenly forced a turnover and a basket for the Huskers. With only a minute before halftime, I didn't want to use a timeout. I hoped that we could avoid another turnover and regroup in the dressing room. In the '60s and '70s, a coach's management of timeouts was especially critical, because there were no media timeouts. However, not calling a timeout proved to be a tactical error on my part, as Nebraska scored two more baskets off of turnovers and we went to the locker room trailing by 10 points. A 10-point deficit—on the road against a solid team, before the introduction of the three-point shot—is a lot for a team to overcome.

> **Coaching Lesson:** *Avoid panic*
> *In allowing Nebraska to score two baskets off turnovers in the half's final minute, I had violated a basic principle of basketball coaching: When the team loses the ball against pressure in a road game, immediately call a timeout before one error leads to another and panic sets in. I should've called a timeout and reinserted either Ron or Al, the key ball-handlers.*

Although we fought valiantly to get back into the game, Nebraska was too much and we lost a tough game, 83-75. Even so, I was proud of the team's second-half effort and I came away feeling good about our chances of improving in the second semester. I will never forget seeing co-captain Delvy Lewis afterward, so totally exhausted that he was lying on the floor, his uniform soaked with perspiration. I knew then that we had a team with pride.

The team responded well to the defeat at Nebraska and committed to improving its defensive intensity and execution against full-court pressure as we approached games against Kansas State and Missouri. Kansas State's Tex Winter had recruited Nick Pino, a seven-footer from New Mexico, and wrapped the "triple-post offense," also known as the triangle offense, around the giant. But the Wildcats had trouble handling Walt, who led us to a hard-fought home win with 26 points.

To Jo or not to Jo

After a win over Missouri in Columbia, it was time to make a decision about JoJo. We were a very good team without him, but his presence on the team would give us a chance to be even more special and make a run at the conference and national championships. I went to my co-captain, Riney, a starter and team leader, and explained the situation. I told Riney that if Jo joined the team, someone would lose a starting job—and that it might be him.

> *"I didn't even think about [losing my starting job to JoJo]. I also put myself in Coach Owens' shoes and thought about what I would*

do if I were him. I would have made the same decision. Winning was more important to me than starting. In fact, if JoJo would have been with us all year, I really feel that we would have been undefeated going into the Texas Western game. We were a good team without him but a great team with him."
> *— Riney Lochmann, University of Kansas, forward, 1963-66*

In response, Riney said he felt that Jo could help us compete for a national championship and that it wasn't a big deal to him whether he started or came off the bench. Meanwhile, JoJo had already told me his preference was to play right away. So, armed with Riney's unselfish act and Jo's desire, we activated Jo for the spring semester.

"I remember every last one of [the practices] like it was yesterday. I just wanted to play. I was doing very well in practice. I was playing the point and that gave me even more incentive."
> *— JoJo White, University of Kansas, guard, 1966-69*

"There were no ripples [when JoJo started playing], no repercussions. We were prepared. We wanted to win the national championship and anything that would help us, we were grateful for. We were a very close unit and we saw JoJo as an asset, not a liability. We all needed to sacrifice to do this and we realized we had to share the wealth. JoJo brought speed and quickness to the team. ... I guess it was a tough decision, though. We were not losing—we had only one [conference] loss when JoJo came aboard."
> *—Walter Wesley, University of Kansas, center, 1963-66*

Our next game was against Coach Iba's Cowboys, and they were never an easy opponent. When I talked to the team before the game, I purposely did not mention Jo's name or that it was his first outing. I was apprehensive about starting Jo in his first game as a varsity player, even though he had clearly won the starting job in practice, and I tried not to show my emotions. As the team left the dressing room, the last player to come by me was JoJo, who slapped me on the leg and said, "I'm all right, Coach, don't worry." Could my emotions have been that obvious?

"I wanted to play—absolutely I wanted to play. I was ready. It was a smooth transition. I loved Coach Owens because he knew how to handle young men like myself, by sitting down with the players to discuss issues that were going to affect the team."
> *— JoJo White, University of Kansas, guard, 1966-69*

But Jo quickly proved that he was "all right." When we secured the opening tip, he went down the court, picked up his dribble and took a mid-range jump shot that sailed right through the net. What a start! Even better, we controlled the game from the beginning, which was critical against Coach Iba, whose teams were masterful at ball control and shot selection when they had the lead. When the game ended in a 59-38 victory, it was obvious that our team could be special, and much more versatile, with the addition of JoJo.

The team now had all the ingredients to contend for a national title with Jo and Delvy in the backcourt, Al the swingman and forwards Ron, Riney and Bob Wilson. Rodger, our backup center, was also starting to blossom, giving relief to Walt.

After demolishing Missouri, 98-54, with 11 Jayhawks scoring, we made the annual weekend swing through my home state, coming away with victories over the Sooners and Cowboys. We swept both games handily and really started playing as a cohesive unit. The team was starting to execute effectively and their half-court trap was disrupting opponents. The trap resulted in a number of steals at half-court, which led to high-percentage shots.

The road trip was even sweeter because I was able to return home to Oklahoma, which was always special for me. I had great respect for Henry Iba, and the trip to Norman gave me a chance to visit with Bruce and Myrtle Drake, the beloved coach and first lady of OU basketball. I always knew where they sat, but I also knew that they couldn't pull against their Sooners.

Myrtle, better known to the OU players as Momma Drake, was an astute student of the game. Even during my tenure at the University of Kansas, I would receive postcards from her with encouragement and Bible verses. She always ended her remarks by saying, "Teddy, you need to work on those free throws more." Interestingly, as I reflect on the losses that I incurred, I find that they were often the result of poor free-throw shooting.

On a roll

After the swing through Oklahoma, we returned home with four days to prepare for the No. 10 Cornhuskers, our chief rival for the conference championship. Nebraska's press tried to force an opponent to catch the ball in the corners of the backcourt, where their traps were more effective. To counter the press, we decided to put JoJo down the court and throw over their first line of defense. Even when we threw to the corners, it was to bait the defenders toward the trap, and we would throw the ball over the top to Jo, who would penetrate quickly, either shooting or passing to the open man. It worked perfectly.

Prior to the Nebraska game, I had begun to receive calls from NBA coaches and general managers wanting to know all about Walt, and I had only positive things to say about his character, ability and interaction with teammates and coaches. Ever since the day I met him in Ft. Myers, Florida, Walt has had a special place in my heart. His modesty and sincerity had made him especially popular with his teammates. The way they responded to him after his 40-point games against Loyola and St. John's with standing ovations as he entered the dressing room is something that I hadn't seen until then—and haven't seen since—in an athletic locker room.

On the night of the Nebraska game, the stands were packed. A large media contingent was on hand, along with a sizeable number of NBA scouts and executives. I was really hoping for a great night for Walt and our seniors. Unfortunately, Walt picked up three fouls in the first half and I had to go with Rodger, our sophomore reserve. Fortunately, Roger was on top of his game and scored 17 points in the first half. With our press-breaker working to perfection, we were scoring at will.

Late in the game, when I inserted Walter so that the pro scouts could see him play, Coach Cipriano thought I was running up the score but that wasn't the case at all. I simply owed it to Walt to give him a chance to demonstrate his talents for all the scouts. We ended up with a 110-73 victory over an outstanding Nebraska team, and in retrospect, I consider it to be the greatest game played in Allen Fieldhouse during my time as head coach. For a number of years the 110-point tally was a record for the arena.

The Nebraska victory aside, we still had some work to do to nail down the conference championship. We went to Kansas State and beat the Wildcats by 13 points, 68-55, which proved to be our closest margin of victory in the second semester.

> *"We dreaded the Kansas State week. We would always hope to play them on a Wednesday after having a game on Monday because Coach Owens and Coach Miranda went crazy in K-State week. Excuse my expression, but K-State week was hell ... extra running, extra shooting, extra yelling. You had to beat K-State."*
> — *Walter Wesley, University of Kansas, center, 1963-66*

After K-State, a victory at home against Colorado was all that stood in the way of Kansas' first outright conference championship since Wilt's 1957 team of NCAA finalists. (The 1960-61 team had tied K-State for the championship and then advanced to the NCAA tourney with a win in a playoff at Manhattan.)

In 1954, I played in the National Industrial Basketball League with Houston's ADA Oilers.

The farmhouse in southwest Oklahoma where I was born and raised was captured in a painting by Mary Zoe Owens, the wife of my late brother, Fred.

In 1958, I led the Cameron College baseball team to one of the most unlikely national championships in the history of the game. (Left to right, standing) Trainer Bub Smith, Tony Owings, Don Hendricks, James Ray, Dexter Rolette, Homer Watkins, Pat O'Dell, Sid Griffin, Ted Hankey, and Fat Sinclair; and (kneeling) Wayne Tedder, Jackie Martin, Toby Tillman, Jim Marr, Terry Byrd, Bill Short, Earl Tankersley, Don Goza and me.

A collage of my days at Cameron College, from 1956-60, presented to me by the university when an endowed lectureship was established in my honor in 2006.

Bud Stallworth (center), with me on his right side, was swarmed by fans after scoring 50 points against Missouri in 1972.

In 1967, Dr. Phog Allen (left) awarded the MVP trophy, named after him, to JoJo White (center) and Ron Franz (middle center).

In front of a portrait of Dr. James Naismith, KU's first coach, I held the game ball from the university's 1,000th win in 1979.

Photo courtesy of Lawrence Journal-World

After the team gave me a celebratory shower, I continued celebrating my first conference championship in 1966 with (from left) Riney Lochmann, Walt Wesley, assistant coach Sam Miranda, Al Lopes, John Carter and Bob Wilson. I consider the victory to be one of the finest moments in my coaching career.

Artist John Martin captured Dave Robisch (left) and Roger Brown (right) celebrating the team's 21st consecutive win—and the 1971 NCAA regional championship in Wichita.

Photo courtesy of Lawrence Journal-World

When my 1974 team earned the NCAA regional championship in Tulsa, there was cause for celebration: Going 8-18 in the previous season, the team had rebounded in fine fashion, earning a trip to the Final Four. (From left) Tommy Smith, Dale Greenlee, Danny Knight, Tom Kivisto, Norm Cook, Roger Morningstar, Rick Suttle and Paul Werner.

At the Final Four in San Antonio, my son, Teddy, and I visited with John Wooden. Toward the end of Wooden's unparalleled career at UCLA, Wooden and I had established a strong-enough friendship that we exchanged notes at the beginning of each season.

134

The McCarthy golfing group at Muirfield in Scotland (left to right): Greg Duvall, Jay Boddicker, me, Jay Hepler, Grant Donovan, Greg Gurley, Brian Wilkinson, Steve Brown, Teal Dakan, Bill Self, Kent McCarthy and Brad Shoup.

When my daughter, Taylor, married Nick O'Connell, the event was truly a family affair as my players from over the years—my basketball family—joined the Owens clan. (From left) Al Lopes, Gerald Hertzler, Joey Graham, me, Walt Wesley, Stephen Graham, David Magley and Tommy Smith celebrated the wedding.

Photo courtesy Michael Dickson/Rich Clarkson and Associates LLC

In 1966 against Texas Western in the Midwest regional final, JoJo White hit this potential game-winner at the end of the first overtime, only to have the referee say his back foot was out of bounds—even if the shadowing makes it appear that his heel might have hovered over the line without touching it. My Jayhawks couldn't recover and lost the game in the second overtime. At their 40th anniversary, the Texas Western players—who went on to win a national title over the University of Kentucky—said that our KU team was the best they had faced.

Artist Ted Watts captured me with my Kansas All-Americans: Walt Wesley, Darnell Valentine, JoJo White, Bud Stallworth and Dave Robisch.

In my early days at Kansas when sideburns were popular.

I recently shared a few words with my friend John Calipari, the University of Kentucky head coach who was a voluntary assistant for me at Kansas in the 1982-83 season.

Photo courtesy of the KU Alumni Association

When his jersey was retired in Allen Fieldhouse, Walt Wesley had some kind words for me in front of the crowd.

In front of the 18th green and the Royal and Ancient Golf Club at St. Andrew's in Scotland, I was joined by friends (from left) Kent McCarthy, Jay Hepler, Brad Shoup and Brian Wilkinson. On this green, I honored my late brother, Fred—who loved golf—by using his putter to finish the round. Telling my friends what I was doing, I couldn't hold back the tears.

Here I am on the eighteenth green at St. Andrews with my brother Fred's putter and the Royal and Ancient Club in the background.

I married Michelle Mazikowski Nelson in 1979.

On the Hollis, Okla., farm on which I was raised, I showed my son Teddy how to pull cotton.

My beloved parents, Homer and Annie Owens, on their 60th wedding anniversary.

Photo courtesy Julie McAlester

The Owens boys—(from left) Charlie, Arthur, me, Layton, Teddy and Nick—over the Christmas holidays in 2011.

Photo courtesy Julie McAlester

The Owens girls—(from left) Nancy, Kelly, Michelle, Taylor and Ashley—over the Christmas holidays in 2011.

My most prized picture is of my entire family. (First row, from left) me and Michelle; daughter-in-law Ashley, grandson Layton, and son Teddy; (second row, from left) daughter Nancy and her husband, Charlie; and daughter Kelly; and (third row, from left) daughter Taylor and her husband, Nick; and grandson Arthur (Nancy's son).

In a painting by John Martin, I'm shown in my Kansas coaching gear.

Our team was really on a roll. All five starters scored in double-figures in a 85-65 defeat of Colorado, and we won the conference title outright. In the seven games following Jo Jo's arrival, this powerful team had averaged a margin of victory of more than 26 points per game. In the celebration following the game, the players threw their coaches into the showers. It was truly a wonderful moment to see those fine young men, especially the seniors, rewarded for all of their efforts, from sprints up the Campanile Hill to a conference title and an NCAA tournament berth.

Texas Western and our place in history

In the '60s, the tournament seeding system was far different. Teams were assigned to their geographic areas, in the Midwest, the West, the South and the East, and the best teams in each region had to play in those areas. At the end of the 1965-66 season, we were sent to Lubbock, Texas, to play against Southern Methodist University, the champions of the Southwest Conference, with the winning team to play Cincinnati or Texas Western.

The winner of the Midwest regional would advance to the Final Four to play the West regional winner at Maryland's Cole Fieldhouse. It was an exciting time for our Kansas players, who hadn't played in the NCAA tournament before, and for the same reason, it was just as exciting for the coaches.

SMU coach Doc Hayes had done a tremendous job at his school, and they were no strangers to the tournament. They didn't back down and fought us to the end, but we came away with a 76-70 victory and found ourselves one game away from the Final Four.

The Cincinnati program, under Coach Tay Baker, had recent experience in NCAA play. Texas Western, on the other hand, was a newcomer to NCAA play, coached by an Oklahoman named Don Haskins.

I had known Don when he played for Coach Iba at Oklahoma A&M. I was OU's freshman coach in 1951-52 when Coach Drake sent me to Stillwater to scout the Aggies. When the Aggies won the tip and advanced the ball to Don, the shooter from Enid, Oklahoma, he let a shot fly from quite a distance out on the court. Now, it was unheard for an Aggie to shoot without passing the ball several times, especially on the initial possession. I looked over at the A&M bench and Coach Iba had already jerked the warm-up off of a substitute to get Don out of the game. To those who knew Iba's disciplinary methods, it was no surprise that Don didn't return to the game.

Now here Don was, years later, coaching a Cinderella team that he had put together in a short period of time. As Don's team beat Cincinnati, I was quite impressed with the Texas Western guards, Bobby Joe Hill, Arsten Artis and Willie Cager, and big guys David Lattin, Neville Shedd and Harry

Fluernoy. We knew that we were in for a battle.

The Midwest regional final could have been a national championship game. I believe the two best teams in the country played that day. Years later at their 40th anniversary, the Texas Western players said that KU was the best team that they had faced. In a tight game, we gained a slight edge in the second half but lost the lead and ended regulation tied. In the first overtime, when Texas Western jumped out to a six-point lead, we went to our half-court trap, resulting in two steals for JoJo, who converted lay-ups and free throws to forge another tie. We entered the last minute with Texas Western holding the ball for the last shot.

When Al Lopes, our senior forward, forced a charge, we gained possession. With seven seconds remaining in overtime, we prepared to inbound the ball from the sidelines, just a bit into the backcourt. Although we had developed plays to run in just such a situation, we decided to get the ball to JoJo and put everyone along the baseline, letting him penetrate and, if they doubled him, to step into the open spot for a shot.

Jo caught the ball in bounds and started to penetrate, but he was driven to the left sideline by an aggressive defense. With time running out, he pivoted quickly and shot the ball beyond what is now the three-point line. He nailed it, and we stormed the court to celebrate the victory ... but an official, Rudy Marich, had been trailing the play. He blew his whistle and said that Jo had stepped out of bounds, so the game had to go into a second overtime.

"There are certain stories that I do not bring up because I do not want to take years off of my dad's life. One of them is the loss to Texas Western, where JoJo White hit the game-winning shot and the official called it no good. Official Rudy Marich prevented one of the greatest Kansas teams from playing for the NCAA national championship. He is like a shunned family member."

— Teddy Owens, son

I reunited with former KU captains (from left) Riney Lochmann, David Magley and Delvy Lewis when I was inducted into the Kansas Sports Hall of Fame in 2009.

After that, it was difficult to settle the team down. We thought we had just won. We lost in the second overtime, 81-80. For many years KU fans believed—and probably still believe—that Jo didn't step out of bounds. From the bench on the other side of the court, it was difficult for us to tell. With all of the camera angles that we have today, the ruling would have been much more obvious. Viewing the sequence of photographs, though, it appears that Jo may have pivoted his foot over the line without letting his heel touch down. The photographs also indicate that the official, with his eyes on the flight of the ball, couldn't have seen the positioning of Jo's foot when he jumped for the shot.

> *"It is one of the memories that I try to erase but it keeps popping up every year. It is a catch-22 because it is a fond memory, but it is not a fond memory."*
> — *Walter Wesley, University of Kansas, center, 1963-66*

> *"I have no regrets about the way things turned out ... except losing the double-overtime game to Texas Western, which still hurts to this day."*
> — *Riney Lochmann, University of Kansas, forward, 1963-66*

> *"I didn't personally get into that. My job was to do what we had to do on the floor. After you do your job, it is all you can do. Everything else was someone's opinion. There is nothing you can do about it. I did what was asked of me and enjoyed every minute of it. Just someone else's opinion, that's all. The officials aren't going to change their minds. Play through it and keep on going. We absolutely should have been playing Kentucky [in Texas Western's place]. But I try not to talk about any of that because it was out of our hands."*
> — *JoJo White, University of Kansas, guard, 1966-69*

No one will ever know for sure whether his foot hit the line or not, but it confirms a simple message: There is a small margin between failure and success, and that margin makes a huge difference in people's lives. Texas Western went on to the national finals and won the championship over an all-white University of Kentucky team. Texas Western made history when they started five black players in the championship game (they started four against us). The 2006 movie, "Glory Road," tells the story of the Texas Western team, with some added Hollywood flair and some inaccuracies.

In the film, Don Haskins was credited with pioneering the opportunity for black players in college basketball. What is factual, however, is that in 1960 the Jayhawks were already starting four black players, and even in that historic 1966 game, we started three black players. Don himself, in his book, "Glory Road," wrote that he never intended to be a pioneer in the

147

civil rights movement—he just wanted to find the best players and build a winning program. After all, that goal is how it always should have been for any program.

That team could have, and I believe would have, won the national championship in Maryland, as Texas Western did. If they had, they could very well have been judged as KU's greatest team. But as Coach Wooden always told me, there is a great difference in "should have and could have and would have." What a difference a small margin makes.

What I do know for sure is that Don Haskins did an incredible job of assembling a championship team in such a short period of time. I also know that the performance of the 1965-66 Kansas team brought honor to the university and restored the program to national prominence. Those players were a credit to the university and they still hold a warm spot in my heart after all these years. I am honored to have played a part on that team, alongside Coaches Sam Miranda and Bob Mulcahy and trainer Dean Nesmith.

In the NBA draft, Walt Wesley was taken with the sixth pick by the Cincinnati Royals and became teammates with Oscar Robertson and Jerry Lucas. He was later traded to Cleveland. Al was drafted by the Baltimore Bullets and, after a brief professional career, he finished his law degree and is now an attorney in Lawrence. Fred Chana had a successful engineering career with McDonnell Douglas, while Riney, after a short career in the American Basketball Association, became the head of promotions for the Converse Rubber Company. Delvy was the envy of all of them when he married Karen, his college sweetheart and KU pom-pom leader.

> *"The transition to the NBA was a learning experience. The entire game was a bit different; the coaching was different. I was a young and my first feelings were like a boy in a candy store, but you quickly learned that it is a business and you had better get on your horse to succeed and stay in the league."*
> — *Walter Wesley, University of Kansas, center, 1963-66*

Ron, Bob, JoJo and Rodger played significant roles in the success of 1965-66, and they gave us hope for the future. Reserves Pat Davis, Ralph Light, John Carter, Ron Lang, Bo Harris and George Yarnevich provided consistent excellence in practice and prepared the team well for games.

While I never liked to pick my favorite team or favorite player because they are all special to me, I think any coach will agree that his first championship team will hold an important place in his heart and mind for the rest of his life.

148

Chapter 12

Back-to-Back Titles

Coach's Life Lesson: *It is important to play each game with passion and energy. While it is important to compete with heart, the team that plays with their heads will ultimately succeed.*

When I started at Kansas, Kansas State was the team to beat. Tex Winter and his teams would always have Ahearn Fieldhouse rocking. As an assistant, I'd watch both teams in the first 10 or 15 minutes try to force plays on both ends of the court and jam it down the other team's throats. What I passed on to our players is that in an emotional game, their heads would win the game. I'd tell them they could play like Leon Spinks or Muhammad Ali. Spinks would duck his head down and plow in, swinging as many times as he could. Ali would move, move, and more some more, and then strike. Float like a butterfly, sting like a bee. I wanted my players to play with the passion of Spinks and the savvy of Ali. Coach Winter called this attitude the "happy warrior" philosophy: play with the passion of a warrior, but be at peace with yourself at the same time. That's what he always wanted his players to do.

On Mount Oread on KU's campus there is a recurring theme each fall: spectacular beauty. The fall of 1966-67, as the leaves changed colors in October, was no exception. Meanwhile, we prepared for another basketball season.

With the loss of All-American Walt Wesley, Al Lopes, Delvy Lewis, Riney Lochmann and Fred Chana, we faced a challenge with a young team. Although we returned starters JoJo White and Ron Franz and reserves Rodger Bohnenstiehl, Pat Davis, Bob Wilson and George Yarnecich, we would have to rely on a solid core of young sophomores to fill in the gaps: Vernon Vanoy, a 6'7" athlete from Kansas City, Missouri; Bruce Sloan, a 6'5" swingman from Kansas City, Missouri; Howard Arndt, a 6'7" forward from Republic, Missouri; and Phil Harmon, a shooting guard who played at Tulsa Central High School under Eddie Sutton, who later became a renowned college coach. Other promising sophomores included Jaye

Ediger, Rich Thomas and Ron Lang. With such a young and inexperienced team, we had an enormous task in front of us if we hoped to continue the road back to national prominence.

Our schedule included the usual tough non-conference slate, the conference holiday tournament in December and the always-tough Big Eight regular season race. Because we knew we were hosting the NCAA regional in Allen Fieldhouse, we set our season goal: the chance to play at home to advance to the Final Four.

Opening the season against the Arkansas Razorbacks in Fayetteville, Rodger and Ron led us with 25 and 18 points, respectively, toward a 73-57 victory. JoJo's effect on a game could never be measured by scoring, because he could dominate a game through his defensive pressure on the opposing point guard and through his ability to initiate the offense with passing and penetration. As with most great leaders, Jo led by example. He didn't have much to say, but when he did speak, the words were meaningful.

Our first home game was a blowout of Xavier, 100-52. We were off to an impressive start, but the schedule would get tougher with the Ohio State Buckeyes coming to Lawrence. Fortunately, one of our defensive weapons, the 1-3-1 half-court trap, had become considerably more effective with JoJo at the point of the press. His athleticism and defensive instincts allowed him to disrupt most opponents.

Although Ohio State shot more than 60 percent from the field, we forged a big halftime lead by forcing 19 turnovers, most of which resulted in lay-ups at the other end, and won, 94-70. JoJo led the way with 23 points and numerous steals, while Ron scored 19, Rodger scored 15 and Phil added 10.

Texas Western rematch

After a string of victories over Florida State, Baylor and the University of the Pacific, we hit the road for Chicago—and a match-up against Texas Western, the defending NCAA champions. In preparation, JoJo spent hours and hours studying film of our previous encounter with the Miners, in which Bobby Joe Hill had played extremely well. Jo, an intense competitor, was determined that Hill would not dominate again. Still, Texas Western had returned many of the previous year's outstanding players, and we knew we were in for an epic battle. JoJo was tremendous, scoring 19 points and holding Bobby Joe to just two points, but the experience of the Miners held up and we lost again, 71-67.

Coaches and mentors will advise that one mistake can't affect a team in such a way that the players follow it with another letdown, but that is exactly what we allowed. Disappointment over the loss in Chicago impacted our next game, versus St. John's in New York City, and we lost, 68-44, in the only game that season in which we played poorly. I felt that I failed the team by not helping them respond to the Texas Western game in a more positive manner. Players will often react in the same manner as their coach, and I think that I let disappointment linger for too long in my own thoughts.

Fortunately, we had nine days before the Big Eight tournament in Kansas City, giving us time to make some changes and rebuild the young team's confidence. (Remember, we had only one senior, Ron Franz, on the roster.) The time obviously was well spent because we entered the tournament with renewed confidence and improved execution.

Our rotation of substitution was in place, with JoJo paired with either Phil or Bruce in the backcourt and Ron joined by Rodger, Vernon, Bob and Howard up front. As a coach, I was never one to rotate 10 players in competitive games, feeling that an eight-player rotation provided better continuity. Any player of mine knew that he had to make the top eight in order to get substantial playing time and be on the floor in critical situations.

The team responded well to the Buffaloes' competitiveness, with seven players scoring in our win, and then we dispatched a solid Sooners team, 86-73, with nine players scoring. Now the young team had an opportunity to win the conference tournament for the third straight year. The Cyclones, led by Don Smith, proved to be a worthy opponent, opening with a zone defense in an attempt to shut off our potent inside game, but outside shooting allowed us to pull away for a 63-57 victory. It was a sweet moment for senior Ron Franz, whose teams were undefeated in the conference tournament in his hometown during his career.

Always recruiting

While we made progress with the current team, the coaching staff was also spending time on the road, visiting prospects and building for the future. Because there wasn't an early signing period for recruits, a coach had to stay in contact with recruits throughout the year. We made a number of trips to Kansas City to see Pierre Russell, a 6'4"athlete who played for Walt Shublom's tradition-rich Wyandotte Bulldogs. We also had made some inroads into the Chicago public schools the year before, already picking up Richard Bradshaw, Marshall High's outstanding 6'3" guard, and now we were focused on Roger Brown, 6'10" center. Lastly, one of the most sought-after big men in the country was Dave Robisch, a prolific scorer from Springfield, Illinois.

Coach Miranda and I had visited the Robisch family in the summer and Dave had come to visit campus during football season. Hosted by another Illinois freshman, Chester Lawrence, Dave enjoyed meeting the team and we felt that Kansas was very much in the picture when it came time for him to make a decision.

I visited the Robisch family early in the conference season. Dave's dad, a former engineer in Cincinnati, had decided to enter the Lutheran ministry at the age of 55 and the family moved to Springfield, Illinois. Reverend Robisch was a straightforward man who didn't care much for recruiting, only wanting Dave to get a good education and play in a solid basketball program. He didn't have time for any "smoke-blowing." After a short visit, the reverend handed me my hat and coat, saying that it was his son's bedtime and it was time for me to go. Although I felt the visit had gone well, I wondered if I had said something to upset the family, and the trip home was filled with doubts.

> *"I wanted to be part of a great basketball tradition, and I also wanted to play baseball in college. There were lots of schools interested, like Michigan and Kentucky and Illinois. Because of baseball, I considered Southern California, Arizona State, Cincinnati and Kansas. It came down to where I would be happy, which school had a great tradition, and where I could play basketball and baseball. A big player in the decision was Coach Miranda, the KU assistant, who was raised in Illinois and had lots of contacts there. ... I visited KU and stayed at the Sigma Nu fraternity house. I enjoyed the football game and the meetings with the players and coaches a great deal. I fell in love with KU right then. It was a beautiful campus, a really special place. The decision, at least for me, was pretty easy."*
> — *Dave Robisch, University of Kansas, forward, 1968-71*

Defending the conference crown

We returned to Lawrence to prepare to defend our conference championship in an opening game at Allen Fieldhouse against the Sooners. I was concerned because Rodger, our leading scorer, was out with an injury. But the Sooners couldn't match the balanced scoring of Jayhawks, with all five starters in double figures, and our conference championship aspirations got off to a good start.

We then traveled to Brewer Fieldhouse in Columbia. Five on our roster were Missouri natives, so the game meant a lot to them—and anyway, any Kansas-Missouri contest is a big event. In a solid team performance, the four veterans led the scoring while Ron and Bob added nine rebounds each. Figuring that each possession of the ball is worth approximately one point, a player who captures rebounds, picks up loose balls and forces turnovers can add significantly to a team's chance of success. Missouri competed hard but we came away with a 70-60 win.

We headed to Boulder next for the usual struggle against the Buffaloes. The arena was poorly lighted and had an elevated floor, and beyond that, I never quite solved the altitude problem. We would try to run the players quite a bit the night before the game to become accustomed to the change in altitude, but there was no avoiding the wall the players would hit after a few times up and down the court. If they pushed through it, though, the effect was not as pronounced.

Despite a great effort in the second half, we lost to Colorado, a loss that proved to be our first and last conference loss of the season. And we didn't have much time to lick our wounds because Iowa State and Don Smith were coming to Allen Fieldhouse.

Don couldn't be contained and scored 30 points, but the Jayhawks' balance was too much for Iowa State, and we won, 73-65. Sophomore center Vernon Vanoy was becoming a factor on defense with his shot-blocking and rebounding. He was also becoming a crowd favorite, thanks to his dunking exhibitions in warm-ups, a practice permitted under the rules at that time. At 6'8" and about 260 pounds without an ounce of fat, he would also display his jumping prowess when defending against the inbounds pass. The passer would try to find a way around all of Vernon's moving arms and legs to throw the ball in, and it was quite a sight to see.

In a unique bit of scheduling, our very next game was against the Cyclones in Ames, and we came away with another win. However, we returned home to learn that Bob Wilson was an academic casualty and we would not have his services the rest of the year, so a real burden fell onto the team's younger players.

Joe Cipriano brought his capable Nebraska team to Lawrence on February 7, and we knew we had to be prepared to handle their full-court defensive pressure. A packed house was expecting a competitive game, and what they witnessed was the Jayhawks' best outing of the year. Utilizing JoJo's ball-handling and passing skills, we broke their pressure defense early and balanced scoring from our upperclassmen and youngsters led to a 84-58 victory. It was becoming more and more obvious that we had a good Kansas team.

Our next hurdle was in Manhattan's Ahearn Fieldhouse, one of the toughest and loudest arenas in the country. As a player at OU, I recall watching them open the fieldhouse doors so that students could make a run for the choice seats near the court, and it was like a stampede. With my players, I would always talk about the emotion and natural rivalry of the KU-KSU game—that both teams would play with their hearts, but the team that plays with their heads would prevail.

The first half was so intense and emotional that Wildcat center Joe Smith fielded a jump ball and then scored a bucket on our basket. I was glad that he did, because we were having a ton of trouble getting shots to fall on our own and we trailed 36-33 at halftime. In the second half, our man-to-man defensive pressure changed the game and we earned a 60-55 victory.

Two nights later we hosted the Cowboys in Lawrence. The game in Manhattan had been so emotional that I worried about the team's mental sharpness, and it was so vital to control the game early against Coach Iba's disciplined teams. Fortunately, we got off to an early lead and controlled the game throughout, winning 52-39. JoJo had only four points, but as usual, his presence on both ends of the court controlled the game.

Heading south, our next game was against my alma mater, OU. Bob Stevens' team could really put points on the board. I loved playing in the old fieldhouse where I had spent some of the most memorable times of my life. Joe Holladay, Roy Williams's longtime assistant at KU and the University of North Carolina, was on the OU team. OU played an excellent first half and led, 44-40, at the intermission, but our defensive intensity took over in the second half and we won, 82-74.

The next morning, we bused over to Stillwater for another tough contest against the Cowboys. Gallagher Hall brought back a lot of memories, most of them bad, because of the losses I suffered there as a player and coach. Memories of trailing the Aggies (the name of their mascot when the school was named Oklahoma A&M) and those ringing cowbells were not very pleasant. Although the conference finally outlawed the playing of musical instruments during games, those cowbells used to be a force to be reckoned with.

We were tied with the Cowboys, 28-28, at halftime. Most coaches will say the first five minutes of the second half are critical, and it was especially true against a team coached by Henry Iba. Thanks to JoJo's 22 points, we came away with a 10-point victory. And JoJo must have impressed Coach Iba because when the legend became the U.S. Olympic coach the following year, he picked Jo as a member of the team.

Notching road wins

After throttling the Tigers, 90-55, back in Lawrence, we had several days to prepare for the Cornhuskers in Lincoln. The bus ride from Lawrence to Lincoln in the dead of winter was never one of my favorite trips. With no greenery and a scattering of snow, the scenery on the drive was a downer, a feeling compounded by having to play in the "bowling alley," as some coaches called it. Vendors would walk in front of the bench during the game, asking us to pass food or drinks to the fans behind us, and it wasn't uncommon for a visiting player to have his leg hair yanked while inbounding the ball from the sidelines.

I knew that "Slippery Joe," the Huskers' competitive coach, would have his team ready to play, especially after the blowout we had dealt them in Lawrence. We led by just three points, 26-23, at the half, and the teams' dressing rooms were so close together that we could hear Joe going on a tear. As we prepared to take the court in the second half, we were hidden from the crowd, so Bob Foster, the KU band director, had his musicians begin playing a famous Huskers song, "There is no place like Nebraska." So the Nebraska fans stood and cheered as we took the court, at which point Bob immediately switched to the Jayhawk fight song. I was caught off guard by Bob's ingenuity, and I was certainly impressed. I've often said that our teams were excellent some of the time, but Bob's band was excellent all the time.

On the floor, our balance with all five starters in double figures gave us the edge. After a 64-57 win, that bus ride back down to Lawrence didn't seem so dreary.

Back in Lawrence, we prepared to avenge our only conference loss of the year, hosting the Buffaloes. While we didn't have an answer to Pat Frink, who scored 27, our overall play on both ends of the court led to a 66-59 win. Then in the last regular season home game, we faced Tex Winter and his Wildcats. Despite the close game we had played in Manhattan, we opened the home contest with a strong run and led at the half, 38-20. Our man-to-man defense was proving effective against Tex's triple-post offense, also known as the triangle offense, a system for which he gained deserved fame in later years with the Chicago Bulls and L.A. Lakers.

In an 18-point victory over the Wildcats, I was able to play 11 players—and it's always a great feeling for a coach to be able to send in the reserves against an archrival. Even better, we celebrated a second consecutive Big Eight championship, the first back-to-back titles since the great Kansas teams of 1951-52 and 1952-53.

Hosting in the postseason

Entering the 1966-67 season, our goal had been to win the conference championship in order to qualify for the NCAA tourney, with the regional being hosted at Allen Fieldhouse. We were right where we wanted to be. Regional participants included No. 2-ranked Louisville, led by Wesley Unseld and Butch Beard; our Jayhawks, ranked No. 3; Houston, ranked No. 6 with future NBA stars Elvin Hayes and Don Chaney; and Southern Methodist, the Southwest Conference champions. The stage was set for a great weekend of college basketball.

In the opening game in front of packed house, the Mustangs upset the powerful Louisville team. As we waited to take the court against Houston, I remember a feeling of relief going through the crowd and our dressing room, knowing that the Cardinals had been eliminated. A coach, though, wants his team to stay focused on the task at hand and I was afraid we would allow the arena's celebration over the upset negatively affect our concentration.

Because of the distraction or because of Houston's athletic ability in their 1-3-1 zone, we didn't get off to a good start. Coach Guy Lewis ran a spread-out gap zone with Don Chaney at the point, and the tactic slowed the rotation of the ball. It takes an unusually gifted athlete to play the zone's point position, and Chaney did it well.

Against most 1-3-1 zones, the key is to rotate the ball quickly and make the defense's baseline chaser cover both corners. In Guy's scheme, however, he left Elvin Hayes around the basket to zone that area and covered the corners with his wing players. Such a defense will give up corner shots, but on this particular night, we couldn't find the range from the corners—or the perimeter, for that matter. The zone and their size shut down our inside game and we were unable get our home crowd in the game.

Trailing 32-29 at the half, I hoped for a solid second-half start to bring the crowd to life. As I've said before, the first five minutes of the second half are the most important—and on this night, it was Houston that seized the lead. Zones are even more effective with a lead, and Houston went up by 11. JoJo led a late rally to cut the lead to six, but Houston's guard hit a running bank shot to break our run. We started fouling to stop the clock but Houston defeated us, 66-53, ending our hopes for a national championship.

Additionally, we faced the challenge of playing Louisville in a third-place game the next night. Third-place games had been a part of the tournament format for many years, probably to accommodate fans who had traveled great distances to see their teams play, and probably as a way to secure a crowd. Well, the game sure did secure a crowd, and Louisville and Kansas did not disappoint. The game was a classic.

Louisville's Wes Unseld was one of the best rebounders and outlet passers in basketball, so it was vitally important for us to not overload the offensive boards and get back on defense. The combination of Wes's outlet passes (which would have done justice to an NFL quarterback) and Butch Beard's finishing skills was a tremendous threat. Louisville decided to zone us, probably because we had shot so poorly against Houston. But the new night was a new game, and JoJo hit 11 baskets as the two teams battled for national respect. While we weren't able to stop Unseld and Beard, who finished with 16 and 17, respectively, Allen Fieldhouse had never been louder and we held on to win, 70-68.

As we looked to the future, things were bright indeed. We were losing only one senior, Ron, while expecting good things out of our youngsters, led by freshmen 6'3" Richard Bradshaw of Chicago and Greg Douglas, a 6'8" forward from Keokuk, Iowa.

Coaching Lesson: *On recruiting*

In recruiting, it's important for a coach to be believable and to establish trust. I enjoyed recruiting, probably because of my background in a farm community: We loved our neighbors, we communicated and we lived in a family atmosphere. It felt pretty easy for me, sitting down and getting to know a family. The good players, the ones you really want, are the ones who know they'll have to compete and earn a starting job. They don't want to hear that they'll automatically have a job. That's when trust breaks down. The good players also don't worry about a team having someone else who already plays at their position. The great players don't care; they want to be surrounded by other good players.

Back to the recruiting trail

Shortly after the season, we received more good news as Pierre Russell and Roger Brown committed. Meanwhile, Dave Robisch had just set the individual scoring record for the state tournament in Illinois, averaging 38 points per game, which was a phenomenal feat. I called the next day to congratulate Dave, and visited with Rev. Robisch on the phone.

The reverend said that he would like for me to be there on Thursday. He didn't ask, mind you—he told me to be there. Still, I found that the visit would fit perfectly into my schedule. So Coach Miranda and I headed to Springfield, with the signing date still several weeks away.

We entered the Robisch home and visited briefly before the reverend told his son that he'd like to talk with him back in a bedroom. They emerged several minutes later to announce that Dave was going to become a Kansas Jayhawk. Because I hadn't expected a decision on that particular visit, I was overcome with joy and nearly touched the ceiling with a leap out of my chair. Sam and I had a very pleasant ride home.

"Coach was coming to visit and was not expecting an announcement. Coach sat down with Dad and me (Mom was there, but stayed in the background) and began to make small talk. I said to Dad, 'Can I speak with you?' and we went to an outside porch and I told him that I wanted to commit to Kansas. We left Coach sitting there.

When we came back into the room I said that I wanted to come to KU. Coach about fell out of his chair and said, 'I didn't even get into the best part about coming to KU!' My dad and I had done our homework, and it was a no-brainer. I will always remember the look on Coach's face and him coming out of his chair."
— *Dave Robisch, University of Kansas, forward, 1968-71*

The 1966-67 season, marked by a third consecutive Big Eight tournament championship and back-to-back conference titles, was somewhat unexpected because of the youthfulness of our team, but the year was one of my most satisfying as a coach. In two short years, this group of young men had re-established Kansas as one of the nation's great basketball powers, continuing a tradition of excellence first established by the efforts and sacrifices of so many former coaches and players.

Chapter 13

Campus Unrest and the Race to 1,000 Wins

Coach's Life Lesson: *Do not make quick judgments about the potential of individuals. The human will and spirit can be very strong. It is not the potential but the production that counts.*

Two players of mine were great examples of this. One came to us from out of state, and I remember talking with our coaches about how carefully we would have to monitor his grades to keep him eligible and allow him to graduate. But he earned his bachelor's and went on to get his master's. The human will and spirit, while not initially apparent, can be very strong. Another player, Dale Greenlee, was someone we rated as the seventh-best player in his freshman recruiting class, but he went on to play more minutes than any of his teammates who had seemed to have greater potential. You can't judge the inner will a person has.

The late 1960s were a period of change in the country and on campuses across the land. As the Vietnam War heated up, Selective Service was instituted but many of the nation's youth resisted the call to duty. And although the war wasn't the only controversy facing the nation, it seemed to be the catalyst that caused general discontent in many other areas, including gender and racial inequities. Nowhere was the discontent more evident than on college campuses, including KU's. In the late 1960s and early 1970s, KU would suffer through events that brought national attention to Lawrence.

Change was occurring in the athletic department, as well. The charismatic, longtime football coach, Jack Mitchell, was no longer heading the program, making way for Franklin "Pepper" Rodgers, a former Georgia Tech football player and UCLA assistant who started his first year as KU head coach in fall 1967. During my 23 years at the university, there were six chancellors, six football coaches and eight full or interim athletic directors, so change was the norm. Even so, it was difficult to see old friends leave.

I liked the football coaches a great deal and ultimately developed lifelong friendships. But I was disturbed when they convinced my starting center,

Vernon Vanoy, to play football. Ron Franz's graduation had already left a big hole on our team, and now the loss of Vernon, a superb 6'8", 260-pound athlete with a special defensive presence, dampened our hopes for a third consecutive championship. The football coaches had told Vernon that he could have a long run as a professional football player, but not as a basketball player. I'm not convinced that this was true, but I don't begrudge the football program for wanting such an excellent athlete to come out for their team.

We had another change in the basketball program when Bob Mulcahy left to become the head basketball coach at South Dakota University. I searched the East for a recruiting coach and decided on Gale Catlett, who was at Davidson with Lefty Driesell, a Hall of Fame coach who later had enormous success at Maryland.

Starting a summer camp

One day Gale asked me if we were going to host a summer basketball camp for youngsters, which was a fairly foreign concept to those of us in the Midwest. Ed McCauley had run a successful camp in St. Louis, but to my knowledge, no other camp existed at the time in the Midwest. I asked to meet with Chancellor Wescoe and his right-hand man, Raymond Nichols, and told them that the basketball staff would run the camp for the university and take a salary for each member of the staff.

I was disappointed to learn that we couldn't use university facilities, including Allen Fieldhouse, because other employees might want to use the facilities for summer activities, but Dr. Wescoe suggested that I run a camp privately and lease local school facilities. So Sam, Gale and I leased Naismith Hall, a private dorm, and we leased high school and junior high gymnasiums from Lawrence public school officials, who were so helpful for many years.

Without knowing what kind of interest the camp would draw, we sent mailers to Kansas schools and schools in states bordering Kansas. We agonized over what to charge the youngsters, finally deciding that $90 per week would be fair. We were pleasantly surprised when 600 young people enrolled for the first summer.

Over the ensuing 16 years, we developed the most successful basketball camp in the Midwest. The friendships that we developed have continued; I run into people all of the time who attended the camp—and more recently, the comments have become "my dad" attended the camp, and even "my granddad" attended.

Some youngsters would stay for all four weeks of the camp. I believe that Mark Turgeon, the present-day Maryland coach, attended for eight or nine years. Many other coaches and players had their start in fundamental training there. Members of the KU coaching staff taught at the camps alongside the high school and college coaches and players we hired, and KU players and alumni also worked the camps. Even during JoJo's years with the Celtics, he would return to help us every year. Chancellor Wescoe once told me that the camp was one of the best new-student recruiting successes on the campus.

The 1967-68 season

Our staff was anxious to build a new team for the 1967-68 season and compete for a third straight conference championship. Sophomores Rich Bradshaw, Greg Douglas, Jim Hoffman of Chicago and sweet-shooting Chester Lawrence of Dietrich, Illinois, joined our returning upperclassmen, while Dave Nash, a 6'10" junior college transfer, competed for the center position.

When I was recruiting Wes Unseld, I had scheduled Louisville in a home-and-home series, thinking that Wes would be wearing the crimson and blue and he would have an opportunity to play near his family, but now we faced a Louisville team led by Wes. So although we experienced some early-season success with a big win at Louisville and a sweep of the Sunflower Doubleheader against Stanford and Texas A&M, we also encountered disappointing losses at Loyola and to Louisville at home.

Over the holiday break, our run of three consecutive Big Eight tournament championships came to an end when we were upset by Oklahoma A&M. As the conference race got under way, we still weren't in sync as a team. Vernon Vanoy joined the team after the football season, but his absence during our skill-development program in early-season practice took its toll and he never became quite as effective as he was toward the end of the previous season.

Norm Stewart, a former player from Missouri, had recently taken over the Tigers' coaching reins. He would prove to be a tough competitor in future years, leaving the university as one of the greats in Missouri basketball history. Hosting Missouri, we had a one-point lead with two seconds to go, but we fouled on the in-bounds pass and they hit a one-and-one with no time on the clock. Later in the season, an overtime loss at Kansas State sealed our fate in the conference race. Although we finished the conference race with three straight wins, it was too late to stop Kansas State, and Tex Winter's patience and work with big Nick Pino paid off with a conference championship.

As the regular season came to an end, we were rewarded with an invitation to the NIT championship in New York City. At the time, the NIT comprised 16 of the best teams in the nation that hadn't qualified for the NCAA tourney as conference champions. So a trip to Madison Square Garden meant we would face teams that were nearly as good as NCAA participants (with the exception of UCLA, of course, which had started its dominating run.)

We defeated a couple of Eastern powers, Temple and Villanova, to reach the semifinals. We thought we would play Duke, but they were upset by St. Peters of New York and Elnardo Webster. The coaches of the four semifinalist teams were invited to the Metropolitan Writers' luncheon. After the luncheon, the coaches were interviewed by a young reporter by the name of Howard Cosell, who went on to say that St. Peters was the greatest Cinderella story in New York City since Jimmy Braddock defeated Max Baer for the heavyweight championship. So Madison Square Garden would be packed with Eastern fans, who always supported an underdog.

Well, we quieted the crowd, beating St. Peters in the semifinals, but then we lost in the finals to a Dayton team led by Donnie May and coached by Don Donoher. Although the season had some satisfying moments, not securing another conference title was hugely disappointing.

The spring and summer of 1968 were very busy, because we knew we had a big void to fill in the second semester of the 1968-69 season when JoJo would graduate. On the recruiting trail, we landed a junior college guard from California named Tim Natsues. In addition, we attracted two guards: Aubrey Nash of DeMatha High in Maryland, whose team had just won the national championship, and Bob Kivisto, who played for his dad, Ernie, in East Aurora, Illinois. Neal Mask, a promising 6'7" forward from Tulsa, committed to the Jayhawks after his state tournament appearance.

Scouting the music camp

Neal, Aubrey and Bob were joined by a young fellow from Hartselle, Alabama, named Isaac Frank "Bud" Stallworth, who came to us almost by accident. One summer day, JoJo came into the basketball office and asked if we had been over to KU's Robinson gym in the last several days. (In the offseason, our players played in Robinson.) Well, JoJo had spotted a 6'5" trumpet player who was on campus for a band camp. The musician might've kicked his feet up behind him on his jump shot, but he could really stick it.

NCAA rules didn't allow us to watch our players out of season, so we didn't go to Robinson very often. What we saw of Bud, though, we liked very much. We encouraged him to consider KU, which he did—and it helped immensely that his sister, Harriet, was a KU student.

"It wasn't an ordinary recruiting visit. The first call Coach made was to my music camp counselor to find out who I was. I wasn't even supposed to be playing basketball while I was there. That was my father's rule. My parents wanted me to concentrate on music during my summer music camp. I was skipping the 40-minute

lunch each day and going to Robinson, across the street from where the rehearsals were, and playing basketball. So for me to not let my parents down if something happened, I asked Coach Owens to wait until I returned home. Several weeks later, he called to say he had heard about me. After a second phone call, an assistant coach scheduled a trip to see me play in a high school game."
— *Bud Stallworth, University of Kansas, guard, 1969-72*

In the Olympics

Besides spotting recruits in Robinson, JoJo's summer of 1968 had other highlights. Coach Henry Iba had been selected by the AAU to coach the Olympic team, which he did for three consecutive Olympic Games. (While it was rare for a coach to be picked more than once, Coach Iba commanded great respect.) When Coach Iba asked JoJo to compete for a position on the team, we were delighted.

Now, social and racial unrest were prevalent throughout the country in 1968, especially among college-aged youngsters, and some players had decided not to participate in the Olympics. But that thought never entered Jo's mind because he had been dreaming of playing in the games in Mexico City. JoJo and Spencer Haywood formed the nucleus of an underdog Olympic team that surpassed all expectations, posting a 9-0 record and defeating Yugoslavia in the finals. The gold medal was one of Coach Iba's greatest achievements.

"Spencer Haywood and JoJo White exploded for 26 points in a space of 12 minutes at the start of the second half tonight to break open a hard-fought battle and give the United States its seventh straight Olympic basketball championship with a 65-50 victory over Yugoslavia. ... White, who scored six points in the first half, added eight in the second half and played an outstanding all-around game."
— Los Angeles Times, *Mexico City, Oct. 25, 1968*

"I never thought that I would have that chance. I was proud to be in that position, to represent the United States in the Olympics— proud to be there and proud to be able to win the whole thing. The gold medal is packed away—my wife kind of hides things."
— *JoJo White, University of Kansas, guard, 1966-69*

"In terms of business, Mr. Iba was on top of all things day to day, but you seldom saw him smile. Ted Owens had a smile every day

with the same kind of energy. Coach Owens' demeanor was what should be shared on the floor."

— *JoJo White, University of Kansas, guard, 1966-69*

The Olympic Games were held in October, so when JoJo returned to Lawrence, practice had already started. Meanwhile, the football was experiencing one of its finest seasons. The team lost only once during the year, in a close game at Oklahoma, and they were invited to the Orange Bowl to play undefeated Penn State. Any Kansas fan can tell you the rest of the story: The Jayhawks stopped Penn State on a two-point conversion to win the game, only to be flagged for having 12 men on the field. Given a second chance, Penn State scored on the two-point conversion, capping one of Joe Paterno's best years.

The 1968-69 season

Prior to the 1968-69 season, the basketball team had lost Rodger Bohnenstiehl to graduation. Finishing with one of the highest shooting percentages in school history, Rodger was also a positive influence on the rest of team. Sophomores Dave Robisch, Roger Brown, Pierre Russell and Fred Bosilevac would add their considerable talents to that of the upperclassmen, but it would take a while to blend together the new and old talent—and we faced the loss of JoJo in the second semester.

Three memories stick out vividly in my mind about the 1968-69 year. First, the nation took great joy in JoJo and the accomplishments of the Olympic basketball team. Everywhere we went, when Jo was introduced the ovations were thundering.

Second, there was a great deal of chatter in the media about which college program would first reach 1,000 victories, and Kansas and Kentucky were neck-in-neck in the chase. Two West Coast December victories, over Utah State and Stanford, gave us a lead in the race, and I remember telling our team how important those two road games were. The players responded beautifully; Dave "Robo" Robisch tallied 20 points and 12 rebounds against Utah State and JoJo dropped 28 points at Stanford.

In Kansas City, we defeated Nebraska, Colorado and Oklahoma State to collect our fourth league-tournament title in five years, and I could tell that we were becoming a cohesive team. After a win at home, we lost another one-point game to Missouri at Columbia. (Notching three consecutive one-point victories against the Jayhawks really got Norm Stewart's program going in the right direction.) We followed the Missouri loss with a two-overtime loss to Iowa State, but we were still in position to beat Kentucky to the 1,000-win mark if we could win at Kansas State and beat Colorado and Oklahoma State at home.

After our players did their job at Manhattan, it was time to win No. 999—JoJo's last game in a Kansas uniform. The game was my third vivid memory of the season, as an enthusiastic crowd and Jo's parents watched him explode for 30 points, his career high. As usual, though, his defensive pressure and passing influenced the game more than his points.

> *"The biggest thing that I remember about my time playing Kansas basketball was the losses. We only lost two games at home in my career. The most serious loss for me was not a game, but the loss of JoJo during my sophomore year. We lost our final two games against Missouri and Kansas State, which meant we did not get to tie Colorado for the Big Eight Championship. In my mind, we would have had a complete team. We would have won the Big Eight and had a chance to go the Final Four. JoJo was a huge influence on me and my growth and when he left, a part of me left with him. I wasn't the same player after he left. It affected me."*
> — *Dave Robisch, University of Kansas, forward, 1968-71*

JoJo names an agent

JoJo's success at KU and in the Olympics had made him a hot pro prospect—not only in basketball but in football as well. Gil Brandt, a discoverer of talent for the Dallas Cowboys, called me to say that the franchise was interested in signing Jo to an NFL contract as a defensive back. I took the idea to Jo, but he was adamant about playing professional basketball. Knowing that, we considered his need for an agent. I didn't know any agents well enough to recommend one to Jo, so I contacted a friend of mine, Judge Roy Holiday, and asked if he would help me negotiate a contract for Jo without compensation.

Helping Jo with his contract was important to me. One of our earlier players had taken bad advice and hadn't received the appropriate value in his contract, and I was determined that I wasn't going to let a Jayhawk get ripped off again. We were under a lot of pressure to finalize the agreement, though, because Jo had completed his four years of school and the military draft board in St. Louis was breathing down his neck. We agreed to meet with Carl Scheer, representing the NBA, and Max Williams of the ABA's Dallas Chaparrals.

We met with Scheer and Williams at the Kansas City airport's Holiday Inn, talking to one and then negotiating with the other. Finally, Williams sensed that he was being used as a pawn to increase the NBA offer, and made a smart decision: He told us that Jo had to name the price it would take to get him to play in the ABA, and if Williams met the price, Jo would have to sign. In response, Jo told us he definitely wanted to play in the NBA, so we asked

Scheer for his best offer—and he came up with a figure that he said was the best-ever offer for an incoming guard, and he added in a guaranteed three-year contract. We agreed to the offer, but warned Scheer that the league had to place Jo with a team that had a military reserve unit nearby so that JoJo could immediately join. That team was in Boston, and Jo joined a Marine unit there and he served on active duty for a period of time. So that's how JoJo White became a Boston Celtic.

> *"Leaving in January wasn't fun for me. I left what came next in Coach's hands. He had a better understanding of what was going on. I really appreciate the decisions that he made for me and where my career went from there. To this day, I appreciate all that he did. It was absolutely tough, not knowing the conclusions or what they would bring ... an entirely different arena, college to the pros or even the Marines. I was ready for anything."*
> — JoJo White, University of Kansas, guard, 1966-69

Three years later, after much success with the Celtics, Jo called and said it was time to negotiate a new contract. I told him that while we would be glad to help, we knew little about comparative salaries for veteran players and our lack of information might ultimately cost him money. So Jo asked Red Auerbach, whom he trusted, to recommend an agent, and Jo managed to land a highly satisfactory contract. Sometime later, Cathy Gurtler, the longtime secretary for the basketball program, buzzed my office and said that Jo was on the phone. Jo said he wanted me to be the first to know that he had signed a four-year contract for more than $1 million (a handsome payday in the early '70s, or today, for that matter). When we ended the conversation, I told Cathy how touched I was to be the first person Jo told of his good fortune. She said, "Coach, do you know he called you collect?" I suppose Jo must have listened during our discussions about being frugal.

A thousand wins

Sports Illustrated magazine was preparing to come to Lawrence to compile a story about the first team to win 1,000 college basketball games when Kentucky's sports information director, Russell Rice, suddenly announced that they had discovered two victories from the early 1900s, games against the Lexington YMCA, that hadn't been recorded. So after their 998th win, Kentucky marked its 1,000th win with a big cake and celebration. To avoid any controversy, *Sports Illustrated* cancelled their trip to Lawrence.

So, on the night of Feb. 3, 1969, our Jayhawks took the floor against Oklahoma State, a traditional rival with their own rich history in the game. While Henry Iba's teams were never an easy out, nothing on that night would deny our team the honor of winning the storied program's 1,000th game. Robisch led all scorers with 23 points and Roger gathered 13 boards, and it was an incredible thrill to be a part of the KU family on that memorable night.

After winning our next two contests, we lost yet another one-point game to Missouri at home. We then notched two wins over Nebraska and Oklahoma but followed with losses to Colorado and Kansas State, costing us a chance to share the conference crown with Colorado. We had some difficulty adjusting to the post-JoJo days, even though Richard Bradshaw, in the season's last three games, began to show some flashes of his potential, and our season ended with an NIT loss to Boston College.

Prepping for 1969-70 amid unrest

On the recruiting front, we landed a potentially great front line, with 6'9" Leonard Gray from Kansas City's Sumner High School, 6'9" Randy Canfield from Wichita and 6'8" Michael Bossard from the Washington, D.C. area. In addition, we gained Denver shooting guard Mark Williams, rounding out an excellent freshmen class.

The beginning of the 1969-70 school year started with a change on campus. Dr. Wescoe, the chancellor who had hired me, resigned to become CEO of Sterling Drug Company, and the new chancellor, Larry Chalmers, walked into a hotbed of social and racial unrest on campus. I was serving on the Lawrence Human Relations Commission and was very much aware of the problems that faced the city and campus. The police force and city manager Buford Watson were consistently called out at all hours of the night to deal with civil disobedience.

The Black Student Union had demanded that Chancellor Chalmers give them an opportunity to crown a black homecoming queen at the KU-Iowa game. And female students, who were required to live in a residence hall for three years and abide by a 10:30 p.m. curfew, were demanding more freedom in their living arrangements. Also, opposition to the Vietnam War was elevating daily.

It was difficult for players to concentrate amid so much distraction, but it was in this environment that we started to build a competitive team. Sophomores Bud Stallworth, Bob Kivisto, Fred Bosilevac, Aubrey Nash and Neal Mask joined upperclassmen Dave Robisch, Roger Brown, Pierre Russell and Chester Lawrence, the only senior on the varsity team. Mark Mathews, a walk-on from Shawnee Mission, had finally won a scholarship. I always enjoyed rewarding a youngster who had sacrificed to achieve his goals. After all, that was the American way—using any opportunity available to achieve aspirations.

As coaches, we were beginning to change our scheduling philosophy in an attempt to play more games in front of large crowds at Allen Fieldhouse. One casualty of the shift, however, was the Sunflower Doubleheader. In its place, I had started the Jayhawk Classic, for which we paid three visiting teams a higher guaranteed amount in exchange for forgoing the return games. The inaugural tournament included Southern Methodist University, a perennial Southwest Conference power, and Western Kentucky, a program that would make the Final Four the following year. Still, we won the first tournament with Bud Stallworth scoring 27 and Pierre Russell hauling in 13 rebounds. It was always a disappointing night if Pierre failed to slide off the elevated court at least once with his great hustle.

Our play was inconsistent in the conference season and we ended 8-6 in the league and 17-9 overall. While we had a young team with a great deal of potential, they lacked the defensive toughness it took to become a conference champion.

Our freshmen on the front line also ran into some hurdles, and we suffered several losses that took a couple of years to mend. Randy Canfield developed a problem with his lungs collapsing, which could happen with activity as minor as sneezing or coughing, and he was lost for the season. Leonard Gray, with his vast potential, experienced personal problems that caused him to leave school, and then we discovered that someone in Mike Bossard's high school had altered his class rank to qualify him for an NCAA scholarship, so Mike, too, was lost.

A boiling point

On top of the on-court disappointments, the campus unrest had reached a boiling point. Some of the more radical leaders armed themselves and made their headquarters in the area where the Oread Hotel sits today. In April 1970, shortly after the basketball season, radicals burned the student union. Jerry Rubin, a leader of the attempt to disrupt the 1968 Democratic convention in Chicago, had visited the campus to speak, and some felt he was a catalyst in the destruction of the union. Many of our basketball players were involved in trying to put out the fire and save the union. A month later, the military science building was stoned.

In this tumultuous environment, we were trying to recruit future players. One spring weekend, a promising 6'9" New Mexico player was scheduled to visit. The campus and city were in turmoil over a local policeman's killing of Rick Dowdell, an active member of the black-rights community, and the atmosphere was worsened by the death of a student, Nick Rice. Kansas Gov. Robert Docking implemented a sundown curfew and ordered the National

Guard to take over the campus. Needless to say, the prospect from New Mexico did not have a good impression on his visit, and we lost him to Kansas State.

I remained active with the human relations board in trying to find solutions. In a controversial decision, Chancellor Chalmers cancelled the rest of the semester, sending students home before finals. The minimum grade awarded in classes would be a C, and those who had a higher grade would keep it. No one knows for sure whether the chancellor made the correct decision, but many parents—including my players' parents, who had anxiously called me—were relieved that the school year had come to an end. And I suppose that the students who had failing grades at the time were the most relieved.

> *"At the end of my junior year, school was closed early because of campus unrest. I felt strongly that Kansas basketball had the strength and the position on campus to bring everyone together again my senior year."*
> — *Dave Robisch, University of Kansas, forward, 1968-71*

Chapter 14

Houston in March

Coach's Life Lesson: *The opportunity to influence others is available to all coaches. History is full of successful people who have said they were greatly influenced by a teacher or a coach. A coach must always remember that they are not just teaching a sport—they are teaching young men and women.*

I look back at my own life and know that outside of my parents, the most influential people have been coaches and teachers. The good thing about coaching is that you have a captive audience; most of the people you deal with have a genuine interest in sports, so you have a real opportunity to have an influence on them.

As the 1970-71 year began, we hoped for a more peaceful atmosphere than what we had seen in the spring. But while the governor lifted the curfew, unrest continued on campus and in Lawrence. For counterculture leaders in the national movement traveling from coast to coast, Lawrence became a major stopover. In August, just before the beginning of the school year, a commission on campus unrest formed by President Richard Nixon sent a team to Lawrence to investigate the sources of the violence. But the mayhem continued; in December, the computation lab was bombed.

Although our spring recruiting was damaged by the turmoil, we were still successful in improving our backcourt, adding Tom Kivisto, Dave Taynor and Randy Culbertson. However, we didn't have success replacing the loss of our frontline players, which would prove to be a problem.

I had rules for my players' personal appearance in terms of length of hair, and I suspected that with the number of long-haired individuals on campus, the standard would be challenged. I consulted with fellow members of the Human Relations Commission, and they believed that if I were fair and consistent, the rule wouldn't pose a problem. On October 15, the first day of practice, Pierre Russell walked down the hall to dress for practice and I saw that he had not complied. I called him into the office and stated my case, and he left to go back to the dorm. When practice started, he and another teammate reported with shaved heads. They made their point and I made mine, and we began our journey to build a team that would become one of the university's all-time best teams.

Dave Robisch, after a junior season in which he averaged 26.5 points and more than 12 rebounds, had just arrived home from the World University games in Tokyo. While he had gained valuable experience, he was fatigued from the extra summer work. He did not get off to a great start in our season, but his teammates did.

> *"Practice began October 15 and in those days you did not play until late in November. The coaches had us scrimmaging all the time, full game-like scrimmages, and they would keep stats. I got called into the office and told 'You are horrible.' We always had disagreements about how important practice was. Did I enjoy practice? No. Did I give 100 percent in practice? No. Did I give 100 percent when the ball got tossed up in a game? Yes."*
> — *Dave Robisch, University of Kansas, forward, 1968-71*

> *"We were very well organized and disciplined in practice. I felt our job was to help them learn to function without the coaches in a game. I tried to make the practices very emotional and disciplined so that the game was a piece of cake. In my earlier years as a student-athlete at OU, I remembered Coach Wilkinson's emphasis on preparation. He said, 'The will to prepare is what develops the discipline and the know-how that transforms itself on game day into the will to win. More importantly, preparation engenders the confidence that enables the will to win.'*
> — *Ted Owens*

The 1970-71 team was full of young men who loved and respected one another and truly loved the game of basketball. Both black and white, the members of the team lived together in Jayhawk Towers and shared a mutual goal of playing for the national championship, which would be in Houston's Astrodome. Soon, the rallying cry on campus became "Houston in March."

Preparing for a season opener against a powerful Long Beach State team coached by Jerry Tarkanian, we saw on film that they employed a 1-2-2 zone, so we decided to start the game switching back and forth between man-for-man coverage and a 1-3-1 zone. It didn't take too long for us to see that they were having trouble against the zone, because our team was big and athletic, with 6'10" Dave Robisch, 6'10" Roger Brown, 6'5" Bud Stallworth, 6'4" Pierre Russell and 6'1" Aubrey Nash as the five starters.

Nineteen minutes into the first half, we had held Long Beach to four points. We had a 32-4 lead when an administrator came to me on the bench with the news that someone had called to say that a bomb had been planted in Allen Fieldhouse. The game was delayed for 30 minutes while the authorities combed the fieldhouse, but they found no sign of a bomb. Still, they had to take precautions because of the university's recent history with the computation lab bombing, the stoning of the military science building and the burning of the student union.

I met with Coach Tarkanian at mid-court and he was shaking his head, partly because of the bomb threat but also at the thought of scoring four points in the first 19 minutes of the first half. At least they scored four more points before halftime to make it a 32-8 game. Television viewers across the country must have wondered if the score was correct when it was posted. Even though Long Beach started to play like a nationally ranked team in the second half, we prevailed, 69-52.

After victories over Eastern Kentucky, South Dakota State and Loyola at home, we faced a strong field in the Jayhawk Classic, which included Houston and two Philadelphia schools, Villanova and Saint Joseph's. Fred Schaus, the general manager of the L.A. Lakers, attended the KU-Houston game in order to see Dave Robisch play. What he saw instead was Roger Brown recording 23 points and 21 rebounds in the greatest game of his career, and Schaus ended up taking Roger in the draft. Sports history is full of examples of youngsters taking advantage of the opportunity to display their own talents while a teammate is being scouted, and it certainly worked for Roger. In a physical and emotional game, we beat a solid Houston team, 89-73.

The day after the Houston game, we traveled to Louisville for a Monday night game in Freedom Hall. I had tried to schedule Louisville on Tuesday but the arena wasn't available, so we had to play a third game in four days. Fatigue and a solid Cardinal team led to our first and only regular-season loss of the year.

After a short rest, we arrived in Kansas City for the annual conference tournament. We opened against Norm Stewart's Missouri Tigers, the team that had beaten us by a single point in the previous three contests. This time, though, we were on our game, blasting the Tigers, 96-63. We then defeated Iowa State and Nebraska to earn our fifth tournament championship in my tenure as head coach.

Before the conference season began, we headed to Atlanta to play Georgia Tech. Championships are usually won by teams that can win tough road games, and I saw this road trip as an opportunity to prepare the team for the conference season. Rich Yunkus, a player from Illinois we had actively recruited, led Tech with 24 points, but the Jayhawks had too many weapons as Pierre and Bud led the scoring with 22 and 27 points.

Rallying around the 'Hawks

After a home win against Abe Lemons' Oklahoma City University team, we were ready for the Big Eight regular season. However, we were worried that Dave, our primary scorer and rebounder from the previous year, had yet to hit his stride. Coach Miranda, Coach Catlett and I called him in for a frank discussion. We told him that he was playing good basketball, but he wasn't playing to his potential—and that if we were to reach Houston in March, he would have to furnish more leadership in every aspect of his game, from rebounding and defense to hustling for loose balls. He responded beautifully, and his leadership and performance provided just what we needed for a tremendous run.

> *"After a tough preseason and prior to going into the Big Eight games, I was called into the office to visit with Coach Owens and all the assistant coaches. He told me that for the team to reach its goals, I had to play better. I was still struggling to reach the goals that Coach Owens set after the last meeting, and now this. Looking back, I understand why he did it. Basketball was a passion for me and being a Kansas player is what drove me. When people told me I wasn't doing it right, it hurt. Coach was always trying to be the motivator and tried to get the best out of my ability."*
> — *Dave Robisch, University of Kansas, forward, 1968-71*

Photo courtesy of Lawrence Journal-World

After a win in Allen Fieldhouse, I addressed the team.

Meanwhile, the campus started to rally around the team. Whereas racial tensions had divided the student body, this team of black and white players—who obviously loved and respected one another—bound our students together and set an example for people of all races to join together for a common purpose. One day, Chancellor Chalmers told me, "This team has saved our campus." Well, there were certainly other factors that contributed to the restoration of peace on campus, but there was no doubt that the team's success and brotherhood was a unifying force.

We opened the conference season at home against Iowa State, a team that had played us closely in Kansas City. This time, though, wasn't a contest at all. Dave scored 21 and simply dominated the boards, collecting 20 rebounds. In fact, Dave would lead the team in either rebounding or scoring in every game left on the schedule.

> *"The meeting that I had with the coaches motivated me. We only lost one game all year and we were ranked in the top five in the country. If you talked to my teammates, you would learn that I did whatever the coaches wanted me to do. Basketball is a team sport, and Coach told me numerous times that in crucial situations, if the team needed a basket, I would get the ball and good things would happen. In that regard, when there were crucial situations, Coach had the ball go through my hands."*
> — *Dave Robisch, University of Kansas, forward, 1968-71*

Scoring aside, this was a team built on defense and rebounding. For the season, we held opponents to 39 percent shooting from the field, we out-rebounded opponents by eight rebounds a game and we held a wide margin in turnovers. All championship-caliber teams have strong defenses, and these Jayhawks were no exception.

Bud gave us an added scoring punch, averaging 17 per game, while Roger led the rebounding effort with 11 per game. Pierre punched in 10 points and eight boards a game, and Aubrey and Bob gave us leadership, ball-handling, and rugged defense at the point. Mark Williams came off the bench to shoot most teams out of their zones, and reserves Randy Canfield, Greg Douglas, Mark Mathews, Neal Mask and Jerry House all made their own vital contributions to the team's success.

After a home win over Oklahoma State, we rolled over Iowa State in Ames, and returned home to face the Wildcats and Coach Jack Hartman. We prevailed, 79-74, with Mark netting 13 points with long-range bombs against Jack's always-tough zone. Arriving next for a game in Lincoln, the team asked the coaches to leave the bus, and they emerged from a players-only meeting to drill the Huskers, 81-67. And then Mark, a Colorado native, scored 22 points off the bench in a win against the Buffaloes. The team's confidence was growing.

The annual road trip to my native state, Oklahoma, was always a special time for me. We pulled away from OSU in the second half for a victory in Stillwater before heading to Norman and OU. The Sooners had a future pro in Clifford Ray and two other fine players, Scott Martin and Bobby Jack. Although we trailed at halftime, we ended with five players in double figures and a 71-68 victory.

We handled Missouri again at home with Bud scoring 30 points (he always seemed to play his best against the Tigers) and Pierre adding 19. Next up, at Ahearn Fieldhouse in Manhattan, the students were at their best again, roaring in like a herd of cattle when the doors were opened. When we were introduced, someone threw a chicken, painted crimson and blue, onto the floor. Their zone squeezed our inside game and held Dave to just eight points and Roger to only four, but Bud and Pierre picked up the slack with 23 and 16 and Greg Douglas added four with two big buckets. Better yet, our defense was superb.

The team to beat

As the team to beat, the rest of the conference took their best shots against us. We played nothing but close games the remainder of the schedule and gained ourselves a nickname, the "Cardiac Kids." True to form, we had an epic battle in Boulder against the Buffaloes. Trailing by two with just seconds to go, Dave muscled his way to a game-tying basket, drawing a foul on the way. Dave might've been an average free-throw shooter under normal circumstances, but with the game on the line, he was one of the best clutch-shooters I coached. He nailed his free throw, keeping our undefeated conference record intact. We returned to Lawrence with an opportunity to clinch the championship by defeating the Oklahoma Sooners. The Sooners played us down to the wire, but sharp-shooting Mark Williams came off the bench to tally six points at a critical time. We were totally ineffective at the free-throw line, going 12 for 25, but our worst free-throw shooter, Aubrey Nash, nailed two at the line to secure the Big Eight conference championship.

A trip to Columbia and a home game against Nebraska were all that stood in the way of the league's first undefeated conference team since Kansas State accomplished in the league's inaugural year of 1959. In Columbia, however, we found ourselves on the short end of a 37-28 halftime score against Norm Stewart's well-prepared team. In the second half, we tightened our defense and battled back to send the game into overtime. Reserves Greg Douglas and Randy Canfield played important roles in the comeback. As the team had so many times during the 1970-71 season, the team found a way to win, prevailing 71-69.

> ## Coaching Lesson: *On Believing*
> *The difference in psychology between a winning year and a losing year is simply amazing. In winning years, the players believe they're going to win, and they find a way to do it. In losing years, players are doubtful of a positive outcome, and most of the time, they'll find a way to lose. If a coach can find a way to convince his players to not think about the game's eventual outcome but to concentrate*

instead on performing their best within each possession, the results will be overwhelmingly positive. A coach has to set the tone from the beginning by not talking about future events, but about the next play, possession, or game.

On Senior Night in Allen Fieldhouse, we honored three terrific young men who had given the Jayhawk Nation some great memories—Dave Robisch, who would go down in history as one of the program's best scorers and rebounders; Roger Brown, a solid rebounder and defender, and Pierre Russell, one of the most tenacious competitors to ever wear the crimson and blue. Before the celebration, though, we had to take care of the business at hand. It wasn't easy, but we survived the Cornhuskers, 59-54, finishing an undefeated conference season with our 19th consecutive victory.

> *"He was really proud of us. We knew we had a good team, but it was basically unheard of to go undefeated in conference play."*
> — *Bud Stallworth, University of Kansas, guard, 1969-72*

Hopes and dreams

The campus was buzzing with the possibility of a national championship. Buttons popped up across campus, displaying the cry of "Houston in March" and mottos for individual players, such as "Robo Wash Them," "Rebound with Brown," "Mash with Nash," "Better Buy Bud," and other catchy phrases.

Wichita State University and its "Roundhouse" arena hosted the regional NCAA tournament. Alongside the Jayhawks, the other contenders were the Missouri Valley-champion Drake Bulldogs; Notre Dame and scorer Austin Carr; and Houston, a team we had beaten earlier in the year. There were predictions that if Houston won its way to the Astrodome, as many as 50,000 might attend the Final Four.

After a stunning upset of Notre Dame by Drake, we took the floor against a fired-up Cougars team. Houston was led by Poo Welch, a junior college point guard I had actively recruited. Poo was at his best, dropping 28 points on us, but Dave and Bud countered with 29 and 25 of their own. We managed a slim victory, 78-77, and positioned ourselves just one game away from the dream of all college teams, a trip to the Final Four.

In the way, however, was Drake, a team that posed real problems for us. While we were big and strong, they were quick and fast. To take advantage of a team's size, the key was to get off to a good start and dictate the tempo of the game. Prior to the shot-clock era, a quick, active team with good ball-handlers could set the terms of a game. Our worst nightmare came to true when Drake sprinted out of the gates and took a 38-30 halftime lead. They forced me to play small ball, and I only played one big man for much of the first half. We were having a tough time guarding the Bulldogs, and Pierre and Bud were in foul trouble.

Many basketball coaches will agree that the first five minutes of the second half are the most critical minutes of the game, and I subscribe to that theory. I decided to risk foul trouble, inserting our starting lineup to start the second period. With risk comes reward, and with Roger and Dave playing together, we were able to pound the ball inside. Roger went 6-for-6 from the field and contributed 15 points and Robisch led the way with 27 points. The risk was realized, however, when Bud and Pierre fouled out of the game. Even though we had switched to our 1-3-1 zone with the bigger lineup, we had failed to protect Bud and Pierre from foul trouble.

Fortunately, our bench was up to the challenge. Bob Kivisto handled the ball extremely well and scored nine points while Mark Mathews became the baseline chaser in the zone. We outscored Drake by 10 points in the second half to pull out a 73-71 win. Dave was voted the regional tournament MVP, and off we went, to Houston in March, carrying the hopes of our campus and fans.

Off to Houston

As the Midwest regional winners, we were set to play UCLA, the West Regional champ. The East was represented by Villanova and their scorer, Howard Porter, pitted against Southeast Regional winner Western Kentucky, and their star, big Jim McDaniels. Leading up to the games, Long Beach coach Jerry Tarkanian, who had lost to UCLA by one point in the West Regional, was asked to compare the Jayhawks and Bruins. He said that if the game was an alley fight, Kansas would win, but if the game was one of finesse, UCLA would prevail. I took that as a great compliment, because the comment explained exactly what we were—a hard-nosed defensive and rebounding team whose margin of victory depended on those areas.

The day before the game, we arrived for a workout and were startled to find an elevated court with no ramps at the ends to catch players going after loose balls. I could picture Pierre Russell sliding for a loose ball and falling six feet down to the floor. The depth perception for shooting was also huge adjustment for players. And even though the benches were built up from the ground, my waist was about level to the elevation of the court. The Astrodome was simply not built for basketball. The court was stuck out in the middle of the dome, while modern domed arenas are planned with basketball tournaments in mind. The 1971 Final Four was the first in a large dome, and now all of the Final Fours are held in the large arenas.

UCLA may have been in between Lew Alcindor (Kareem Abdul-Jabbar) and Bill Walton, but they still had a talented team, led by forwards Sidney Wicks and Curtis Rowe. While Steve Patterson didn't have the notoriety of Alcindor or Walton, he was a solid center, and Henry Bibby led their guards. The Bruins were going to be a great challenge.

Because we were scheduled to play the second game of the semifinals, we awaited the ending of the Villanova and Western Kentucky game. We had given our instructions and pre-game talk to the team and the players were emotionally ready to hit the floor. Unfortunately, the first game went into overtime, and then a second overtime. After 30 minutes of waiting, we finally took to the court in front of 31,000 fans.

We started the game as flat as we possibly could have and trailed by as many as 13 points. We closed the gap to seven by halftime and then made a run in the second half, using a full-court press and tying the game. The acoustics of a traditional gym would have made the noise level incredible, but in such a gigantic arena, the noise wasn't a factor. With the score knotted up, Dave executed a perfect crossover step and scored, giving us our first lead, but an official called him for traveling.

> *"I remember a jump shot. It was off our fast-break transition game, a shot that I had made hundreds and hundreds of times. This time, the referee called me for traveling, and the shot would have put us ahead for the first time in the game. We would've gone ahead in the game, and momentum is so important. Lots of great memories, lots of games, but the losses are what I recall."*
> — *Dave Robisch, University of Kansas, forward, 1968-71*

UCLA scored to regain the lead and the momentum, and we couldn't catch back up. We lost, 68-60, in part because of our Achilles' heel—shooting 12-for-23 from the free-throw line—denied us an opportunity to close the gap.

> *"I'm not blaming those overtimes [in the preceding Villanova-Western Kentucky game]. You either win or lose. But there was also the Wooden factor. We can't blame the loss on the referees, but it was hard to overcome, and there's simply no margin for error."*
> — *Bud Stallworth, University of Kansas, guard, 1969-72*

> *"It is the losses that I remember the most. My senior year we were 27-1 and UCLA was 27-1, playing in the Astrodome in Houston. It was the Final Four and a chance to play for the national championship was on the line. I thought we would win ... we were*

one of the best teams in Kansas basketball history ... we would win the championship."
  — Dave Robisch, University of Kansas, forward, 1968-71

I went back to the Astroworld Hotel, trudging down the hallway with profound sadness. Our quest for a national championship had vanished, our 21-game winning streak broken. When I entered my room, daughters Nancy and Kelly, then 11 and 8, met me at the door. "Too bad about the game, Dad," Kelly said. "Do you want to play some cards?" It was a great lesson in sports and in life: When faced with disappointment, pick yourself up and forge ahead with new goals and plans for the future. Sometimes those lessons come from unexpected sources.

> *"Coach Owens wasn't unusually disappointed, any more than any other loss. We felt like that team had the ability to win the title. When it was over, there wasn't any 'could've, would've, should've.' Once we were back in the locker room, everyone realized our season was over and the seniors realized that their college careers had ended. He wasn't one to get excited or disappointed about it. We were in a position to win and we simply didn't get it done."*
> *— Bud Stallworth, University of Kansas, guard, 1969-72*

Two nights later, our team was faced with playing the dreaded third-place game. We played a good Western Kentucky team, losing at the gun, 77-75. Dave led the way with 23, but a 15-for-27 performance at the free-throw line doomed us once more.

The 1970-71 season was incredible, with the first Final Four for members of the team and the coaches, an undefeated conference season, and a winning streak of 21 games. As I look back, though, the team's most remarkable achievement was unifying a campus and city in a common cause. Our players demonstrated that people from divergent backgrounds and ethnic groups can set aside their differences and, by loving and respecting one another, can exceed expectations. Today, the team group continues their special bond, and they held a touching reunion in 2011.

> *"I am most proud of running the table in the Big Eight my senior year. Not many teams in the league did that. We were 17-0, but I still feel like we missed our chance to be remembered as one of the greatest Jayhawk teams of all time."*
> *— Dave Robisch, University of Kansas, forward, 1968-71*

Chapter (15)

Persevering

Coach's Life Lesson: *Sports do not automatically build character in athletes. Some players will finish their careers without learning to be self-sufficient and will have difficulty adjusting to life on the outside. It's our responsibility to develop the values that they'll need in life. It is true that sports provide the opportunity to teach the value of hard work, skill development, teamwork, competing fairly, responding properly to winning and losing, and gaining confidence, but these lessons will only be realized when they are presented in the correct manner.*

The University of Kansas and the community became less turbulent in the early 1970s. After overseeing the dramatic events for several years, Larry Chalmers resigned as chancellor to manage the Chicago Art Institute, and he was replaced temporarily by one the university's most loyal and dedicated servants, Raymond Nichols, who had long served as an advisor to university leaders.

On the sports side, when Pepper Rodgers left to become the head football coach at UCLA, the vacancy was filled by Don Fambrough, a friend of mine who became one of the school's most beloved coaches. Don was a talented recruiter and gifted storyteller. Good recruiters come in many different packages, but there is a quality identified in the most successful ones: whether the coach is believable and whether he can be trusted. Parents found Don, with the drawl he brought from Longview, Texas, to be both entertaining and trustworthy.

On the basketball court, the combination of graduation, minimal recruiting success during the turbulent times on campus and the unexpected loss of Leonard Gray and Michael Bossard left us with only Randy Canfield and Neal Mask returning on the front line. Mark Williams, the outside shooter, transferred back home to Colorado State. Bob Kivisto, wanting to enter the coaching profession, asked if he could forgo his senior year of competition and join us on the coaching staff. He had a deep love for his brother, Tom, who was eligible to enter varsity play, and Bob didn't want to take playing time away from his brother. At the other guard position, Aubrey

Nash returned. At the time, we ran a two-guard offense system, but in retrospect, I wish that I had changed to a three-guard system, playing small ball with Bud Stallworth and another big man in the starting lineup. The smaller team would've allowed us to play a pressing, up-tempo style fairly well. Of course, everything looks better in hindsight.

The 1971-72 season did not have many highlights, although it was certainly an eventful year. Gale Catlett, who had been our assistant coach for four years, and was replaced by Bob Frederick, former graduate assistant at KU during the 60s returned to Allen Fieldhouse. He was the new assistant for the University of Kentucky under the legendary Adolph Rupp.

On the road, we played at Indiana University, a team coached by a new face in college basketball, Bob Knight. Coach Knight was in his first year at a program that he would lead to three national championships. As a player, he was a member of some of Ohio State's finest teams, and had been the head coach at the U.S. Military Academy.

Unfortunately, in a rebuilding year for the Jayhawks, we played one of our most difficult schedules. Indiana, Kentucky, Louisville, Notre Dame, Brigham Young, Southern California, Georgia Tech and Xavier were not huge confidence boosters in December.

> *"He cared so much about the players and that we represented the university in a positive way. I didn't finish my sophomore year the way he thought I could, and that summer, I missed class. So he called me in and he demoted me—first time that had happened to me in my playing career. He told me I had to prove to him that I wanted to be a player and earn my playing time back. This was after I had started most of the previous season. So he put me on the second team and I had to play my way back into the starting lineup. I was playing as well as I thought I could play, but he thought I could do better. It takes a lot to bench the leading scorer. Even if I believed I was doing my best, he was bold enough to say I wasn't. That discipline carried over into classroom, too, and I became an Academic All-American."*
> *— Bud Stallworth, University of Kansas, guard, 1969-72*

An on-court tackle

Nevertheless, the players put forth great effort and earned several significant wins. One win was in Lawrence against Jack Hartman's outstanding Kansas State team. Playing with an ankle sprain, Bud led us with 28 points, and we were leading, 64-61, when Kansas State scored to cut the lead to one point with less than 20 seconds remaining. Jack took a timeout and inserted a football player, Lindbergh White, whom everyone in the house knew would go after our ball handler, Aubrey Nash, to foul him, because he was having a bad year at the free-throw line.

I was faced with the decision of taking out one of my best ball-handlers or taking a chance at the line. We devised a play to give Aubrey a running start, and he took the ball with Lindbergh in hot pursuit. He finally tracked Aubrey down and practically tackled him at mid-court and Aubrey crashed to the floor. After Jack took a timeout, Dean Nesmith worked feverishly on Aubrey, spraying his right elbow with a freezing compound to prevent swelling. I was ticked off at what I perceived to be the unfairness of injuring my player and placing him at a disadvantage at the line, so I told the referee that I was substituting Mark Mathews for the injured player, Aubrey.

Jack came unglued and protested, but to no avail. Mark went to the line and nailed both free throws to ice the game. The press questioned me after the game, as though I had bent the rules by substituting Mark at the line, so I suggested that they watch my television show the next day to see exactly what had happened.

The next morning, I arrived at the office and started to put together the highlights for the evening show. I couldn't wait to reach the part where Aubrey was injured, and sure enough, I watched on film as he crumbled to the floor and banged his elbow on the floor. I would have been perfectly justified in pulling the injured player, were it not for the fact that it was Aubrey's left elbow that hit the floor. As you might imagine, there was not a single comment about the incident on the television program that evening.

When we returned to Kansas State and Ahearn Fieldhouse later in the year, we saw a locker trunk, painted red with a cross on it, titled with an inscription: "Aubrey Nash First Aid Kit." I had to laugh at their cleverness. Kansas and Kansas State usually kept their kidding in good taste.

A second notable win was against Nebraska Coach Joe Cipriano. His Cornhuskers led by one point with two seconds left and they had possession of the ball. As they looked to inbound the ball in the backcourt, on the side, I put 6'7" Neal Mask into the game to guard the sideline and try to deflect the inbounds pass. When the Nebraska player threw the ball in, Neal tipped it just enough to slow the pass and Fred Bosilevac alertly intercepted it, dribbled once and laid it in for an incredible win.

In the last home game of the year, we were playing our old rivals, Missouri, on national television, and we were celebrating the 20th reunion of the 1952 national championship team. A festive crowd witnessed one of the greatest shooting exhibitions in KU history. Bud Stallworth scored 50 points, a conference record, and I took him out late in the game so that he could receive a standing ovation. Then someone sent me a note saying that he was just two points from tying Wilt Chamberlain's Allen Fieldhouse scoring record.

I put Bud back into the game and he was fouled with a few seconds to go, giving him a chance to tie the record. Unfortunately, one of his teammates stepped into the free-throw lane early, ending his chance. Thirteen of his shots that day were beyond the present-day three-point line, meaning that he would've scored 63 points by today's standards. The nationally televised game opened more doors for Bud in professional basketball.

> *"Sixty-three? He used to call it 70. But it was 50. Those were the rules at the time. And being against Missouri, that adds a lot more importance in this part of the country."*
> — *Bud Stallworth, University of Kansas, guard, 1969-72*

Bouncing back

Going into the 1972-73 season, we had lost All-American Bud Stallworth, competitor and defender Aubrey Nash, Neal Mask, Fred Bosilevac and Randy Canfield. Our class of freshmen—Rick Suttle, Danny Knight, Dale Greenlee, Tommie Smith, Marshall Rogers, Mike Fiddelke and Glen Russell—were now sophomores and added more depth. We were a young squad, with two seniors, junior college transfers Dale Haase and Wilson Barrow, two juniors in Tom Kivisto and Dave Taynor, and the remainder as freshmen and sophomores.

Another difficult schedule awaited us, with Vanderbilt, Indiana, Murray State, Iowa, Xavier, Texas Tech, San Francisco and Notre Dame highlighting our non-conference competition. Our young team struggled throughout the year. In good years, teams believe in themselves and find a way to win, but in down years, teams have doubts and find a way to lose. The latter was certainly the case with this team, and we ended at 8-18, my worst record at KU. We knew that we had some good young players, but we needed to supplement them with additional talent.

In the offseason, we were successful in recruiting four first-rate players: 6'9" Norm Cook from Lincoln, Illinois, 6'9" Donnie Von Moore from Chicago, 6'4" Rueben Shelton from St. Louis, and 6'6" Roger Morningstar, a junior college transfer who could really shoot the ball. The biggest problem that we faced at the beginning of the 1973-74 season was getting the players to believe that we could be successful. Fortunately, the previous year's top five scorers returned for the new season.

Duncan Reid, an outstanding high school coach from Lincoln, Illinios, had joined Sam Miranda and me on the coaching staff. A superb teacher of the game, Coach Reid also turned out to be an excellent recruiter. Faces on campus were changing, too, with the arrival of a new chancellor Archie Dykes, formerly chancellor of the University of Tennessee, while Clyde Walker replaced Wade Stinson as athletic director.

Preparing for the 1973-74 basketball season with a nucleus of veterans and promising newcomers, we knew that we would be much improved. It was critical that we experience early-season success in order to give the players a reason to believe in themselves and the system. We also knew that we would have to be in superb condition to tackle a non-conference schedule that included Kentucky, Indiana, Vanderbilt, Iowa, Washington State, Oregon and Notre Dame.

I remember two things about our opening 103-71 victory over Murray State. The win was freshman Norm Cook's coming-out party, as he shot 9-for-9 from the field and scored 21 points. The other thing I remember was the Murray State coach wanting to know if we had a handball court that he could use on game day for a workout. At first, I thought that a coach can't be taking the game seriously if he's more concerned about working out than concentrating on the game. After all my years of sitting and stewing about every game on game day, it finally occurred to me that exercising on the day of the game took away the day's stress and left a coach more alert and energized for the battle.

Coaching Lesson: *Exercise*
I highly recommend exercise to all young coaches—work out, and not just on game days. Stay in prime physical condition. It will give you a different perspective on the task at hand and you will be more relaxed and more positive. Young coaches shouldn't misunderstand, however, that they can't be relaxed and positive if they haven't prepared in advance of the game.

Our old nemesis, Kentucky, was next on the schedule. To our growing team, the game was vital, a barometer of where we were in our hopes of returning to a championship-caliber program. Newcomer Roger Morningstar led the way with 20 points, Norm Cook made his first two shots to start his career 11-for-11 from the field, Danny Knight delivered 17 points on the inside and Rick Suttle added 12 off the bench.

As good as we felt after winning against Kentucky, a trip to Bloomington, Indiana, reminded us that both the players and the coaches had work to do. It was already apparent that Bob Knight, early in his tenure, was establishing a top-tier program. We came away with a 72-59 whipping, and our eyes were fully opened.

Learning to respond

A 94-60 victory over Northern Iowa at home was much needed, restoring our confidence. We had settled into a lineup with Team Captain Tom Kivisto at the point-guard position, Dale Greenlee at shooting guard, Roger Morningstar at small forward, Norm Cook at power forward and Danny Knight in the post. Our bench rotation included Rick Suttle and Tommy Smith (we called them the "super subs"), shooter Dave Taynor, Nino Samuel, Rueben Shelton and Donnie Von Moore.

In the Northern Iowa game, Dave Taynor scored 17, his second-best effort in a Kansas uniform (his best was 27 at Georgia Tech in an earlier year). Our bench accounted for 39 points, with Nino, Rick, Donnie, Rueben, Jack Hollis and Bob Emery contributing. It's so rewarding for a coach when the reserves, who sacrifice so much for the good of the team with their effort in practice, are able to receive playing time.

The Jayhawk Classic was our next challenge, with Coach George Raveling's Washington State team and Coach Dick Harter's Oregon team coming to Lawrence. Against Washington State's match-up zone, we did far too much analyzing, which led to the players standing instead of moving, and we only led by a point at halftime. In the second half, though, the players passed and cut quickly, and the movement opened up opportunities for the shooters. On defense, our half-court man-for-man pressure held the Cougars to 22 points in the second half, and we came away with a 66-51 victory.

Dick Harter had a reputation as one of the very best defensive coaches in the country, and he later became one of the NBA's top defensive coaches. His players prided themselves in their toughness; the team brochure proudly displayed all five players on the floor fighting for a loose ball. Preparing for them, we challenged our players to measure up to Oregon's defensive intensity. Well, the Jayhawks outdid themselves, holding the Ducks to only 15 points in the second half. For our team, the victory against such an excellent team was a statement win.

After the Jayhawk Classic, we took to the road, where championships are won. We had yet to prove to ourselves that we had matured enough to compete against good teams in front of hostile crowds. Vanderbilt was a complete team, and they jumped ahead by 10 points at halftime in front of a packed arena. Although we responded with a great effort in the second half, with Danny Knight scoring 24 points and Norm Cook adding 19, we fell short, 83-72. The team still had some growing to do.

Choosing to believe

The Big Eight conference tournament presented some real challenges. Our first game was against the Colorado Buffaloes. Coach Sox Walseth had initiated a new offense, a continuity offense with interchangeable positions that he had learned from a junior college coach in California. The offense didn't yet have a name, but it later evolved into the "flex" offense. The problem that it created for most opponents, us included, is that the system forced post players to defend on the outside as well as on the inside, and it occasionally forced guards to defend players in the post. The Buffaloes also had two versatile players in the 6'5" range, Scott Wedman and Dave Logan, who became successful professional athletes (Scott in the NBA and Dave in the NFL). Zoning Colorado wasn't an option for us because they shot the ball so well.

Battling in old Municipal Auditorium in Kansas City, both teams played well, but Colorado prevailed, lifted by Wedman's 30 points. The loss disappointed our squad and doubts began to surface. In a team meeting, we allowed the players to air their concerns. It was a productive meeting, especially with the leadership of team captain Tom Kivisto.

Tom had been a scorer in high school, but as our point guard, he was willing to sacrifice his scoring in order to keep the team moving and distributing the basketball. Like JoJo before him, Tom couldn't be judged by the statistics he produced. He was a tenacious defender, an excellent ball handler and an extraordinary leader. He led by example, as all great leaders do. He wasn't the fastest player, but he always led the conditioning sprints. The Bible teaches that we as individuals must lessen ourselves so that the cause can become greater, and the same holds true for a basketball team.

It was a critical time for the team, a time to make a choice: Either revert back to the previous year's mentality of not believing or become a team that would find a way to succeed. On the afternoon following the Colorado loss, we faced a consolation game against a Sooners squad led by Alvan Adams. I told the Jayhawks what I've told other youngsters over the years: When your back is against the wall, your only choice is to fight your way out. Most of the time, that fight won't mean beautifully executed plays. It will mean fighting for loose balls and rebounds and defending every possession as though that trip down the floor would determine the outcome of the game.

That afternoon, with a sparse crowd and nothing to play for but pride, we grew up as a team. Seven Kansas players shared the scoring and a substitute, Tommie Smith, led the way with 24 points, earning him a spot in the seven-man rotation that held for the rest of the season. We played with grit and determination and defeated a solid Oklahoma team.

We finished the tournament with a 75-66 win as Roger Morningstar and

Dale Greenlee lit up the Nebraska zone with 28 and 23 points, respectively. We emerged with renewed hopes for a competitive conference regular-season run.

Growing as a team

What we needed before the conference race started, though, was a meaningful road victory over a good opponent. We traveled to Iowa City, Iowa, in quest of such a win. A hard-fought game against the Hawkeyes ended 72-71 in our favor when Tom Kivisto fed the ball to Danny Knight for a bucket. Danny scored 23 and Norm Cook grabbed 14 rebounds, and the team began to believe that they could win close ball games.

In the conference race, the home-opener against Nebraska was critical for the team. Four players scored in double figures in a balanced attack—which became a feature of this team—and we won, 79-64. After a win at Iowa State in the new Hilton Arena, we returned home to host Oklahoma State, a team coached by Guy Strong, my fellow artillery officer in Korea. After a successful stint at his alma mater, Eastern Kentucky, Guy came to Stillwater to resurrect OSU's fortunes. His team was ready to play and took the fight to us from the beginning. With three minutes to play, we were down 10, positioned to lose a home game—a crushing blow to our hopes of a conference title. Many disappointed fans headed for the exits, but our team responded and tied the game. With only a few seconds remaining, Tommie Smith stole the ball. In a timeout, I designed a play to free up Rick Suttle, whom Tommie would feed. Rick wasn't open, though, so Tommie nailed a bucket that would've been an NBA-distance three-pointer, and we won, 68-66. The shot was the first of several historic moments for Tommie on the season.

Coming into Allen Fieldhouse next was a Notre Dame team that had just ended UCLA's 88-game winning streak and grabbed the No. 1 national ranking. Coach Digger Phelps, who had taken over the Irish reins in the 1971-72 season, had quickly built a strong team, which included Adrian Dantley, John Shumate and Gary Brokaw. A packed house was treated to a great game as Notre Dame jumped out to a 14-point lead at the half. Our comeback fell short by just two points, and the Irish held onto their top ranking. Still, Rick was becoming the offensive force we had hoped for, nailing 27 points off the bench.

Gut check

The following week offered our team a gut check as we went on the road against Oklahoma and Missouri. Coach John MacLeod had done a fine job rebuilding the Sooners. We had recruited their talented player, Alvan Adams, an Oklahoma City native. Tied 43-all at the half, Rick came off the bench in the second period, his guns blazing, and poured in 31 points. Seven players participated in the scoring and we eked out a three-point win over a tremendous OU team, giving us the confidence that we could win on the road.

We traveled to Missouri that Saturday to face the Tigers. One thing we could count on with Norm Stewart's teams was physical defense and rebounding, and no Missouri player epitomized their style more than Al Eberhard. My high school coach always told us that playing in such a manner would gain opponents' respect, and that certainly happened with Eberhard. However, our frontline players—Norm, Roger and Rick—led an offense that produced 80 points and another road victory.

Back in Lawrence, we were prepared for the Buffaloes' flex offense, beating them 81-66 as Rick scored more than 20 points for the fourth straight game. And then a visit Stillwater yielded an 80-71 win over the Cowboys, with Danny Knight dominating the paint and scoring 34 points while Norm Cook added 14 boards.

The stage was set for a showdown in Manhattan between the two conference leaders and rivals. Lon Kruger, a tough guard from Silver Lake, Kansas, was the heart of the Kansas State team—and the league MVP for two consecutive years. Larry Williams, the 6'9" player we had recruited until his visit was interrupted by the turmoil on KU's campus, played extremely well and led the Cats in scoring while Lon added 18. Their zone shut off our inside scoring, and although we played hard, we lost, 74-71. We shot four free throws to their 24, and it was a difference we couldn't overcome.

Fortunately, this team responded well to the loss, blowing away a good Iowa State team, 72-57, and then dropping Oklahoma, 98-80, with Danny's 24 points leading the seven scorers. We were right back in the conference race.

On the dreary winter trip to Lincoln, we knew that Joe would have his troops ready to go. Both teams had high-scoring offenses, but this game turned out to be a grinder. Not only did we shoot poorly from the field, we couldn't buy a free throw, hitting five of 18. We were forced to rely on our patented half-court defense and with Tom Kivisto and Dale Greenlee initiating the pressure, we held Nebraska to 46 points. We managed 51, adding one more badly needed road win.

Things wouldn't get any easier as we journeyed to Boulder to play Colorado for the third time, with each team having won once. As it happened so many times in my years at KU, we went down to the wire, but we stuck it out for a 70-68 win that served as a reminder that in good years, when teams believe, they find a way to win.

'Dance with what brung you'

We returned to Lawrence for the conference title game against Kansas State. Even though we were in first place with one defeat and Kansas State had two, they could tie us with a win and gain the conference championship in a tie-breaker. With an NCAA bid on the line, the stakes were high.

With only a couple of days to prepare, we decided to try to trick Coach Hartman and his players by showing one defense and shifting to another. I had studied the Wildcats enough to know exactly what they would do in such a situation. The game started with my cleverly designed defense confusing no one but my own players.

After we dropped behind, 8-2, I called timeout and told them that we would, as Texas football coach Darrell Royal once said, "Dance with what brung you." In our case, that meant tough man-for-man defense. Guards Tom Kivisto and Dale Greenlee led an inspired defense that contained the Wildcats' fine guard play. In one of those beautiful, pressure-cooked games between KU and K-State, Allen Fieldhouse rocked every possession, and we held the Cats to 20 points in the first half. Kansas State fought back with pride, but we held them off for a 60-55 win to clinch the conference championship and an NCAA bid.

On a gorgeous March night, Jayhawk Boulevard was filled with celebrating fans. After three seasons without a championship and NCAA bid, this basketball-loving campus enjoyed the moment.

Meanwhile, I learned an important lesson from the Kansas State game: Don't ever try something new in an emotional game without having several days to work on the tactic. Coaches think about an upcoming game around the clock, but the players spend an hour or so on a new approach before their thoughts go to their studies or social life.

On senior night the following Saturday, it was fitting that we were playing the Missouri Tigers as a farewell to seniors Dave Taynor and Tom Kivisto. We played loose, having already clinched the championship in the Kansas State game, and it was a night of celebration as we routed the Tigers, 112-76. The game was a tribute to a team that overcame the doubts of the previous year's losing season and persevered.

We were successful in turning the season around because of several factors—Tom's leadership, our players' willingness to assume roles that benefited the team as a whole, well-balanced scoring (with our leading scorer in the conference, "super sub" Rick Suttle, playing as a reserve), a defense that held our opponents to 41 percent shooting and a rebounding margin of plus seven in conference play.

'Expect a miracle'

As we prepared for the NCAA tournament to begin in Tulsa—only a four-hour drive from Lawrence—we knew that we would have a large following. Because of the Big Eight's previous success in the tourney, we had a bye, and awaited the Creighton vs. Texas winner while Louisville awaited the Syracuse vs. Oral Roberts winner.

In those days, being an independent school like Oral Roberts had some advantages. Rather than having to win a conference championship, an independent school could qualify on the basis of their season record, although they had to play an additional game to qualify for the Sweet 16. Another bonus for Oral Roberts was the Mabee Center, a state-of-the-art-facility with cushioned seats and a practice court below, a luxury that few schools had. The arena seated 10,000 and proved to be an attractive site for a regional tournament. Oral Roberts had been a member of D-I basketball for only a few years, and the short period of time it took them to enter the national picture was pretty phenomenal. I recall feeling like it was just yesterday that Ken Trickey had brought his staff to KU to learn about our athletic organization and methods.

Coached by Eddie Sutton, Creighton had advanced. As we prepared for them, every indication was that we were in for a difficult game. Coach Sutton's teams played good defense and minimized errors on offense, so every possession counted. We played a sound game, escaping with a 55-54 win with 18 points from Roger.

The second semifinal game was between Louisville and Oral Roberts, who had upset Syracuse in a first-round game. The game was just the opposite of our Creighton contest as Oral Roberts prevailed 96-93 in an offensive shoot-out. The stage was set for a game to determine the Midwest region representative to the Final Four, the dream of all college players. We went back to our hotel knowing that we would face a terrific offensive team.

What we didn't know was what would hit the *Tulsa World* headlines the next morning. ORU Coach Ken Trickey had been picked up on a DUI complaint the night before and had been suspended for the game. (Earlier in the season, Ken had announced his resignation in order to pursue other jobs.) When we went to practice on Friday, Ken's assistants were running practice. Early on Saturday, I went over to the Mabee Center to tape an interview with *NBC*. When I arrived, I was surprised to see Coach Trickey standing there. I went over to offer my condolences, only to learn that he was awaiting his interview time. After visiting with the university president during the night, he had been reinstated.

We knew that we were in for a fight. The ORU team was big, strong and mobile, and extremely talented. Their frontline was imposing and their backcourt even better. They had a freshman, Anthony Roberts, who could really light it up, and he became one of ORU's all-time greats. We knew that we could only hope to slow them down, not stop them.

To this day in Tulsa, the KU-ORU contest is still called "The Game," as one of the best athletic events the city has ever seen. Knowing they fronted the post on defense, we cleared the weak-side area and had early success lobbing the ball to our post men, and we got off to a 20-5 start. We knew they'd make a run, though, and they certainly did, pulling within one, 45-44, at the half. They took control as the second half started, and with three minutes to go, we trailed by nine. I looked down at the floor by our bench and the bold wording read, "Expect a Miracle." We were about to witness one. Our players kept their poise and our press rattled ORU. Shooting with deadly accuracy, we tied the game, 81-81, at the end of regulation.

The momentum was all ours in overtime. When Tommie Smith tipped in a missed shot with a few seconds to go, we went up three. The 93-90 victory—and a trip to the Final Four—was an incredible turnaround for a team that had gone 8-18 the previous year. We were headed to the Final Four for the second time in four years, thanks to a remarkable group of young men.

The Final Four

The bus ride back to Lawrence seemed much shorter than the trip down. We were making plans for a trip to Greensboro, North Carolina, and a meeting with Marquette and Coach Al McGuire. UCLA, with one of their most talented teams, would meet North Carolina State.

When I arrived home, I was surprised to receive a phone call from ORU President Oral Roberts. I thought he was calling to congratulate us, but instead, he said that he wanted to fly up and talk to me about the open coaching position at ORU. He said that he liked the way I coached and thought I was perfect for ORU. I told him that I was preparing for the NCAA finals and that I couldn't possibly interview. Besides, I loved coaching at KU and had no desire to change. He kept insisting that if I would give him just a little time, he would fly into Topeka. (Those who knew him will agree that he was quite persuasive.) Fortunately, on the day that he planned to fly in, thunderstorms formed between Tulsa and Topeka and he couldn't make the trip.

In Greensboro on the night before the games, *Sports Illustrated* hosted a dinner for the Final Four coaches and their spouses at the Greensboro Country Club. I didn't like the idea of the dinner because I didn't like to mingle with an opponent the night before the game. Still, we arrived to meet Coach and Mrs. Wooden, Norm Short and his bride and Al McGuire and his wife, and the worst possible thing that could happen did happen: Al charmed everyone, including my wife, which she reminded me of on the way back to the hotel. I cut off her remarks about "how witty that Al was" and told her I didn't wish to hear anymore.

The 1974 Final Four teams were loaded with future first-round draft picks, such as the Bruins' Bill Walton, David Meyers, Silky Wilkes, Marcus Johnson and Rich Washington; Marquette's Maurice Lucas, Bo Ellis and Earl Tatum; and North Carolina State's 7'4" Tom Burleson, David Thompson and Monte Towe. Few Final Fours have ever had the quality of that 1974 field.

Even though we led by one point at halftime, Marquette's full-court pressure uncovered our Achilles heel. We were not a team of great ball-handlers, and Marquette trapped Tom, our point guard and leader, and kept him away from the ball. The tactic took its toll, as did poor shooting, which had been a strength of ours, and we lost. Coach McGuire said after the game that their strategy was to keep the ball out of Tom's hands. As he put it, "If you cut off the head, the body dies."

> *"It was the end of the 1974 Final Four in Greensboro, North Carolina. My sister and I were happily swimming at the hotel pool. Despite his disappointment, Dad decided to have a little fun. He pushed me in, so without hesitation, I pushed him back. His good-luck jacket rose to the top of the water, circling his head like a flotation device. At that moment, I realized what I had done. Given our loss, he must have already picked out a replacement jacket. The wet dog-drenched jacket wasn't upsetting him. It was the newly acquired water-logged Final Four watch he was holding over his head that he found most disturbing."*
> — *Nancy Owens Wilde, daughter*

To make matters worse, we had to play UCLA, upset by NC State, in the third-place game. On Sunday, at a press conference with all four coaches, Coach Wooden announced that he did not believe in the third-place game and was going to give his seniors the option of whether to play or not. My wheels were spinning. I immediately thought that the UCLA underclassmen—Rich Washington and Marcus Johnson (both of whom were No. 1 picks in future drafts), 7-footer Ralph Drollinger, and guards Pete Trgovich and Andre McCarter—were capable of beating nearly any team in the country, and I knew it wouldn't look good if we lost to UCLA's second team.

When it was my turn to speak, I told Coach Wooden that the Jayhawks would be honored to play UCLA's first team, and it was our hope that their seniors would play. When Monday rolled around, UCLA fielded their entire team, and we played well enough in the first half to lead by eight points. But the Bruins were too gifted and too deep. They finally wore us down, and we lost the last game of a miraculous season.

Chapter 16

Ups and Downs
in the '70s

Coach's Life Lesson: *Do not ever forget your obligations to others. Let them know that they have a part in your success. Then follow the example of others and "pay it forward."*

Even though success requires an individual to make a commitment and develop his or her skills, all of us were assisted along the way by others. We should let them know we appreciate their support, and then support others. I've always done this with youngsters, whether in Tulsa or Florida. They've always known that they can come to me to work on their basketball skills. I never charge them anything, only requiring that some day, they pay it forward and help someone else. It comes from an awareness on my part that as I progressed as a player and a coach, it would've been impossible to achieve any level of success without the help of my parents, coaches, teachers, and teammates. We wouldn't have survived the Depression without help. It's the reality of my life.

The excitement of the beginning of the 1974-75 school year was dampened with the September passing of Dr. Phog Allen at the age of 88. His vision not only influenced the athletic program at KU but also went far beyond. He helped lay the groundwork for the National Association of Basketball Coaches so that coaches could join together as guardians of the game. He was a leading proponent of basketball becoming a part of the Olympics. Even today, his presence hovers over Kansas basketball. Visiting teams are reminded of his legacy when they enter Allen Fieldhouse and see a banner that reads "Pay Heed, All Who Enter: Beware of the Phog."

I first knew Dr. Allen when I was an opposing player from OU. While I had limited contact with him while I was at KU, I always enjoyed the response he received from the Allen Fieldhouse crowd as he entered the arena. On the golf course, my locker at the Lawrence Country Club was close to Dr. Allen's. His golf group, known as the Doc Allen group, always walked when they played. One day as our groups passed, I hit a terrible shot with my two-iron and angrily slammed the face of it into the ground. Dr. Allen just calmly said, "A person at certain levels of skill should not expect a perfect shot every time." I never forgot that bit of advice.

Following the 1974 Final Four season, it appeared that we would be solid again in the '74-75 season with all but one starter returning. We added several freshmen in 6'10" Ken Koenigs; guards Milt Gibson, Clint Johnson, Rueben Shelton and Marc Fletcher; and a junior college transfer, Rick Bussard, who had been a teammate of Roger Morningstar's. The one starter we lost, however, Tom Kivisto, had exceptional leadership qualities and basketball skills. We never quite replaced him on the court, although we experimented with a variety of possible solutions.

We struggled in December, for the most part, although we did play one outstanding game, a 35-point win against a University of Iowa team led by a new coach, Lute Olson, who later found great success—and a national title—at Arizona. We lost an overtime game, 74-70, to an Indiana team that racked up a 29-0 record before losing to Kentucky in the regional finals. We also lost to that Kentucky team, which then advanced to the national championship game against John Wooden's UCLA Bruins.

During the previous summer, I was recruiting in L.A. and dropped by the UCLA athletic building to see Terry Donahue, who had been an assistant football coach at KU before taking the head coaching job at UCLA. I told him that I didn't want to be in the building without saying hello to the Wizard of Westwood. Coach Wooden took me to lunch at his favorite deli in Westwood and told me that the season was going to be his last. He asked me not to mention it and, naturally, I honored his request.

Our other December losses were to two outstanding teams, Notre Dame and Washington. Although we entered the conference tournament in Kansas City with a 4-4 record, we won by 20 over Oklahoma State in the opening game followed by one-point victories over Nebraska and Iowa State to win the sixth Big Eight tourney title in my time as head coach.

A road comeback to remember

After a win at St. Louis, we returned home to begin the conference season with a win against Missouri. We then lost to Iowa State in Ames, beat Oklahoma State and Colorado at home, and lost on the road at Kansas State. Donnie Von Moore was giving us solid play and freshman Clint Johnson, a track-and-field high jumper from Leavenworth, was adding to the team's depth.

After wins against Nebraska, Oklahoma, and Iowa State, we were right back in the race for the championship. In a crucial road game at Stillwater, we prevailed, 59-57. But then a loss in Columbia meant that we had to win a home game against Kansas State. Rick Suttle ignited the crowd with his dance steps in an emotional player introduction, and the team delivered their best performance of the year and stomped the Wildcats, 91-53.

Now we faced what all contenders must face: the challenge of winning road games. Our first venture was to Boulder to face Sox Walseth's Buffaloes. After leading at halftime by six points, we held off their rally for a 78-76 win. Rick continued his dominance, scoring 30 points.

The conference race's most important night came down to March 5, when we visited Nebraska in Lincoln as Kansas State traveled to Missouri. We needed to win our own game, but we also hoped for a Wildcat loss, which would put us one game ahead in the race.

The Cornhuskers were certainly ready. We ran into a buzz saw and trailed by 19 points with three minutes to go in the first half. When we challenged the players to close the gap before the half, they delivered an 8-0 run and we went into the half down 41-30. I spent the break convincing our players that we needed to be patient on offense, explaining that 11 points represented only six possessions. I told them they had to tighten their defense and take pride in wearing the KU uniform—and for effect; I slammed my fist into a locker. I didn't want to flinch, but man, did it ever hurt. I thought that I had broken something with that display of passion.

Whether it was my speech or simply that the team's motivation came from within, they responded in the second half. This team was a special group of young men, led by seniors Dale, Roger, Danny, Tommie and Rick. We gradually trimmed the lead, but Nebraska wouldn't give in too easily, and with 40 seconds to go, we still trailed by five. After Rick went to the line and hit his first free throw to close the gap to four points, we called a timeout and told Rick to purposefully miss the second one. We told him to position his feet slightly to the right of his normal free-throw position and to bank the ball off of the rim. We put Norm, at 6'9," and Danny, at 6'10," in the second spots on the lane. Many times, our players had practiced the footwork to free themselves from the second spot on a missed free-throw. Rick banked his second shot off the board and rim, and Norm captured the rebound and hit a short shot, cutting the lead to two. A coach always feels that he has to prepare his players for any and all situations that might occur in a game, and that preparation certainly paid off against Nebraska.

On behalf of the national rules committee, the Big Eight was experimenting with a 30-second shot clock for all conference games, so we knew that we would get the ball back again with at least 10 seconds left, if not more. Unfortunately, we fouled their ace scorer, Jerry Fort, with 16 seconds on the clock. But he missed the front end of a 1-and-1 and Rick nailed a jump shot to send the game into overtime. The first overtime was a battle, with each team scoring eight and one of our best players, Roger, fouling out.

Before the second overtime began, trainer Dean Nesmith whispered to me that Kansas State had lost in Columbia. I told the team that I knew they were tired, but they could win the championship with a win in the second overtime and a home victory over Oklahoma. They played inspired basketball and we won, 79-77, in what I consider the greatest road comeback against a worthy opponent in my career. Overcoming a 19-point deficit without the three-point shot was a near impossible feat, but those guys pulled it off.

We returned to Lawrence to play Oklahoma, led by All-American Alvan Adams. Alvan finished with 32 points, but our balance was too much for the Sooners, and we pulled out a victory, 74-63. Our seniors had honored Kansas basketball with their accomplishments in the last two years, including two conference championships, a conference tournament championship and a Final Four appearance. It was a great night for them in Allen Fieldhouse.

The next week, we traveled to Tulsa and ORU's Mabee Center, where we faced Notre Dame and forward Adrian Dantley. We didn't get off to a great start and trailed at the half, 44-32. We made a run in the second half but soon ran into severe foul problems. We outscored Notre Dame by 20 points from the field, but the Irish shot 50 free throws to our 13, and we lost 77-71. Seven Kansas players were eliminated by fouls, which still stands as an NCAA tournament record.

A few weeks after the season, I made a trip to Las Vegas to provide commentary for the Pizza Hut All-American game on *CBS*. The West team's coach was Arizona State's Ned Wulk. I asked him how his recruiting was going and he told me that they were about to sign Paul Mokeski, a 7-footer from Encino, California. What Ned didn't know was that we had developed a relationship with the Mokeski family and Paul planned to sign with our assistant coach, Duncan Reid, the next morning. I didn't give Ned any indication of our interest, and I became a little more anxious to hear from Duncan that Paul had indeed signed with us.

Elsewhere in recruiting, one of the country's most highly sought-after high school players was Darrell Dawkins of Orlando, Florida. I called JoJo White, who in just a short period of time had become a star with the NBA's Boston Celtics, and asked if he would meet me in Orlando to visit with Darrell.

As I gave my pitch at the Dawkins home, I noticed that I had attracted a crowd outside the living room window, and the fans were listening to me talk to Darrell and his family. As we left the house, I told Mark and JoJo how impressed I was that the adoring fans had assembled outside the house on my account. Jo told me he didn't want to rain on my parade, but he had been signing autographs and passing them through the window to the kids outside. We all need a little humility every once in awhile, but does it have to be so painful?

The decisions players face

That summer, Norm Cook was selected to become a member of the U.S. Pan American Olympic team and played extremely well. At the time, the ABA and NBA were in a fierce battle for college talent. When Utah Jazz staff members offered Norm a contract, he called to tell us and we dispatched a person who was knowledgeable on contracts. While he concluded that the offer was legit, there were many indications that the ABA wouldn't last and the Utah franchise would fold.

Norm decided to come back to school, but he continued to wonder if he should have accepted the contract. At the conclusion of the 1975-76 basketball season, the Boston Celtics assured me that if Norm was still available for their first-round pick, they would take him. When I presented Norm with this information, he decided to forgo his senior year and begin his professional basketball career.

Trials of the late '70s

The period of 1975 to 1977 was difficult for me in my coaching, in my family, and in my faith. On the court, the Jayhawks struggled in 1975-76, finishing 13-13 and 6-8 in the league. The 1976-77 team made considerable progress (18-10 overall, 8-6 in the Big Eight) with the maturation of Paul Mokeski, Ken Koenigs, Donnie Von Moore, Clint Johnson, Milt Gibson and Herb Nobles, and the addition of Hasan Houston, Mac Stalcup and John Douglas. John, a junior college transfer, scored 46 points against the Cyclones in Ames, a total that stands today as the most scored by a Jayhawk on the road.

In the 1976-77 season, the conference held its first postseason tournament. The winner would be declared the league's NCAA tourney representative, and other league teams could qualify on the basis of their overall seasons. Our season ended in the tournament semifinals with a loss to Kansas State.

In the spring of 1977, assistant coach Duncan Reid left to become the head coach at Dodge City Community College, and my longtime assistant coach, Sam Miranda, left the program to go into private business in Lawrence. Sam had been with me for 13 years, since the beginning of my tenure as head coach, and he had a major influence on the program. To fill the open positions, I hired Bob Hill, an experienced assistant coach at the University of Pittsburgh, and Lafayette Norwood, a successful high school coach from Wichita.

Family and faith

On the home front, my 19 years of marriage to Nana came to an end with a divorce in 1977. In the termination of a long, shared life between two people, there are simply no winners. And those two people aren't the only ones who suffer. Our precious daughters, Nancy and Kelly, 14 and 17 at the time, felt the pain as much as we did. It was an incredibly difficult time for all of us.

On top of all of this, I faced another challenge that consumed my thoughts and caused many sleepless nights. I had started to question my Christian faith and my purpose in life, questions for which I had neither the knowledge nor information to answer acceptably. I had always harbored a childlike faith, a product of the beliefs and experiences of my beloved father and mother. But I had not been a dedicated student of the Bible, nor had I established a consistent, daily prayer life.

Throughout these difficult times, many friends told me they could see that I was troubled, and they shared their faith with me. Dick Harp, who was then the Fellowship of Christian Athletes deputy director, sent me many books that would encourage me in my struggle. I searched for answers to the questions that have troubled humans for centuries: Who created the universe? Who created life? Are there natural explanations for the origin of the universe and life on earth, or are there supernatural forces at work? If there is a Creator, did He come to earth as a human to teach us His purposes and plans for us? Is the Bible an accurate record of the Creator's word? In our lives, is there a supernatural force that guides us in our decisions? My search for these answers truly began during that period of my life, and the studies have continued in a more comprehensive manner later in my life.

On a positive note, my daughter, Nancy, was a member of the Lawrence High School volleyball team's second-straight state championship team. It was a wonderful experience for me to sit in the stands as a parent and watch my child perform. In all of my coaching and playing, I was never more excited about a victory than when Nancy's serve for the final point in the championship dipped over the net without a return.

Renewed hope in 1977-78

Heading into the 1977-78 season, recruiting had gone well with the addition of freshmen Wilmore Fowler, Darnell Valentine, Booty Neal and John Crawford, and junior college All-American Chester Giles. With a strong nucleus of returning players including John Douglas, Ken Koenigs, Paul Mokeski, Donnie Von Moore, Hasan Houston, Brad Sanders, Clint Johnson, Mac Stallcup, Scott Anderson and Milt Gibson, our hopes for an improved team were high. Even with an improved outlook, though, we were picked to finish no higher than third or fourth in the conference. Defending champion Kansas State had returned two quality performers and added Rolando Blackman, a future NBA player, and the Wildcats were heavily favored to win the league again.

In preseason workouts, we emphasized conditioning so that we could play an up-tempo game. This was a team with solid depth and rebounding potential. We had speed and skill in the perimeter players, and inside players Paul Mokeski, Ken Koenigs and Donnie Von Moore had strong potential as scorers.

In the first five games of the season, our team averaged more than 100 points per game. In our sixth game, we played a veteran Kentucky team that proved to be the top team in the country. It was a tremendous battle, but Kentucky prevailed, 73-66, with an edge at the free-throw line.

After wins over St. Louis and Oral Roberts, we journeyed to Little Rock to take on an Arkansas team that later played in the Final Four in St. Louis. Arkansas's trio of Ron Brewer, Sidney Moncrief, and Marvin Delph—known as the "Triplets"—edged us, 78-72. Although we had proven that we could compete with the best teams in the country, we had to prove to the league and to ourselves that we were of championship caliber.

The Big Eight Holiday tournament had been moved from Municipal Auditorium to Kemper Arena, and a crowd of more than 16,000 saw 13 KU players score in a 96-49 rout of Missouri. Darnell Valentine led with 20 points and Donnie Von Moore came off the bench to score 11. In a hard-fought semifinal game with Oklahoma, we managed a 79-76 win. Donnie gave another great performance with 18 points to lead all scorers.

Up next, it was time to battle the defending conference champions, the Kansas State Wildcats. Taking a 38-26 halftime lead, the Wildcats still looked like the best team in the league. But our Jayhawks, thanks to the effort of two bench players, Donnie and Clint, delivered a huge second-half performance and KU won, 67-62, for its seventh conference tourney title in my time as head coach. Even better, the game was a tremendous victory for a team that had struggled the past two years.

The conference quest

In our quest for the regular season conference crown, we opened at Missouri, knowing that Coach Stewart would have his team ready for the crushing defeat we had delivered in the tournament. Not surprisingly, they put up a fight—but they succumbed in the end, 71-67. Donnie was still on a roll, scoring 25 points on 10-of-15 shooting. We followed with another road win at Stillwater.

We were starting to hit our offensive stride, drilling Oklahoma, 91-61, in Lawrence, and exploding for a 100-82 win at Iowa State. Then we came home to face Kansas State. The teams knew each other well, and Jack Hartman was an excellent defensive coach, so we were prepared for a grind-it-out game. Our shooting was horrendous as we went 22-for-62 from the field, but our defense held up, and we secured a four-point win against the league's preseason favorites.

Curtis Redding was an outstanding player for Kansas State, and he loved to trash-talk with our bench and fans. During a timeout toward the end of the game, a fan threw a link of hot dogs toward the Wildcats' bench, in honor of Curtis. We would pay for that when we traveled to Manhattan.

Almost every Big Eight championship team over the years had to fight through a battle against one of Joe Cipriano's teams in Lincoln. This season, his Huskers would win 22 games. The league had also added some outstanding arenas, and the advantages Kansas and Kansas State once held were a thing of the past. As a matter of fact, with our dirt indoor arenas, we were falling behind. In Lincoln, a Devaney Center crowd of more than 11,000 saw the Huskers beat us, 62-58.

Defeat is often difficult to swallow, but out of trials, a coach makes adjustments that, many times, led to future success. We decided to quit juggling our lineups and committed to a set starting team and a rotation off the bench. Ken and Paul started inside, backed up by Donnie Von Moore, while John Douglas, Clint Johnson and Darnell Valentine started on the perimeter, backed up by Wilmore Fowler. Others also filled in off the bench, including Milt Gibson, Brad Sanders, Booty Neal, Mac Stalcup and Scott Anderson.

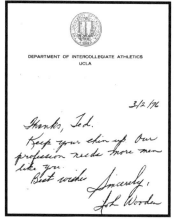

Toward the end of John Wooden's unparalleled career at UCLA, Wooden and I had established a strong-enough friendship that we exchanged notes at the beginning of each season. Wooden sent this note to me in the first year of his retirement.

Thanks to the schedule, we were fortunate to test out the new lineup in home games against Colorado and Oklahoma State, and the rotation worked well. The perimeter players were on fire in both games, with much of the production coming out of our transition game, and we won handily in both contests.

Heading to Norman to take on a Sooner team coached by Dave Bliss, we had difficulty defending, but the balance of scoring across our seven-man rotation was sufficient to produce a hard-earned 69-68 road win. We returned home to host Missouri, and Ken led us to victory with 20 points. For the season, Ken shot better than 60 percent from the field.

Bananas in the Little Apple

In the week preceding our next contest at Kansas State, a friend of mine who lived in Manhattan notified me that the students were ripening crates of bananas to throw at the Jayhawks, most likely when we were introduced. I didn't tell my players, but devised a plan to negate the effect of a banana bombardment. I told the team that as they were introduced, I wanted them to go over to the Kansas State bench, shake hands with Coach Hartman, and simply stand there until the introductions were finished. They looked at me quizzically but followed my instructions. When I was introduced, I followed them over, shook hands with Jack, and stood there. Not a banana was thrown.

Our fast break was highly effective, with John Douglas and Wilmore Fowler both scoring 18. Late in the game, with the Jayhawks leading by 15, a barrage of bananas hit the court. Our team escaped without being hit, but the game was delayed for 30 minutes while crews tried to restore the playing surface to an injury-safe condition. Order was finally restored, and we finished off the win, 75-63.

With two of our last three games at home, we were in position to claim a conference championship. Playing awfully well in his senior season, John Douglas led our team to a win over an inspired Iowa State team, 80-70. Then a full house awaited the Cornhuskers, who had given us our only conference loss, but our balance and depth were the differences in a 75-70 victory.

We clinched the title by winning in Boulder. What a season it had been. A team picked to finish fourth in the league won the league instead and only lost a total of three games to date. Two of those losses came against Kentucky and Arkansas, teams ranked in the top five that would advance to the Final Four.

Looking ahead, realizing the dream of a national championship was a real possibility with the first- and second-round games scheduled in Wichita, the regional games in Allen Fieldhouse and the Final Four in St. Louis. First, though, we faced the Buffaloes in the Big Eight tourney. Fortunately, the same seniors who had led us to the holiday tournament title and a regular-season record of 13-1 had another solid night, and we advanced to the tourney semifinals in Kansas City.

In our path was Kansas State, and we would have to beat them for the fourth time in the same season. We outscored the Wildcats from the field, but a 15-point advantage at the line was more than we could overcome, and our dream of playing in Wichita and at home in the NCAA tournament vanished.

An unwelcome postseason opponent

In those days, the NCAA tournament didn't have seeding. Had seeding been in place, we most likely would have been assigned to the Midwest region, keeping us at home because on the strength of our season's performance. As it was, the Missouri Tigers, who had upset Kansas State in the finals of the conference tournament, represented the conference in Wichita, even though the Tigers had a losing record on the year.

We were quite surprised to learn that we were headed to the Western regional in Eugene, Oregon, to face UCLA, the Pac-10 champion. That's right—two conference regular-season champions had to play in the first round. After moving past the disappointment of the loss to Kansas State, we started preparing for the Bruins. Calling several coaching friends, I learned that UCLA had an outstanding backcourt, a good center, and depth, with such players as Kiki Vandeweghe, a future NBA standout. But of all things, my friends said, don't let UCLA get its running game going.

To be certain that we stopped their transition game, I decided to send only our two big guys in for offensive rebounds and keep the three perimeter players back to try and disrupt the break. I made sure our big guys, Ken, Mo and Donnie, understood that the responsibility for offensive rebounds fell entirely on them. Our preparation went well and our practices were uplifting. The team had not lost their hopes of a national championship, even if the road was much rockier after the loss of a home-state, home-court advantage.

The first half was a classic. We were successful in our own transition game and led at the break, 45-42. Mo was playing his best game of the year, and he would finish with 18 points and 12 boards. Up by 10 points with nine minutes to go, Darnell picked up his fourth foul. Ordinarily, I would have substituted for him, but the momentum was ours and I couldn't allow the UCLA guards to take over the game. I decided to leave him in the game ... and on the very next possession of the ball, he was called for a charge. I must have looked like the dumbest coach in America—and I might have been. But if I had to do it over, I would do the same. (They say that insanity is doing the same thing over and over again and expecting different results. Maybe it fits.)

The game went down to the last minute or so, but UCLA came away with a win. We played well, for the most part, and scored 12 more points from the field than they did, but the Bruins had a 27-8 advantage at the line.

The memories of the 1977-78 team have remained a source of joy for me, even if the thoughts of what might have been remain. Because of the players' efforts, I was selected by *Basketball Weekly* magazine as their National Coach of Year. Any coach knows that personal awards are simply the result of the accomplishments of your players and your staff, so I am indebted to them for that.

Chapter 17

The End of a Christmas Tradition

Coach's Life Lesson: *Be patient and recognize the differences in people. Every individual is important in the eyes of God, and a parent or a friend. Coach Wooden always said, "We can disagree without being disagreeable."*

Thomas Jefferson said that a difference of opinion is not necessarily a difference of principle. If you look beyond the initial disagreements when you're working with someone, you'll find that Jefferson is right. As my dad would say, there are a whole lot of ways to skin a cat.

With the loss of seniors John Douglas, Ken Koenigs, Donnie Von Moore, Milt Gibson and Clint Johnson, we were faced with rebuilding a 1978-79 team anchored by seniors Paul Mokeski and Brad Sanders. Darnell Valentine returned from an outstanding freshman year along with classmates Booty Neal, John Crawford and Wilmore Fowler, while juniors Mac Stalcup and Randolph Carroll were joined by a group of promising freshmen including Tony Guy, David Magley and Mark Snow. (Due to the generosity of my good friend Jamie Coulter, who allowed us to use his personal jet, we managed to sign all three freshmen in one day—Tony in Baltimore, Maryland, David in South Bend, Indiana, and Mark in San Diego.) Chester Giles, who would have been a senior, received a medical hardship after undergoing knee surgery due to a mishap his junior year.

Clyde Walker, the KU athletic director from 1974 through 1977, had tried to solve the dirt problem in the fieldhouse by installing an artificial surface throughout the building, including on the track and basketball floor. Many athletic departments had bought into the idea that the new product would be easily maintained. Regrettably, those of us who tried the surface found that traction was difficult to control. The composition that covered the cement base was just over a half-inch thick, insufficient to absorb the pounding that a basketball player's knees, ankles and feet endure.

As a consequence of our five-year experiment with the surface, we encountered more knee problems, shin splints and ankle injuries than we saw over my entire tenure at KU. Chester Giles, a sought-after 6'9" junior college All-American, had been one of those casualties in his freshman year, although he returned from surgery to start the 1978-79 season. The good news was that plans were being made to install a wooden surface for the following season.

After opening with four victories at home, we were beginning to develop a solid starting lineup, with veterans Paul, Darnell and Wilmore, freshman Tony, and sophomore John. When we traveled to Lexington to take on the undefeated Kentucky Wildcats, the crowd of more than 23,000 was anticipating a great game, and they were not disappointed.

> *"My freshman year, we were watching game film. Coach was always frustrated because he could never run the projector. In one particular stretch of bad play he couldn't get the film to move so he said, 'I simply cannot understand why you all won't compete better,' and marched out of the film room."*
> *— David Magley, University of Kansas, forward, 1978-82*

Darnell played one of his finest games, and we led by six with 40 seconds to go. In one of the most frustrating defeats of my career, our team, which had played a beautiful game up until that point, made several mistakes—not blocking out a free-throw shooter, not rolling to the ball on a screen-and-roll and missing a free throw that would've iced the game. As a consequence, we lost to Kentucky in overtime, 67-66.

The dressing room was the most emotional I have ever entered. The players were unable to hold back the tears, knowing they had let a tremendous victory slip away. I made an error in that I let them vent their emotions for too long. In retrospect, I should've pointed out that while we played a great game, we made several fundamental errors that cost us the victory. I should have stressed that it wasn't fate or our opponents that cost us the game, but our own failures in execution—and those could be corrected.

(From left) Donnie Von Moore, John Douglas (with his arms in the air in the background), Darnell Valentine and Ken Koenigs after a win in Allen Fieldhouse.

The Kentucky loss had a lasting effect on our team and its confidence. Even though we won our next game at home against Southern Methodist University, we did not play well. The lack of confidence was evident on a trip to the West Coast, where we lost to the University of Southern

California (despite the thrill of having Wilt Chamberlain at the game) and San Diego State.

The last holiday tourney

We returned home to prepare for an historic event, the last conference holiday tournament in Kansas City. Given the addition of the postseason tournament, a majority of conference members determined that two tournaments and regular-season competition was too much, so the grand holiday classic that began in 1946 was coming to an end.

Back in 1946, the conference, then named the Missouri Valley Intercollegiate Athletic Association, had taken notice of the country's first holiday tournament, the All College tournament in Oklahoma City. Seeing its success, the conference's six members—Kansas, Kansas State, Missouri, Nebraska, Oklahoma and Iowa State — started their own tournament.

I fondly recall my own history with the tournament. In 1948, I was a member of the Sooners team that won it. In 1962, I was an assistant for Coach Dick Harp when the Jayhawks won a four-overtime classic against Kansas State. As KU's head coach, I had the privilege of winning eight championships.

In the final tournament, the Jayhawks defeated Iowa State, Oklahoma and Colorado on our way to the championship. The wins were bittersweet, though, because ending the tournament was like saying goodbye to an old friend.

After splitting road games with OU and OSU, we returned home to play the Missouri Tigers and lost a close game, 58-55. Coming so early in the season, the home loss was a terrible blow to our conference hopes.

A positive approach

In the middle of the conference season, we journeyed to East Lansing, Michigan, to take on the Spartans' Magic Johnson, Greg Kelser and Jay Vincent on national television. We had no answer for Jud Heathcote's zone and lost to the eventual national champions.

Instead of ripping the team for a bad performance, I took a more positive approach and told my players to put the game behind them and prepare for a trip to Columbia early the next week. Tom Osborne, the former Nebraska football coach, once told a story about a loss in the Fiesta Bowl that decided the national championship. As Tom walked to the dressing room, a writer asked, "I'll bet you're really going to rip them when you get to the dressing room, aren't you?" Said Tom, "What can I possibly say that would make them feel any worse than they already do?" Although there are times that correction is warranted, many times encouragement is the tonic that players need. In this case, the team responded with an 88-85 win in Columbia.

After a 74-62 victory over OU at home, we lost two nail-biters to Iowa State and Kansas State that ended our chance to defend the league championship. Even so, we rattled off two wins against Nebraska and Colorado before we traveled to Kansas City for the conference tournament and beat Iowa State in the first round. Facing Missouri in the semifinals, Paul and Darnell both scored 19 to secure a 76-73 win. Against Oklahoma, though, we shot 30-for-89, and the Sooners won the league's NCAA tournament berth.

New Orleans and the Sweet Sixteen

Coach's Life Lesson: *Effective teaching requires patience. If a player has bad habits or techniques that require change, it will take some time to change. The need for patience should be understood by both teacher and pupil.*

In today's society, with all of our technology, we're spoiled with quick solutions. All of the world's information is right there on my computer. Unfortunately, that doesn't work when you're teaching skills to players. It takes time to break bad habits and then it takes time and repetition to establish good habits. Working with a big man is one of coaching's biggest challenges, because his skills haven't kept pace with his growth. Walter Wesley is the best example. He could run, but he carried his arms below his waist and didn't bend his knees. Every day, we made a little progress, and every day, we would say, "Bend your knees, Walt," over and over. But then, all of sudden, he got it. It's hard to describe the enormous satisfaction that a teacher or a coach has when he sees all of the effort put into a project or a person come to fruition. It's that satisfaction that makes coaching and teaching worthwhile.

The spring of 1979 brought new faces to the program when we signed 6'6" Ricky Ross from Wichita South High School, 6'2" Keith Douglas of Quincy, Illinois, 6'7 Kelly Knight of Salina and 6'10" Art Housey, from a junior college in Tyler, Texas.

Another new addition in 1979 meant even more to me on a personal basis. That summer, I married Michelle Mazikowski Nelson. After meeting on a golf course, we had been dating for some time. She is a wonderful wife, mother and grandmother, and she remains a talented elementary school teacher in Tulsa.

Michelle and I were settling into our new house near campus, a house that, incidentally, we had bought from Bud Moore. (Don Fambrough, whose career was resurrected when he returned as the head football coach, replaced Bud.) Michelle had secured a position in the Lawrence School District as an elementary teacher. We loved our home and enjoyed being near campus. Just behind our back porch, there was a bird sanctuary. Even with the activity of a bustling campus nearby, we could sit on the porch and the sanctuary provided the feeling of being out in the woods.

In the fall of 1979, we had some talented youngsters on the team, but at several positions, particularly in the post, our players had limited experience. We hoped that in time, Art Housey, the 6'10" junior college transfer, would be effective in the post. He certainly had the strength and stamina and his work habits were excellent. We had three seniors on the roster, Mac Stalcup, Randolph Carroll and Chester Giles, and although they had limited experience in varsity games, they had good attitudes and were a big help to the incoming players, Art, Ricky Ross, Keith Douglas and Kelly Knight. Juniors John Crawford, Darnell Valentine, Booty Neal, Mark Knight and George Thompson and sophomores Tony Guy, David Magley and Mark Snow completed the 1979-80 roster.

The year was marked by some phenomenal basketball performances but more than our share of excruciating losses. In the backcourt, Darnell, Tony, and Ricky were performing well, and we won a home game before leaving for West Coast to take on Pepperdine, Arizona State and Arizona. After two losses, the players responded against Arizona, delivering their best game of the year. As we returned home to prepare for the conference race, we may have been 5-5, but we had had chances to win in every game.

After a win over Wisconsin-Oshkosh, a non-conference opponent, we won our conference opener, 69-66, against Missouri. Close losses at Ames and Lincoln put us in a poor position in the conference standings, though, and then a good K-State team beat us in Lawrence, 61-52. In a league that had some great teams, no victory was a certainty. We managed to beat Oklahoma in Norman and the Buffaloes in Lawrence before dropping a four-point loss in Stillwater, which was a blow to any hope of staying alive in the conference race. After a win over Iowa State, we suffered another home loss, this time to Nebraska. Coach Joe Cipriano was battling cancer, and in his last game in Allen Fieldhouse, he accomplished what he had failed to do so many times: defeat the Jayhawks. Although it was a stinging defeat for us, it was a proud moment for Joe.

The Nebraska loss was followed by a narrow defeat at the hands of Iona, coached by Jimmy Valvano, in Madison Square Garden, and we followed that up with our worst performance of the year at Missouri, getting waxed, 88-65, by the Tigers. Despite the losses, it was at this point that the players began to unite as a team. Facing a talented Sooners team at home, the perimeter players combined for 41 points and we emerged with a victory.

An odd double-team

In Manhattan, against the team that had beaten us in Lawrence, I encountered one of the strangest finishes in my coaching career. Jack Hartman's aggressive 1-2-2 zone caused most teams problems, and we were no exception. Without an answer for the zone, we trailed the entire game, and the televised Saturday afternoon game had the packed crowd in Ahearn fired up.

Their zone was spreading out to cover our perimeter shooters, so I put another shooter into the game and placed the point guard in the center of the zone, so that he could penetrate and score or pitch to an open man. The scheme worked perfectly because Darnell and Keith both executed well, and we crawled back into the game. Although we didn't shoot a high percentage, our defense was strong and we out-rebounded the Wildcats, 38-26.

Trailing by three with about 30 seconds left, Ricky Ross stole the ball and drove in for a lay-up and a foul, and we tied the game. When Jack called a timeout, I knew that they would play for the last shot, but we managed to force a turnover near mid-court. With seconds to go, I called a timeout. We set up a play to get the ball to Darnell, who would penetrate to score or pass to the open man.

Much to our surprise, Kansas State double-teamed Darnell, but he was so strong with the ball that he forced a pass through the defenders' outstretched arms to Booty, who was wide open under the basket with two seconds left in the game. Booty scored and we pulled out a miracle win. The entire crowd and Kansas State team were stunned; they had led the entire game. Our players picked me up on their shoulders, which turned out to be a mistake. Cups of ice started peppering my head, and I looked down and a little old lady had come out onto the court with a rolled-up program and was whacking me on the leg. I reached the dressing room with welts on my face, but I was thrilled. With patience, determination, defense and rebounding, the Jayhawks managed a win against a solid Kansas State team that included two future NBA standouts, Ed Nealy and Rolando Blackman.

Several years ago, when former Kansas State player Tim Jankovich was on Bill Self's coaching staff at KU, I talked to him about the game. I told Tim that I was surprised that Coach Hartman had opted to double Darnell at the end of the game, because Jack came from the Henry Iba school of straight man-for-man defense. Tim smiled and told me that he had never told anyone the real story: that while he was guarding Booty Neal, he decided on his own to double Darnell, and when Darnell's back was turned, Tim rushed up to double the ball-handler. We laughed about it, because for years I had wondered why Jack had abandoned his defensive principles and double-teamed the ball. Tim, after all those years, was able to muster a smile.

A few weeks before the Kansas State game, my assistant, Bob Hill, had encouraged me to spend more time on special and end-game situations. So when we had possession of the ball with a few seconds left to play, we were well prepared; his advice had been prophetic. As he and I left the facility after the game, I was driving and I looked over a couple of times at Bob, who had a smug, satisfied look on his face. It was obvious that he was very pleased with himself. What I said to him is not printable, but we have laughed about it many times since.

After a loss in Boulder to a team coached by Bill Blair, who had replaced Sox Walseth, we came home to host the Cowboys, who had upset us in Stillwater earlier in the season. We needed a win to secure a home-court game in the quarterfinals of the conference tournament, which we would have to win to get an NCAA bid. Our perimeter players were exceptional. One highlight was the emergence of Salina freshman Kelly Knight, as he shot 4-for-5 from the field and 4-for-4 from the line. We badly needed some inside scoring punch, and Kelly filled the need. We defeated the Cowboys, whose roster included future football coach Houston Nutt, by a score of 84-74.

An end-of-year surge

In the conference quarterfinals, we entertained the Buffaloes once more. On fire from the field, we shot 67 percent. That'll win most games, and it did on this night, sending us to Kansas City to take on the Tigers, who had whipped us earlier in Columbia.

Since the Missouri loss, though, we had won four out of five games and become a much more consistent team, especially because of Kelly's production in the post. Despite a year full of close defeats and inconsistent performances, we had high hopes of earning a berth in the NCAA tournament. Before a crowd of 17,300 in Kemper Arena, we continued to perform, grabbing a 40-32 halftime lead over a strong Missouri team.

The outstanding shooting continued, both from the field (59 percent) and from the line (24-for-27). Darnell delivered outstanding play, as usual. His work habits were among the best I have ever had in a player, and his defense against the league's opposing point guards was impressive. His impact on a game could never be judged by only scoring, because his defense and ball-handling always factored in. In the end, we beat Missouri, 80-71.

The stage was set for a battle with Kansas State. After splitting two regular-season games, we felt good about our chances. Unfortunately, our streak of hot shooting turned frigid, and we couldn't throw it in the ocean and we were soundly defeated. It was a disappointing finish for a team that had started to hit its stride late in the year, but we hoped that our young team had learned the lessons that would lead to a successful season in 1980-81.

'About to get good'

In the spring of 1980, David Magley asked me if I would give him a release so that he could transfer to Indiana State, saying that he wanted to be more of a scorer, as he had done in high school. I told David that I wouldn't release him, explaining that he would only be running away from the reality that he needed to become a more complete player. He was not a good athlete, and he needed to become stronger and much quicker.

Sometimes a coach makes a decision that he feels is correct, but it doesn't work out the way he hoped. In this case, though, David accepted the challenge to become a better athlete, running many miles per day and hitting the weight room with a passion. By the time school started in the fall, he had made remarkable progress and was running one-mile times in the preseason workouts that were outstanding for a 6'8" player. He went on to have two excellent years at KU, and in one of them, he was second in the conference in scoring and rebounding and made the league's first team.

In the summer of 1980, Darnell Valentine was invited to the Olympic tryouts and made the team. As I noted earlier, Darnell was one of the hardest workers I ever coached. He brought effort to the court in every single practice. But if he had one weakness, it was that he penetrated with his dribble so deep into the lane that he wouldn't have many passing angles available to him. I had pointed this out many times, with little success. When he returned from the Olympic workouts, I asked him if he had learned anything new, and he said the coaches had told him that he was penetrating too deep and didn't have any passing angles. It was as if he had never heard such advice before. The scriptures are right: "A prophet is accepted in every country but his own."

Unfortunately for Darnell and the other Olympic athletes, President Jimmy Carter decided to withdraw the U.S. from the Games in Moscow as a protest against the Russians' invasion of Afghanistan. In 1984, the Russians retaliated by holding their athletes out of the Olympics in Los Angeles. Who said the Olympics are supposed to be free of politics?

On the hardwood, we were optimistic, with the return of Darnell Valentine, Tony Guy, David Magley, John Crawford, Booty Neal, Ricky Ross and Kelly Knight. We had added Victor Mitchell and Mark Summers from a junior college in Amarillo, Texas. Victor was strong 6'9" center whom we hoped would give us a strong inside presence. The key, of course, was molding the players into a cohesive and effective unit. Early in the fall, though, we lost Ricky when he decided to drop out of school. The promising young player had enormous potential, and after a few years of finding himself, he ended up in Tulsa and played for Nolan Richardson.

A West Coast swing

In the late 1970s, I started making an annual preseason trip to Reno, Nevada, to spend a few days with a group of coaches and talk about coaching situations and strategies. Hosted by Sonny Allen, the coach at the University of Nevada in Reno, the annual gathering was very informative, and I wish I had participated in something similar earlier in my career. The meetings led to a request from Sonny to start a home-and-home series between KU and his Reno team, so we ended up opening the 1980-81 season on the road. Fortunately, we were an experienced team, with only one new player, Victor Mitchell, playing a significant amount of time. Still, I was more nervous about this game than usual. My in-laws, Frank and Terrie Mazikowski, drove from California for the game, and my freshman coach at Oklahoma, Shocky Needy, and his wife, Helen, were also coming to the game. Because Shocky had played such a significant role in developing my philosophy of coaching and my methods of conducting practices, I was anxious for my team to play well.

After a close and competitive game in the first half, our experience and depth surfaced and we broke open the tight game, winning by a comfortable 91-73 margin. I was pleased with the team's level of effort and togetherness, and I hoped that Coach Needy had noticed the same things.

In our home-opener against Pepperdine, Tony led with 23 and Booty scored 16 off the bench, while Victor grabbed 10 rebounds and Darnell led with his defense and ball-handling, and we picked up an 81-67 victory. Two nights later, we lost a home game to Michigan. But we then won five of our next six games, with the only loss coming at Kentucky. The team's play was becoming more consistent.

Winning away from home

In early January, we took the team to Kansas City to play the Tar Heels and Coach Dean Smith, the Jayhawk alumnus who was a member of the 1952 national championship team and the 1953 runners-up. It was a hard-fought, defensive game, with players on both sides getting few open looks. We hung on at the end for a 56-55 win against one of the nation's best teams, a squad that made it all of the way to the NCAA finals against Indiana.

We had barely settled down from the North Carolina game when we had to travel to Memphis. We weren't sharp to begin the game—a carryover from the UNC test, I think—but we did manage to grab an early second-half lead. So I did something I seldom did, which was to go to a four-corner type of offense to pull their big guys out onto the court. The tactic worked well and we spent much of the second half at the free-throw line, where we shot 19-for-23, and we came away with a 59-49 road win.

A 94-64 home win over Iona capped our non-conference play. The win was a good transition to our tough league schedule, in which we jumped out to a 4-0 start with wins over Iowa State, Missouri, Colorado and Oklahoma, but our depth was reduced when Kelly blew out a knee. After that, an unusual schedule put us out on the road for a string of away games. We were 14-2 before the road trip, but we didn't do what championship teams have to do: win on the road. We lost four road games at Kansas State, Oklahoma State, Nebraska and Missouri, sandwiched around one home win against Oklahoma. The stretch didn't offer many bright moments, although Victor Mitchell did have his finest game with 26 points and 13 rebounds against Oklahoma State.

A win at Iowa State stopped our losing streak, and we returned home to host Kansas State. Seven Jayhawks scored while we held their star, Rolando Blackman, to four points in a 58-50 win. After that, though, we went down to the wire at Colorado, losing 53-50 in a well-played game.

The rest of the season, the team really dug in and played tremendous basketball. With Art now starting and Victor coming off the bench, we hit our stride. Defeating Nebraska once and Oklahoma State twice, Art went 19-of-25 from the field in the three games. The second OSU game was a quarterfinal contest in the conference tournament, leading to a final game in Allen Fieldhouse for our seniors, who performed in brilliant fashion for another win.

Off the bubble

We then traveled to Kemper Arena with the knowledge that we had to win the postseason tournament to guarantee a spot in the NCAA tournament. Without a win, we knew were on the bubble with 20 wins and seven losses. In a field of 48 teams, our chances of at-large selection were marginal, even with wins against North Carolina, Memphis State, Missouri and Kansas State.

In the conference semifinals, we faced an excellent team in Missouri. We played near-perfect basketball, committing only four turnovers and shooting 33-for-40 from the line for the game. At the half, we led 34-22. We knew that Missouri was too good to be limited to 22 points in a half again, and they ended the game with 70

An expectant Michelle and I at our home in Lawrence.

points. But we ended with 75, thanks to balanced scoring, ball-handling and free throws. Forwards David and John combined for 26 and guards Darnell and Tony combined for 36, entertaining a sell-out crowd with an incredible game.

Only Kansas State in the tournament finals stood in our way of an NCAA berth in the Midwest region's first round in Wichita. We had split with the Wildcats in the regular season and knew that we would face a determined team. What followed, though, was a coach's dream, especially because we started the season with so many questions about whether the team could become a championship-caliber, cohesive unit. On this night, the players and coaches were rewarded for the long hours of practice and preparation.

Even though Kansas State shot 50 percent from the field and 89 percent from the free-throw line and recorded less than 10 turnovers, we played a near-perfect game, shooting 56 percent from the field and 77 percent from the free throw line, committing just four turnovers, and out-rebounding the Cats, 36-25. Our seven-point halftime lead grew, and we won, 80-68. Darnell and Tony scored 43 together, David and John added 19, and Art recorded his best night as a Jayhawk with 20 points and 11 rebounds.

We looked forward to a return to Wichita, the site of the 1971 regional triumph that had propelled us to the Final Four. In the first round, we faced the University of Mississippi, the SEC winner, with the winner advancing to play the No. 3 team in the country, the Arizona State Sun Devils. On the other side of the bracket, Wichita State faced Southern University before playing Iowa, the surprise champions of the Big Ten. It was going to be a great weekend of basketball in the old Roundhouse at Wichita State.

Mississippi took the fight right to us and proved to be a worthy opponent. We slowed their all-conference player some, holding him to 22 points. The Rebels' point guard, Sean Tuohy, gained a measure of fame in later years as the foster parent of football player Michael Oher, whose story was told in the 2009 film *The Blind Side*. The Jayhawks' balanced scoring and high-percentage shooting carried us to a 69-66 win and a shot at the Sun Devils, who had just defeated the No. 1 team in the country, previously unbeaten Oregon State.

Stunning the Sun Devils

Veteran ASU coach Ned Wulk fielded a lineup of NBA first-round selections including Byron Scott, Lafayette Lever, Sam Williams and 7-footer Alton Lister; the four of them combined to play 35 years in the NBA. The fifth starter was the dangerous Johnny Nash. While we knew that it would take an outstanding performance to defeat them, we were playing awfully well.

Just prior to the ASU game, Lute Olson's Hawkeyes were playing the host school, Wichita State, with the Hawkeyes-Shockers winner playing the Jayhawks-Sun Devils winner in the regional tournament in the New Orleans Superdome. Led by 6'9" twin towers Antoine Carr and Cliff Levingston, Wichita State dismantled Southern, 96-70, and then beat Iowa.

With top seeds Oregon and DePaul losing to Kansas State and St. Joseph, respectively, ASU was the highest-ranked team left in the tournament. We were on top of our game, with Darnell having a tremendous weekend in front of his hometown fans. It was Tony Guy, though, who played like a man possessed, and we led 45-29 at the half.

The crowd was stunned, and so was *NBC*, which broke away to cover a more competitive game. With a few minutes remaining, the pro-Wichita State crowd started chanting that they wanted to play Kansas. Tony scored 36 points on 13-of-15 shooting from the field and 10-of-12 from the line, and all the reserves got into a game that ended in an 88-71 upset.

Three state schools, Wichita State, Kansas State and Kansas, had advanced to the Sweet Sixteen by defeating national powerhouses. It was truly a proud moment for a state whose residents dearly love college basketball. As for me, I was extremely proud of a team that hadn't been highly rated to start the season but had become a solid team.

The Touchdown Play

Against Wichita State, we knew we would have difficulty defending the twin towers, so I decided to stick with our 2-3 match-up zone. Although we weren't as sharp on offense as we had been in recent games, we managed to hold a three-point lead with 50 seconds left when a Jayhawk went to the line for a one-and-one. At this juncture, a five-point lead would have been huge, especially without the three-point shot, but we missed the first free throw and Wichita gained possession.

With about 20 seconds to go, Mike James hit a bomb that would've been an NBA three-pointer today, cutting the lead to one, 65-64. As Wichita pressed us, we had some trouble getting across the half-court line, so I called a timeout. On a sideline inbounds play, we read the defense correctly and isolated the back end of the court, but we missed a lay-up. With possession of the ball, Wichita was having trouble finding a shot until Jones hit another bomb to put them up one with two seconds left.

We had a play called "Touchdown" for just this sort of situation. If the defense jumped the player taking the ball out of bounds, the player inbounding the ball would run along the baseline and blindside the defender with a pick. It worked to perfection as a Wichita player knocked Darnell to the ground, but the official didn't call a foul and we lost a heartbreaker, 66-65.

Many times, a coach walks off the court regretting his decisions. In this case, though, we made the right calls and they just didn't work out. I was awfully proud of a team that had come so far, although I was disappointed because I thought we were playing well enough to advance far into the tourney. Still, I never was more proud of a group of young men, and I knew that our seniors had finished their careers with honor.

Chapter 19

The Final Kansas Years

Coach's Life Lesson: *Time is one of our most important gifts. I find that as I get older, time becomes more precious and I don't want to waste time on things that have no lasting value. To young readers, I'll say this: I wish I understood that at your age.*

When you're six years old, it feels like forever before you'll turn seven. When you're 17, you'll wonder if 18 will ever come. And then when you start to be 60 or 65, all of a sudden you blink your eyes and you're 75. Time becomes so precious when you know that you have a limited time. I wish that I had felt that way when I was younger. There's so much to get done today and there's so much to learn. I believe with all my heart that this life is preparation for the life to come, and I'm more conscious than ever that time is our most precious resource and that we must be diligent in planning to use our time effectively.

After the game in New Orleans, athletic director Bob Marcum rewarded me with a new three-year contract, another one-pager just like my previous contracts. This was in the days before agents and attorneys negotiated a coach's contracts. At least that is what I thought. Maybe I was just out of the loop. The simple truth is that when I grew up on the cotton farm in southwest Oklahoma, my dad taught us that our word was our bond and a handshake was good enough for a contract.

The summer of 1981 was one of great joy with the birth of our son, Teddy, on July 29. Already blessed with two wonderful daughters, Nancy and Kelly, we now welcomed a son into the family. When my daughters were born, fathers weren't allowed in the delivery room, so I had looked forward to participating in Teddy's birth, especially not knowing if we would have a boy or girl. When I walked into the Lamaze training sessions with Michelle, the younger couples looked at me as if I had mistakenly entered the wrong room. There just weren't many 51-year-olds attending the sessions. I must have experienced the feelings of a freshman playing his first college game— uncertain, but hopeful.

For the basketball program, the past two or three years had been disappointing in recruiting. We had spent a lot of time on high-profile players, coming close but not succeeding. Recruiting is much like a hand of poker—you either have a winning hand or a bad hand that causes you to drop out early, and if you have the second-best hand you spend all of your time, effort and resources on a lost cause. One of the players we failed to sign was Scott Hastings of Independence, Kansas, who grew from 6'6" to 6'10" in his first year in college. When I decided I wanted to sign him, I was too late, and on the day after I called, he signed with Eddie Sutton's Arkansas Razorbacks. A coach can't afford to miss on an in-state player, and we paid for that mistake.

Meanwhile, JoJo White had retired from professional basketball and agreed to join our staff. Voted MVP of one of the Boston Celtics' championship teams, Jo was a great addition to our staff. He replaced Lafayette Norwood, who had become the head coach at Johnson County Community College.

We added several inexperienced players and were hoping that Tony Guy, David Magley, Victor Mitchell and Kelly Knight would give us a solid nucleus to build around. Mark Summers and Jeff Konek also returned from the 1980-81 squad. Unfortunately, Victor, a 6'9" senior, chose to drop out of school and return to his home in Amarillo, Texas, so we were really short-handed to start the 1981-82 season.

"My senior year was memorable for many reasons. Coach Owens and I got along and I had worked hard to get in the best shape of my life and he respected me for that. The biggest change was that I had gotten married to Evelyn and since my wife and Coach's wife, Michelle, were friends, we got to be the designated babysitters for Teddy and Taylor. So it was interesting that Coach would get mad at me and then shortly after, he would come home and find me sitting in his lazy boy and eating his fresh fruit and had to deal with me again. This babysitting routine allowed our relationship to grow in new ways. I remember one morning he called me at 2 a.m. to tell me if I could just get a better 'in-between game' I would be a very complete player. After hearing that 'I could shoot from deep and drive well,' I reminded Coach of the time and asked if we could finish the conversation in the morning."
— David Magley, University of Kansas, forward, 1978-82

The new players—Tad Boyle, a 6'4" guard from Colorado; Tyke Peacock, a world-class high jumper from California; Jeff Dishman, a junior college player from Hutchinson; and Brian Martin, Mark Ewing, Lance Hill, Ron McHenry and Tim Banks—were dedicated young men who valiantly attempted to fill the gaps left by the previous year's veterans. Tad, a true student of the game who is now coaching at the University of Colorado, is in the beginning of what I believe will be a long and successful career.

With a roster full of inexperienced players, we couldn't have scheduled more difficult games. We opened at Charlotte against No. 1 North Carolina, and we played the No. 2 Kentucky Wildcats, ranked teams Indiana and St. John's, and such national powers as Michigan State, Arizona and Arizona State. Even the conference was loaded. When we played Missouri, they were No. 1 in the country.

Nevertheless, our preparation for the opening UNC game was solid. We decided that we couldn't handle the UNC front line with straight-up man coverage, so we elected to pack in a tight zone around James Worthy and Sam Perkins and take our chances with the outside shooting of Matt Doherty, Jimmy Black and a freshman by the name of Michael Jordan.

We put up a terrific fight and slowed their shooters some, leading to a 37-all tie at the half. Tony and Kelly were terrific, and David had one of his best performances, while the new guys, Jeff, Lance, and Brian, played remarkably well. We played the Tar Heels to a tie up until about 13 minutes to go, when Kelly drew his fifth foul. We substituted and immediately turned the ball over three times, giving UNC their first lead. Even though we were within three or four points near the end, we had to foul and they converted their free throws. We lost, 74-67, to a team that won a national championship that year, thanks to a clutch shot by that heralded freshman, Michael Jordan.

We returned home and defeated Texas Southern and Arizona State before taking on Jud Heathcote's Michigan State Spartans. Against Jud's match-up zone, we ran a 1-4 offense with our inside men screening baseline defenders. Tad Boyle did a beautiful job feeding the big guys, and we defeated the Spartans soundly, 74-56. Next, we beat the Arizona Wildcats as Kelly continued his torrid pace, shooting 9-for-11. Against Southern Methodist University, we switched

from zone to man-for-man and went on a streak that pushed the lead to 21 points. Tony led with 27 points while David added 19 points and 10 boards.

When Kentucky, ranked No. 2, brought their powerful squad to Allen Fieldhouse, the Jayhawks responded. Tony dropped 31 points,

Photo courtesy of Lawrence Journal-World

I shared my disbelief with an official's call ... even if it was most likely a good call.

David added 21, and Kelly notched 17 with 10 boards. Despite the effort, we missed a shot with six seconds left and then lost in overtime, 77-74. However, we were pleased to see our young team competing so well.

At the Garden

A great field awaited us in Madison Square Garden: St. Johns with Chris Mullin, later a member of the 1992 Olympics Dream Team; Indiana, the defending NCAA champions; and Villanova. We had hoped for a final game against Indiana, but they were upset by Villanova in the first game. Against St. John's, we started slowly before exploding with hot shooting and stiff defense, and we led throughout most the game. Ahead by a point with seconds remaining, we were called for a very questionable five-second count (more like three seconds) while trying to inbound the ball along the baseline under the St. John's basket. They then scored with a second or two left, winning the game.

After such a bitter loss, I didn't want the players to spend the night talking about the five-second (three-second) count, so I banned the press from the dressing room and just started talking about the Indiana game coming up the next night. Even some of the Garden officials apologized for that short count, but I knew that our focus had to shift toward Indiana.

Bob Knight's Hoosiers ran an incredibly tough motion offense. Facing his team's intense preparation and effective man-for-man defense, I knew that we didn't have the practice time, so I decided to zone them and eliminate their motion. On offense, we relieved their defensive pressure by breaking Kelly toward the ball, which drew out the big 7-footer guarding him. The schemes worked well and we led, 29-24, at the half. David was getting down the court in our transition offense, recording a 32-point night against an Indiana team that hadn't recruited him out of high school. Only the five starters saw the court—just the second time in my career I hadn't substituted—and we won, 71-61. Coach Knight took time after the game to congratulate David on his performance, and that gesture still means a lot to David today. As for me, at that point of the season, I couldn't have expected more out of my team.

> *"Coach called timeout [and encouraged me to shoot]. Inspired, I scored 24 points in the final eight minutes and we won by 10. That all came about because I knew Coach believed in me."*
> — David Magley, University of Kansas, forward, 1978-82

Near misses

After a short break, we resumed our preparation for the conference season. To keep us sharp, I had scheduled two non-conference opponents, Rollins and

Evansville, and the wins boosted our record to 9-3. But we were not sharp. We played to our maximum potential in the early part of the season, but we had yet to regain that form as we entered a difficult Big Eight schedule.

With poor play and 35 percent shooting, we lost the conference opener on the road in Lincoln. David went 3-for-3 from the line to extend his Jayhawk-record 23 straight free throws, but that was the sole highlight. Against Oklahoma State, Brian and Lance came off the bench to score a combined 24 points and lead us to a win. Tony scored 17, becoming the seventh-leading scorer (at the time) in Kansas basketball history. On the Cowboys' side, a substitute from Edmond, Oklahoma, a young man by the name of Bill Self, came off the bench to score 14 points.

The rest of the conference season was filled with near misses: two losses to Missouri's top-ranked undefeated team, two losses to Iowa State by two points each, and a narrow loss at Oklahoma when we missed a wide-open lay-up with six seconds left. Even though we had achieved so much in the early part of the season, we couldn't find a way to close games during the conference race.

Still, I was proud of the young men on the team. Tony finished a fantastic career as one of the leading scorers in Kansas history, while David finished second in the conference in scoring and rebounding and was a strong candidate for league player of the year. One of the greatest rewards for a coach is to help players recognize their shortcomings and guide them toward sacrifices to correct those conditions. David acknowledged that he wasn't a good athlete when he arrived in Lawrence, and he took it as a challenge. Through weightlifting, running and skill development, he put in the work to become a fine player by his senior year. Kelly grew as a player, returning from knee surgery to give us all the effort he had. Tad demonstrated the leadership that has made him a successful coach. Jeff Dishman, playing as an undersized forward, competed with all of his heart. Lance, Brian, Mark and Tyke also offered their own positive moments.

While I took pride in the players' development, I was disturbed that we weren't in a position to compete for the conference championship. This was on *my watch*. For the university, for the fans, and for the players, I felt a huge burden to get the Jayhawk program back on course and produce teams that could consistently compete for conference and national honors.

Looking ahead to the next season

Our spring 1982 recruiting efforts were successful, and we managed to land some outstanding high school players and two great transfers, 7-footer Greg Dreiling from Wichita State University and 6'6" Carl Henry from Oklahoma City University. I had recruited Greg since he was a ninth-grader but the Shockers had initially convinced him to stay at home in Wichita. Carl had also initially decided to stay close to home in Oklahoma City, but it didn't hurt our chances that his girlfriend, Barbara Atkins, and sister, Vicki, were on the KU women's team.

In addition to Greg and Carl, our freshmen signees were really talented, including 6'9" Kerry Boagni, of Los Angeles; shooter Ron Kellogg, from Omaha; Calvin Thompson, from the tradition-rich Wyandotte High School program in Kansas City; and point guard Jeff Guiot from Chanute, Kansas. Assistant coaches Bob Hill and JoJo White had helped to search the country for these young men, and we felt good about the future.

On the home front, midway through the season, Michelle and I welcomed the birth of our precious daughter, Taylor LaRaine. The middle name came from Michelle's mother. She has been a blessing to our lives.

The joy of the year was disrupted, though, with the news that Odd Williams, a dear friend and supporter of the university, had died in his sleep. He and his wife were godparents to our son. Odd's brother, Skipper, had died a few years before while doing push-ups in the morning. Both brothers were in their fifties when they died, and both were rocks for KU and the Lawrence community.

The fall season in 1982 was further disturbed by the firing of my dear friend, Don Fambrough, by the new athletic director, Monte Johnson, who had replaced Jim Lessig. We had been thrilled when Jim became the athletic director because we thought that he would assist us in making improvements to Allen Fieldhouse and to the players' living conditions. Much to our dismay, Jim left to become the conference commissioner of the Mid-American Conference within a few months of his hiring at KU.

On the court, I knew that our youthfulness meant we were in for a challenging year but I felt that we were in good shape to restore KU basketball to its stature after two disappointing seasons. Carl Henry was everything we had hoped for, averaging 17 points a game and shooting 54 percent. Back from his knee injuries, Kelly Knight started all but two games and shot 55 percent from the field. Jeff Dishman, Brian Martin and Tad Boyle brought experience to the group. Kerry Boagni, Calvin Thompson, Jeff Guiot and Ronnie Kellogg had great potential, but they needed time to develop into complete players.

Room and board for an aspiring coach

The season had many disappointments, although not without some enjoyable moments. The previous summer, an aspiring young coach named John Calipari had come to campus to work on our basketball camp staff, and we had encouraged him to participate in the Jayhawks' basketball program in the 1982-83 season. With little income, John dished out food at the Jayhawks' training table so that he could have a place to eat. He roomed with Randolph Carroll, our graduate assistant, so that he could have a place to live.

> *"Bob Hill, the assistant at Kansas, saw me work five-star basketball camps as a counselor/coach and asked, 'Why don't you come out and do our camp?' So that next summer, I came out and worked that camp. When the camp was over, Coach Owens said, 'Why don't you stay and be a part of our staff here?' I said, 'What position, Coach?' He said, 'The volunteer assistant.' So then I said, 'Well, how much do you pay your volunteer assistant?' Obviously nothing, but Coach Owens was very generous throughout the camp. I worked at the training table, serving the football and basketball teams their evening meals with the Sinclairs, who ran the training table."*
> — *John Calipari, voluntary assistant, University of Kansas, 1982-83; University of Kentucky head coach*

I found out later that because John and Randolph didn't have enough money to buy a bed frame, they slept on mattresses in their apartment. During the year, a movie called *The Day After*, depicting the day after a nuclear holocaust, was being filmed in Lawrence. Allen Fieldhouse was portrayed as a medical aid station, and film crews had placed beds in the arena. A few days after filming, when the crews returned to pick up the beds, two were missing. There was considerable suspicion as to where they might have gone.

In a season of ups and downs, we showed signs of maturity toward the end of the season with a home win against the Sooners and a road win at Iowa State. In the final game of the regular season, we defeated a good Colorado team. Kelly led us with 27 points, Carl added 21, and the other three starters also played well. However, it was the Colorado native, Tad, who gave us a second-half spark with six huge points to rally the team.

In the conference tournament quarterfinals, we had to travel to Norman to play my alma mater, nationally ranked Oklahoma, led by its center, Waymon Tisdale, a freshman and consensus first-team All-American. With a 17-2 home record, Oklahoma was a huge obstacle. But our youngsters responded beautifully, winning 87-77. Calvin scored 30, Kelly added 20, Carl had 19, and Tad had eight. After the game, several players placed me on their shoulders, and my last memory of coaching a game at my alma mater was being carried up the ramp and looking up to see my beloved college coach, Bruce Drake, and his beautiful wife, Myrtle, smiling at me. What a wonderful blessing it was to have them there for my final game at Oklahoma.

For the semifinals in Kansas City, we had only a short time to prepare for Oklahoma State, a team that had already beaten us twice during the season.

Our players put forth a great effort, and we led midway through the second half. Although we out-shot and out-rebounded them, the difference came at the free-throw line, where we were 5-for-9 and they were 20-for-30, and we lost the game. Still, our young team, without a single senior in the starting lineup, had made tremendous progress late in the season. Kelly had one of his best games with 26 points and 14 boards, while Kerry added 22 and Carl added 21.

The longest week of my life

We felt that the future was bright with the return of talented freshmen Kerry, Calvin, Ron and Jeff. We would also have the red-shirted 7-footer, Greg Dreiling, with three years of eligibility remaining. All-conference player Carl would return along with Kelly, Tad, Brian and Mark. In addition, we had a commitment from one of the nation's top scorers, Curtis Akin of Pittsburgh.

I had assembled a potentially great recruiting and coaching staff, with Bob Hill, JoJo White, John Calipari, Randolph Carroll and a new addition, R.C. Buford, a graduate of Texas A&M. Feeling that we were positioned to be a dominate force in the following season, I hoped that the new athletic director, Monte Johnson, would honor the remaining year of my contract and allow me to return to coach the team.

However, I wasn't overly confident when he called me into his office and told me that he was going to Florida for a week on vacation with his son. While he was gone, he wanted me to prepare an evaluation of my program compared to the history of Kansas basketball. I asked him if we could stick with the modern era, and we agreed to start after World War II.

It was the longest week of my life. Since the war, the Kansas basketball program had achieved a lot, with an NCAA title in 1952 and national championship games in 1953 and 1957. In my time as the head coach at Kansas, we had won 15 Big Eight titles (a combination of regular-season and tournament titles) and advanced to the NCAA Final Four in 1971 and 1974. Fitting Dr. Allen's criteria for a successful team, the players' graduation rate was high and they had gone on to successful careers.

Monte must have known that if he was going to make a change, the timing was ideal, since we were coming off of two seasons that were below the Kansas standards in terms of wins and losses. It was a perfect time to give a new coach the reins to a talented team and allow him to become immediately successful. And that was the decision Monte made.

I was absolutely devastated. I had hoped Chancellor Gene Budig would block the move, but he had been at the university for only the last two years, when our teams weren't as strong as in previous years. Years later, at the 2009 memorial service for longtime KU athletic director Bob Frederick, Gene told me that if he had taken the time to look at my overall record, he wouldn't have allowed me to be removed as the head coach. Even if it was far too late to change matters, I respected Gene and felt good about what he had said.

As numb as I was, I felt the need to talk to my players, and I asked Coach Hill to assemble them. I can't tell you, even today, what I said to them, or if my remarks were helpful to them at all. I also prepared a statement for the media, thanking the many people who had assisted us in the 23 years during which I had the privilege of serving the university as an assistant and head coach.

I fault no one, and I take full responsibility for the decline of the program during the two years that followed our NCAA regional participation in 1981. In the spring of 1983, I had felt that we were positioned to restore the program to its rightful place as a conference power and national-title contender, had they decided to honor the last year of my contract. But we can only speculate about what might have been, and those who have followed me—Larry Brown, Roy Williams and Bill Self—have certainly done great things at the helm of Jayhawk basketball.

> *"I loved the job and I loved being the caretaker of that program. Bill Self said it right—that a KU coach is simply a caretaker."*
> — *Ted Owens*

The chancellor called me to his office a few days later and offered me a position as his assistant for the following year. When I asked him if the job would include overseeing the athletic programs, he laughed and said he thought that probably wouldn't be a very good idea.

So after 23 years, I was no longer a part of Kansas basketball. Those years were a wonderful time in my life. I loved every minute of it, from the joy of successes to the pain of disappointments. I dearly loved the University of Kansas, and I continue to do so today.

> *"I did something some say a coach shouldn't do. They'll say that a coach shouldn't fall in love with the fans and the players. But I did. I loved the University of Kansas. I loved my players. My biggest fault was that I didn't want to disappoint people. When we lost a game or experienced failure, I was really hard on myself. I never blamed anyone else."*
> — *Ted Owens*

Chapter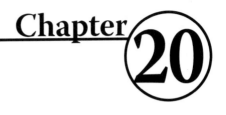

New Beginnings

Coach's Life Lesson: *It is important that we salvage something out of every victory and every defeat. Many of life's lessons are learned from the tough times we are presented with.*

People most often think of success, but it's also good to be reminded of our failures. Michael Jordan has talked about the 26 times he missed a game-winning shot. You're going to fail, but as my mother said, when one door closes another door will open. There is always another opportunity.

For the first time in 23 years, I wasn't coaching at the University of Kansas. I felt an emptiness, but I didn't have the luxury of thinking about it for long. I hadn't made much money coaching at KU, and I needed to provide for my family.

My first thought was to find another position in basketball, since I felt that I had quite a few years of teaching and coaching left in me and that my experiences might be helpful to another university. It had been such a pleasure to teach the game's skills to young people and watch them master those skills, and then test them in competition, and watch their confidence grow as a result. For a teacher, coach, or mentor, there isn't a greater joy than to witness the growth and maturation of someone under your guidance.

Unfortunately, at least for me, no jobs of any significance opened for the next two years. I visited with the University of California at Santa Barbara about their open position, but with the salary they paid, I wouldn't have found affordable housing in that expensive city. My friend Jerry Pimm, the former Utah coach, figured out how to solve the housing problem when he accepted the Santa Barbara job: He lived on his sailboat.

I took an intriguing phone call from the athletic director at Southwest Missouri State in Springfield, a D-II school that planned to become D-1 in two years. Because I had visions of coaching at another large school, I decided against visiting further with them. In retrospect, though, I wish I had considered the position, as Springfield is a nice city and the school, now

Missouri State, is an excellent institution. I have since learned that if a job brings you joy and a sense of accomplishment, the level doesn't matter.

Many times in life, we wonder what might have been. I sometimes think that in the 1970s, I should have gone to Austin, Texas, to see my friend Darrell Royal when he asked me to talk with him about the University of Texas coaching position. Or perhaps I should've accepted Chancellor Budig's offer to stay at KU. Then again, I remember what I wouldn't have experienced if I had made those choices over the years. I wouldn't have met my wife, Michelle, nor would I have Teddy and Taylor. I wouldn't have established the friendships that I have with people in Kansas City, Tampa, Fresno, Tel Aviv, Tulsa and around the world. I can only conclude that a person has to make the best decision possible with the available information, and then live with the choice. As Satchel Paige, the baseball pitcher and philosopher, once said, "Don't look back, or they will be gaining on you."

> *"In 1982-83, I played for the Cleveland Cavaliers and following the season, Coach Owens was let go at KU. Devastated and hurt, he decided to get out of Lawrence for a week and go skiing in Colorado. He asked Evelyn and me to go along and babysit the children. What was a blessing was that I could be with a man that I loved at a time when he was hurting. The relationship that was forged during those four years at KU was strengthened again and will last forever."*
> — David Magley, University of Kansas, forward, 1978-82

Moving on

The choice I made was to accept an offer with a securities brokerage firm in Kansas City. They certainly didn't want me for by business expertise, but I knew a lot of people and they hoped that I could open doors for their business. On October 15, the annual day of excitement for players and coaches when varsity practices started, I was on my way to Kansas City to take my Series 7 exam to qualify for a position in the securities industry.

I fared quite well on the test and felt rewarded for the weeks of preparation. Because it had been so long since I had studied, I had to stay awake during those long weeks by jumping in the shower, riding my stationary bike, or going for a walk. Driving back from the test, I felt a great sense of accomplishment. My joy soon passed, however, when I reached Lawrence and remembered that the basketball team was going through their first practice of the year.

We loved Lawrence and our home there and we loved the university, but Michelle and I knew we needed to move to Kansas City in order to put the past behind us. I went back to a game during the season, just so I could sit there and be reminded that I was no longer the Kansas coach. It was too painful, though, and I didn't go back for a long time—another 10 years, in fact.

Pros and cons

As it turned out, I actually liked the business world. There was a sense of fairness about the rewards. It didn't matter what a person's social background or race was, or whether a person was good-looking or average. Production mattered, and it was rewarded. The firm's top producer got the best parking spot, the best office location and the best vacations. In terms of fairness and rewards, the system was like the sports world. Apart from work, I also thoroughly enjoyed spending the weekends with my family. In all of my years in coaching, weekends always meant practices, games, or entertaining a prospect.

I was frequently asked if I missed my players and staff members, and my answer always was that I did, very much so. But I also missed the managers who took care of many of my needs, such as taking my car to get serviced or picking up sandwiches and drinks ... all of those numerous errands that I now found to be time-consuming and annoying. Thirty years later, I still miss those managers. Boy, were we ever spoiled.

Someone must have sensed that I was missing the game, because Wichita State athletic director Lew Perkins (who was later the Jayhawks' AD) called to ask me if I would do the commentary on the Shockers' telecasts. I jumped at the chance, and my superiors at the brokerage firm were good enough to allow me to travel with the Shockers. Because of our travels that year, I formed a lasting friendship with Lew and his wife, Gwen. And Gene Smithson's team was fun to follow that year, particularly because of the "X-Man" Xavier McDaniel and Aubrey Sherrod. I encountered only one difficulty, when a listener called in to complain about my pronunciation of Aubrey's name as "Arbrey." I apologized, explaining that in southwest Oklahoma we didn't wash our clothes, we "warshed" them.

An opening at Oral Roberts

After a couple of years in the brokerage business, I was contacted by Bob Patterson, a former player for the University of Tulsa, about my interest in becoming the head basketball coach at Oral Roberts University. Bob was a successful businessman in Tulsa and he and Dr. Jim Winslow, an orthopedic surgeon, pretty much ran the ORU athletic department, even though baseball coach Larry Cochell was the athletic director. I replied that I was happy in the business world and wasn't interested. When he continued to call, I gave him a list of things that I would require, including Michelle's studying dentistry at ORU, in order to consider the position. One night, he called to tell me that they would meet all of my requirements.

I had been warned that some members of the Roberts family interfered in the athletic department's operation. I was also reminded that Ken Hayes, an excellent coach, had been fired during the Christmas holidays a few years before. Although I asked for and received a long-term contract, I still had some misgivings. First, the team had been mediocre the previous year and had lost all of their starters except for Willie Irons, a part-time starter.

When I met with President Oral Roberts, I told him that it would take three years to build the type of program in which he could take pride. I also told him that I was a Christian but knew very little about the charismatic and healing beliefs of his ministry. He replied, "Ted, you do the coaching and I will do the preaching." President Roberts and I developed a strong relationship, and I found the ORU faculty and staff to be dedicated people who were loving and strong in their Christian beliefs.

Recruiting proved to be difficult and it took awhile to experience success. In the Midwestern City Conference, ORU competed against schools with solid histories in the game, such as Butler, Xavier, Saint Louis, Loyola of Chicago, the University of Detroit and Evansville. Winning the league would be a challenge, but the conference was so highly regarded that more than one team could be picked for the NCAA tournament. I looked forward to the test.

ORU's crowds had been small in recent years, so we tried to play strong non-conference teams, scheduling such teams as LSU, Arkansas, Oklahoma State, Memphis, BYU and Texas. In the 1985-86 season, we often lost to good teams by 10 points or more. In the following year, we were considerably better and played some close games, but we weren't beating good opponents, and our record in my second year wasn't much improved. Even so, one highlight was beating a great Tulsa University team, 59-55, to break their 13-game winning streak over ORU.

Discord at ORU

We were right on track to fulfill my promise to President Roberts of a strong team in my third year. Haywoode Workman, who went on to play several years with the Indiana Pacers, had finished a successful sophomore season, and he led a solid group of returning players. We also had four good Proposition 48 players who were red-shirting, two of whom were outstanding frontline players, 6'10" Kenzie Scott and 6'9" Marvin Washington.

After my first season, President Roberts had asked if I would consider becoming the athletic director. If I didn't take it, he said, they would give the position to Jack Wallace, a longtime ORU employee. So I accepted the position, not wanting to work for someone I didn't know very well. I was also asked to take on Jack as an assistant athletic director, so he was assigned to oversee the rest of the sports programs while I spent my time working to improve the basketball programs for the men and women.

During the course of my second year, Richard Roberts was being groomed to take over as president of the university and the ministry. He came by the office one day and as we talked, he told me he wanted the team to start scoring 100 points per game, just like in the '60s and '70s. That era was a special time for the university. In the '80s, though, with the financial losses of the City of Faith medical complex (rumored to be more than $1 million per month), the university was forced to close its dental school and shortly after, the law school and the medical school. I suppose it was natural to yearn for ORU's good old days.

I explained to Richard that the game of basketball had changed considerably since those days. The NCAA had tightened up eligibility rules and made both independents and conference schools abide by the new Proposition 48 rules, with required test scores and class ranks. In addition, we were playing in a tough conference that required sound defensive performances in order to compete, and we simply didn't have the outstanding scorers that it would take to win shootouts against good teams. I told Richard that I would rather win a 72-64 game than score 100 points and lose.

After the last home game of the 1986-87 season, President Oral Roberts spoke to the squad and told them "that we have the coach we need in Coach Owens," and he challenged them to work hard in the offseason in order to field a strong team the following year. I felt good about the support from President Roberts and looked forward to the future.

Shortly after, Richard Roberts tried to force me to fire one of my assistant coaches and hire Ken Trickey, the former head coach, as my assistant. Ken and I had long been friends, but we were as far apart in how to coach the game as two people could be, so I told Richard that I was happy with my staff. I was called into many meetings on the matter but I continued to stand my ground, convinced that such a move was not in the best interest of our program or the university. I tried to see President Roberts in the hope that he would stop the madness, but he was never available to see me.

During this period, I was stripped of my title of athletic director and the job was given to Jack Wallace. I was moved out of the head basketball coach's office and placed in a small office down the hall. Then I was excluded from meetings in which the administrators made two questionable decisions—to drop the University of Tulsa from our schedule and to leave the Midwestern City Conference and go independent.

The decisions were questionable for a couple of reasons. Even if Tulsa had dominated ORU in recent years, we had just broken their 13-game winning streak against us, and those Tulsa games were the biggest draw for our fans. Dropping them made no practical sense. Secondly, the advantages of being independent had vanished because conference teams no longer had to win the league to qualify for the NCAA tournament; they could be selected as at-large participants, the same as independent schools. And with the passage of the Prop 48 rules, independents lost another advantage, as they were now governed by the same academic requirements that conference schools faced.

Next, the administration said that my contract didn't give me the authority to hire and fire my own assistants, so they fired one of my assistants and hired the man they wanted. I was even restricted from leaving the building during the day, except for an hour at lunchtime.

Resolve

They did everything possible to break my resolve. I tried to present an optimistic front, but deep down, I was suffering. I closed my office door and read the Book of Job several times, searching for a reason for my troubles. While I certainly don't mean to equate my condition to the magnitude of Job's suffering, dwelling on the book gave me strength as I read about the incredible faith that he kept during his ordeal.

One day, one of my players, Akin Akin-Otiko, dropped by the office to share that he had been thinking about me and wanted to share some Bible verses that he thought would be helpful. The verses were from the Book of Ecclesiastes, where Solomon searched for answers and came to the conclusion that each of us should serve God and follow His commandments, leaving it to God to be the final judge of the actions of those who are good and evil. I found the verses to be sound advice.

When it became apparent that President Oral Roberts would not see me, my only hope to resolve the situation disappeared. There was no way that I could run a basketball program in that environment. I asked my attorney, L.K. Smith, to start negotiating a settlement of my contract. The entire ordeal was a nightmare. We had built a house in Tulsa, as I had intended to coach at ORU for many years. I was not happy with the settlement because, at the age of 58, my chances of coaching college basketball again at a high level were not favorable.

Fortunately today, ORU is prospering under the management of professional administrators. Mike Carter is a first class athletic director, Mark Rutland, who recently retired, was an excellent president. Scott Sutton and his staff are doing a very good job with the basketball program. The Green family has provided the funding to pay off the indebtedness and provide much improved facilities. Ironically, the university, long after Oral Roberts death, is fulfilling many of his dreams and purposes for a the university.

The Fresno Flames

In 1987, I was overly anxious about the future and, as a result, I made a poor professional decision. A new professional league, the International Basketball League (which later changed its name to the World Basketball League) contacted me about coaching one of the teams. I was told the league had good financing for operations and a two-year contract with ESPN, and Bob Cousy, the Celtics star, was going to be the league commissioner. Some of the cities that were committed to the league were attractive to us, including Chicago, Vancouver, Calgary, Las Vegas and Fresno, which was especially attractive because my wife's family lived in nearby Merced, Calif.

The league's plan was to begin in the U.S. and Canada, expand into Japan, the Philippines, and South Korea as soon as possible, and then to someday expand into Europe. I was asked to take a group of all-stars to the Far East to showcase the league.

Our first stop was in Seoul, which was preparing to host the Olympics. I could not believe the city's cleanliness, beauty and growth. It had been more than 30 years since my first visit, on a short R&R leave during the Korean Conflict. At that time, Seoul was far from beautiful.

In a game televised by *ESPN*, the all-star team played the South Korean national team in the Olympic Arena, which was quite a thrill. Next, we traveled to Manila, where I learned that the people of the Philippines loved basketball. Even though the economy wasn't good, fans managed the price of admission and packed the arena for the tournament. The opening ceremonies were conducted in an Olympic type of atmosphere, with each team marching in. In the finals, my team overcame a 20-point deficit to win the championship.

I coached the Fresno Flames at the season's start, and we won our inaugural game in Las Vegas, with the contest televised by ESPN. Everything with the league was going great until one of the paydays came around and the owner didn't meet the payroll. Among other promises that didn't come true, the two-year ESPN contract was nonexistent. Soon enough, the league ended operations.

Even so, with every disappointment or bad experience in life, some good can come about. One positive is that Teddy and Taylor were able to live close to their grandparents, Frank and Terri Mazikowski, for about a year.

"In 1988, I was on the outskirts of professional basketball, playing in a 6'4"-and-under league. I was far, far away at that point from the realities of my career in the NBA as a player and coach. It was there as a member of the Fresno Flames that I met Coach Owens and began a friendship that is now going on 25 years and counting. Coach Owens' resume and pedigree spoke for themselves, so I knew as one

of his players that I was going to learn a great deal about the game. What I learned early on was that some of the greatest lessons that Coach Owens would teach me would come away from the court."

— Scott Brooks, Fresno Flames, guard, 1988; and Oklahoma City Thunder head coach

I also had the opportunity to coach some tremendous players. Kenny Natt played for me in the league before playing in the NBA and coaching the Sacramento Kings. Scott Brooks also played for me, demonstrating the talent and grit that led to a long NBA career, including a championship year with the Houston Rockets. Scott and I became friends, and now that he's coaching the Oklahoma City Thunder, I often go to his games and practices. He remains the same committed and positive person that he was as a player. And Ray Giacoletti, a member of my ORU coaching staff, joined me with the Fresno Flames. Our friendship has lasted for many years during his career at Eastern Washington, Utah, Gonzaga, and now Drake University.

"Prior to the start of the 2011-12 season, I invited Coach Owens to sit in on some of our preseason coaching meetings for the Oklahoma City Thunder. As I sat in the room with our assistant coaches and put together the blueprint for what we hoped would be a deep run in the NBA playoffs, Coach Owens was adamant about sharing one of his favorite plays. As he diagrammed the play on the whiteboard, he had players moving the ball like a hot potato, with a couple of down screens and cross screens thrown in. By his account, a wide-open jumper at the elbow would be the end result. The only problem was that a 24-second shot clock wouldn't allow for what seemed to be a 24-step play. When I reminded Coach Owens of this factor, he adjusted on the fly like the great coach that he is, and replied, "Well, no problem, take out one or two of the cross screens or down screens, and you should be set." Coach Owens has since asked if we've ever used the play, but I like to think that it is our secret weapon. NBA opponents beware."

— Scott Brooks, Fresno Flames, guard, 1988; and Oklahoma City Thunder head coach

Photo courtesy of Layne Murdoch/NBAE/ Getty Images

Scott Brooks, coach of the NBA's Oklahoma City Thunder, played professionally for the Fresno Flames when I coached the team. We remain close today.

Israel comes calling

Following the Flames, I scouted the West Coast for the New Jersey Nets and did telecasting for the West Coast Conference. The scouting and television work kept me close to the game, and I enjoyed the many friendships that I was able to make with college coaches in the west.

Bill Musselman, hired as head coach of the NBA's Minnesota Timberwolves in 1989, the franchise's first year, called me to ask if I would join him in Minnesota to prepare his new team for the Midwest Revue, a four-team summer series with the San Antonio, Denver and Houston teams. An impressive young coach named Tom Thibodeau, then a coach at Harvard and now the Chicago Bulls coach, joined us for the workouts and the revue.

Bill said that while he wanted to hire me permanently, the franchise's management team didn't want to hire the coaching staff until positions on the business side of the organization were filled. Not hearing from him for several weeks, I became concerned about the upcoming season. While I waited, I was contacted by the management of Maccabi Tel-Aviv, an Israeli team playing in European Cup competition, about becoming their head basketball coach. When I flew to Tel Aviv to interview for the position, I was struck by two things: the thoroughness of security on flights going in and out of Ben Gurion Airport and the singing and chants of the passengers on my flight from New York as we approached our landing in their beloved Israel.

I had a good interview with the management team. At the conclusion of our meeting, they asked if I had any concerns. I was quite honest with them and said I was worried about security for my family. They laughed and said that I would never feel more secure than while living in Israel. I found that to be true, largely because of the meticulous care that Israeli officials take in protecting their people.

I accepted the position and made plans for Michelle, Teddy and Taylor to join me after Michelle was able to sell our condo and store our furniture. With the preseason tournaments in Europe starting soon, the best opportunity for my family to join me was later on in Miami when the team traveled to play the NBA's Miami Heat in an exhibition game.

'Coach Evans' goes overseas

As the preseason began, the team management introduced me to the squad as "Coach Ted Evans" instead of Owens. A person needs a little humility, but for them to not know my name was more of a lesson than I required. They later explained that in Hebrew, "Owens" and "Evans" are spelled the same. After a month of correcting people who called me Coach Evans, I gave up.

While we were in Italy for a preseason tournament, I was awakened one night by a phone call from Bill Musselman, informing me that the

Timberwolves had approved my hiring. I told him that I appreciated the offer but that I had signed a contract with Maccabi.

The first trip out of Israel was an eye-opener for me. The precautions that the Israelis took in protecting their athletic teams were truly impressive. After the tragedy that their wrestling team suffered in the Munich Olympics, they were determined that such a thing would never happen again.

The security procedures began at the airport. When we departed, we were accompanied by three security guards. The guards wore jackets to conceal their handguns, and each one carried a case that contained an automatic weapon that could be assembled in seconds. Once we were airborne, they paced the aisles, conscious of any unusual movements by the passengers.

When the team arrived at European airports, we were escorted through the airport and through a corridor of policemen to our awaiting buses. We did not see our luggage until it was loaded on our bus. In the meantime, the three security guards thoroughly inspected the buses for explosives. A police escort accompanied us to our hotel. No other guests could stay on our floor, and security guards were on duty at all times.

If we went out at night, we had to be accompanied by other staff members or players. If a cab pulled over, we were told not to take the first cab—maybe the second one, and possibly the third one. At first, it was a bit scary to witness all of these precautions, but after awhile, it became comforting.

Life in Israel

After a couple of preseason tournaments in Europe, we flew to Miami to play the Heat. I was excited to coach against an NBA team, but I was much more excited to see Michelle, Teddy and Taylor. The Maccabi team had built a great following in Europe and the U.S., and we were often greeted with large turnouts of Jewish fans. The playing of the Israeli national anthem was always a moving event. The team was made up of eight Israeli players and three Americans—Willie Sims from LSU, Kevin McGee from California-Irvine and Lavon Mercer, a big guy from Georgia. Later in the year, Kenny Barlow from Notre Dame joined the team.

The team president sat near me on the bench while the other management team members sat on the other end of the bench, just past the players. The players and management team all spoke English very well—except for the times that they spoke in Hebrew so that I wouldn't understand what they were saying.

The team leased a villa in Ramat Sharon, a suburban area of Tel Aviv, for my family. The children would attend the American International School, where instruction was in English four days a week and in Hebrew one day a week. We decided against sending them to a public school, because Hebrew was a difficult language to master.

The team practiced in the evening so that members of the management team, after working during the day, could attend practice. During the day, Michelle and I often traveled with Major Baker, the U.S. embassy's military attaché and a parent of a student at the American International School, to sites around Israel. Baker had grown up in Israel, where his dad was a missionary, and he was fluent in Hebrew and Arabic, making traveling much easier.

Baker was also a strong student of the Bible. He took us to many of the locations where Jesus had lived and traveled during his ministry. I had been a fairly good student of the New Testament but not of the Old Testament, and as we visited the sites, I regretted my lack of knowledge of the events and characters of the era. In later years, as I did a more comprehensive study of both testaments, I became more frustrated with myself for blowing the opportunity to fully appreciate the historical significance of those names and places.

But even with my limited knowledge, I appreciated the travels to Bethlehem, where Jesus was born; to Nazareth, where He lived for the first 30 years of His life; to Cana, where He performed his first miracle; to the Sea of Galilee and Capernaum, where He spent so much time with the disciples; to Mount Olive and the Garden of Gethsemane, where He was betrayed; and to the Via Dolorosa, the "Way of Grief," the road on which He carried His cross. It was an incredible experience.

Christmas in Israel

Our scariest adventure occurred just before Christmas. We had planned to have the team and management and their children over to our house for an American Christmas. In advance of the party, though, we were desperately trying to find a tree. We read one day in the Jerusalem Post that a nursery not too far from Tel Aviv had Christmas trees, so Michelle and I decided that we would venture out in a small SUV to pick a tree.

That morning, after the school bus stopped by to pick up Teddy and Taylor, we immediately left so that we could get back before the bus's afternoon return. We reached the nursery only to find out that the trees were gone, but the proprietors recommended another nursery several kilometers away. After securing the tree, we drove around collecting pinecones for decoration ... and wandered into the West Bank. When we realized our mistake, we tried to work our way back toward the Israeli border, and we finally spotted a bus full of tourists. Then the tour-bus driver spoke the most beautiful words: "Coach Evans, what are you doing up here?"

We made it home just in time to meet the kids after school. Members of the management team had searched all over for us and scolded us for exploring on our own. The good ending of the story, however, is that we had a great Christmas party. The team trainer even dressed up as Santa Claus and gave out presents.

In turn, our Jewish friends included us in their holidays. Our kids loved the festive holiday, the Feast of Purim, which celebrates Esther and Mordecai's efforts to save the Jewish people from annihilation. We became close to Moni Fanan, one of the team managers, and his wife, Sharon, and their two children, Liron and Regev. Even though Regev did not speak English, our kids always found ways to communicate.

While in Israel, we were fortunate to travel from the northern mountains to the Red Sea in the south, from the Mediterranean Sea to the Dead Sea. We came to realize what a small area the nation covered and, as a result, the concern Israelis have in giving up land and strategic terrain in proposed peace settlements. There is certainly not an easy solution to the problem.

Our family entertainment was pretty limited. We found a video store that offered a membership for 30 shekels, then about 15 dollars, that gave us unlimited access to movies. We selected every available English-speaking title and watched the films many times over. We could speak the words from "Hoosiers" almost before Gene Hackman could voice them.

Years later, Teddy and I journeyed to Indianapolis for the NCAA tournament and had an opportunity to visit Hinkle Fieldhouse, the building filmed in "Hoosiers" as the site of the state tournament where Hickory High School won the Indiana state championship. Teddy and I went to the exact spot where we thought the actor (Bobby Plump) had held the ball and played for the last shot. Teddy replayed the scene, waiting for the last shot, and he nailed it. Meanwhile, a guide led a tour group through the building, and we asked her to verify that we had found the exact spot of Jimmy's winning shot. She replied that she thought it was on the other end of the court ... but, hey, what did she know, anyway?

The European influence

I found European basketball to be intriguing. They observed the game's international rules: a 30-second shot clock (at the time), a three-point line just beyond the American college line, and a widened lane at the base of the free-throw lane. European players were good shooters and ball-handlers, but not nearly as aggressive on defense as the better American players. Also, European big guys didn't play much low-post basketball, partially because of the wide lane. Their style of play is best exemplified by a German player, Dirk Nowitzki, with today's Dallas Mavericks.

The versatility of the European big guys has influenced American basketball. Players here have added the screen-and-pop to the traditional screen-and-roll, and in the NBA, there are few low-post players, a huge change from the era of dominant big men such as Shaq, Kareem, and Hakeem.

Chapter 2?

Back in the U.S.A.

Coach's Life Lesson: *The things that happen to you in life are not ne important as how you respond to them. Responding to defeat or failu positive way is one of the great lessons of sport.*

With our 1977-78 team, we were trying different line-ups and offens defensive combinations, and we lost a game or two. We concluded tha to set a rotation—decide on the starters and the substitutes and stic consistent plan. Once we reached that conclusion, the team took off had a heck of a year. But we had to lose a couple of games in order to reality that we needed to make some changes. As Coach John Woo "Failure is not fatal, but failure to change can be."

Although Israel was a tremendous educational experience for r one that encourages me to return and learn more someday, we w to get back to the U.S. In 1990, we arrived in America without to what my next job would be or where we would live. One call was from Dr. Wanda Hartman, a friend from the First United Church in Tulsa. As the headmaster at Metro Christian Academ Dr. Hartman asked if I would help her raise money. The school had a development director before, and they had discovered what m schools know, that it is difficult to survive on tuition alone. They a coach high school basketball, and they wanted Michelle to teach school while Teddy and Taylor attended school.

We visited the school with some reservation but found the caring and loving and excited about the academy's future. We felt there and thought it would be a good place for our family to set

With school starting in a few days, Michelle and the kic stay in Tulsa, so I headed to California to fetch our vehicle, f cats. Because I had previously given thought to a career in pul I brought along several humorous speaking tapes to accompa

drive. I left Merced, California, with my Suburban, my furniture, my cats, and my tapes, and I started the long haul back to Tulsa. I must've been a strange sight for passing motorists, this odd man driving along with cats in his lap and laughing for no apparent reason.

Our family had a great experience at Metro. The fundraising went well and I felt some satisfaction in helping the school grow. And even though I initially was not excited about coaching high school basketball, it turned out to be one of the most enjoyable times of my life. When I started, the players told me the team had never won a district title or advanced to the state tournament, and I started to get caught up in their excitement. In the next five years, with the help of my assistant, Jeff Hogue, we won five district championships and participated in three state tournaments. I learned that if a coach cares for young people and loves the game, it doesn't matter at what level he coaches. The away games in Paris and Madrid might have become road games in Choteau and Durant, but the thrill—to witness a player's performance using the skills he had developed, and to see your strategies lead to wins—was the same.

Coaching Lesson: *Encourage the players*

When I coached basketball at Metro, Michelle asked if I ever videotaped my timeouts, and said I acted like I hated the kids. My first thought was, 'Hey, what do you know? I've been coaching a long time.' But I started to think about it. They would play tight, and I'd get onto them. In Europe if you weren't tough with them, they'd run right over you—and I carried that toughness over into high school. But nowadays, kids are different. So I started to shift, to become an encourager. I encouraged them—I'd put my arm around them, hug them—and they started blossoming.

If you're happy where you are...'

After five years at Metro, I was contacted by Woody Wolverton, an old friend from my time at the University of Oklahoma and Cameron College. Woody was on the board at Saint Leo University near Tampa, Florida, and they were looking for an athletic director. I thought that spending the rest of my life in the warm climate of Florida wouldn't be such a bad thing. Also, we would be able to see my oldest daughter, Nancy, who lived in Florida, as well as my daughter, Kelly, when she visited from Colorado Springs. Even so, I would warn any aspiring coach or athletic director who is considering leaving a good job in hopes of finding greener pastures: If you're happy where you are, don't try to get happier. I have seen too many successful coaches, whose personalities and skills perfectly fit their current jobs, leave for supposedly

better jobs and never reach the same levels of success again, simply because the new situation wasn't a good fit.

In the mid-1990s, we moved our family to Tampa, and I spent four years as the Saint Leo athletic director. We improved the facilities and improved the quality of our total sports program, but I missed what I loved in sports: the interaction with coaches and players, teaching skills, planning strategies, establishing team goals with the players and being a positive force in their lives.

Paying it forward

Working late one night at Saint Leo, a gentleman knocked on my office door. He said that he had two twin sons who loved the game but had no place to practice at night. As eighth- or ninth-graders, the twins were already more than six feet tall. I told them that they could work out any night that I was at the office. After I spent a few minutes more in the office, I walked down to the gym to see if they had any promise as players, and I saw two incredible athletes who just needed some guidance with their shooting and offensive-drive series. So I embarked on a journey with them that has brought me immense joy.

Joey and Stephen Graham became regular visitors to the gym, and I started training the boys on a regular basis. I have loved following their careers, in the Florida state high school finals, in their 2004 run to the Final Four with the Oklahoma State Cowboys, and in their NBA experiences. More than just players, Joey and Stephen are terrific young men, and the Graham family has become part of my family.

"It was 1996 when we were 14 years old that we had the privilege of meeting Coach Owens. We were blessed to have a father that made time to find a gym and teach us the first mechanics of basketball. While doing our workouts at Saint Leo, we would always wonder who the elderly man was, and one day he approached my father and said 'Hello, my name is Ted Owens. I am the athletic director here at Saint Leo. Do you mind if I show your boys a couple of things?' That first encounter turned out to be a blessing in disguise. From that meeting on, we continued to receive lessons from Coach Owens three or four times a week. Little did we know that he happened to be one of the winningest coaches in University of Kansas history, coaching all kinds of great players and putting them into the NBA."

— Joey and Stephen Graham, Oklahoma State University, forward and guard, 2003-05

Even today, I am contacted from time to time by athletes who have aspirations of playing college basketball or playing in the pros and want me to spend some time with them in reviewing and improving their skills. What a joy to see them succeed in working toward and accomplishing their goals. I tell them that I never charge them anything for my time and efforts, but require them someday to "pay it forward" to someone else.

> *"While I was coaching in high school at Bradenton Christian, each year Coach Owens would fly in for a few days and work with my team. I was consistently shocked with how much he knew and how little I knew. One year we were playing a high-powered team from IMG and Coach was in the stands. My best player was struggling and at halftime, Coach grabbed him and said, 'Relax and get your feet under your shot.' That is it. That's all he said. Then the player, Jameson Tipping, went for 27 in the second half and we won in a big upset. All the kid could talk about in the paper was Coach Owens—who has never let me live that down!"*
> — *David Magley, University of Kansas, forward, 1978-82*

Back to Oklahoma—and Michelle

After four years at Saint Leo, I left to take a job with the same pay and benefits at a firm that specialized in athletic skills camps and small-group instruction, which really appealed to me. Unfortunately, I didn't do my due diligence and soon learned that the firm had very serious financial difficulties. I had invested with the company and with the loss of what amounted to two years' salary, I had wiped out our savings.

As with any marriage, my marriage to Michelle was far from perfect. I think we both respected each other enough to avoid harsh words, unkind remarks or conflict. We both internalized our problems and issues. Both of us had trouble dealing with conflict and as a result, we didn't communicate our concerns— and issues that go unresolved over time will grow into much greater problems. Unfortunately, our issues became such a wedge that Michelle and I ended up separating for a couple of years and getting a divorce that neither of us wanted.

I left the divorce proceedings with my head hanging down and a hole in my heart that I thought would never close. Michelle told me later that it was the hardest day of her life, watching me walk away. I didn't turn to look at her because I knew it would tear me up inside.

I left Florida and returned to Oklahoma to be close to Teddy and begin a new life. Soon afterward, Michelle returned to Tulsa, followed shortly thereafter by Taylor's transfer to the University of Oklahoma. As disappointing as it was to be away from Michelle, the separation afforded me an opportunity to spend time with and get to know Teddy and Taylor in a special way. I was able to be there for Teddy as he worked toward his degree at OSU and support Taylor as she studied long hours for her nursing degree.

"During those two years, Dad and I made it a routine to take weekend trips together to Lawrence to take in Kansas football and basketball. We got to travel to Miami and watch the Jayhawk football team win the Orange Bowl. We got to travel to San Antonio to see the Jayhawk basketball team win the national championship. Those two years living together were some of the most precious memories I have with my father. Ted Owens became more than my dad, he became my great friend. I have never, a day in my life, felt unloved because I know whatever obstacles I may face in life, he will support me and love me endlessly."
—*Taylor Owens O'Connell, daughter*

The best thing is that Michelle and I have since remarried, bringing us both a great deal of happiness. It has been more than 30 years since we took our vows at the beautiful Danforth Chapel on the KU campus. We are learning to communicate more clearly, and I encourage all couples to work to communicate with each other and to never let issues go unresolved.

'The Jimmies and Joes'

One day after returning to Oklahoma, I took a call from Joe Graham, who said that Joey and Stephen wanted to find a university whose basketball program would challenge them to become complete players. I contacted several coaches, including the staff at KU, asking if their programs would be interested in landing two outstanding players who would have to red-shirt one year and then have two years of eligibility left. OU and Oklahoma State were among the interested schools, and I knew that both Kelvin Sampson and Eddie Sutton were both sound fundamental teachers whose experiences would benefit the twins.

"During that time, Coach Owens became our biggest advocate, our biggest promoter, our biggest supporter. He instilled in us the fundamentals that were necessary for us to succeed at every level of basketball. We became inseparable from him in a coach-student relationship. He became another father figure in our lives. We included him in all of our decisions in basketball and life."
— *Joey and Stephen Graham, Oklahoma State University,*
forward and guard, 2003-05

I told Joe that if he could fly the twins to Tulsa, I would take them to Norman and Stillwater for visits. In preparation, I had taken video highlights to both schools. I really thought that they would select Oklahoma because Kelvin had spoken at a clinic of mine in Tampa, and the twins had been very impressed with him. In addition, the Sooners had just been to the 2002 Final Four.

When friend Bruce O'Connor and I arrived in Norman with Joey and Stephen, an assistant told us that he was busy with scheduling and that Kelvin was out of the arena for a meeting. He said that Kelvin would be there in an hour or so to show Joey and Stephen around. I have recruited enough to know that if a coach has a prospect arrive, he drops whatever he's doing to tend to the lifeblood of the program: the players. As the old saying goes, "It's not the X's and O's, but the Jimmies and Joes that win games for you."

Well, after waiting an hour for someone to take the twins around, I took them on a tour myself. When Kelvin arrived, he did a good job with them and tried to reconcile a bad situation, but the damage was done. I had really expected Joey and Stephen to decide, that day, to attend OU.

The next day as we traveled to Stillwater, Kelvin called to tell me that they wanted both Joey and Stephen, and I told him that I would pass it on to them. I told the twins the news and asked if they still wanted to visit OSU, and they said that they did. In Stillwater, we met with the coaches, an academic adviser and the weight coach, and the twins were made to feel wanted. On the way back to the Tulsa airport, I asked them which school they would choose if they had to select one right then, and they said OSU. I talked later with Kelvin and told him that the Sooners had some work to do if they wanted the Grahams. He tried, but Joey and Stephen stayed with their decision.

The Grahams had two solid years with the Cowboys, winning a regular-season conference title and two conference tournament titles and making a trip to the 2004 Final Four in San Antonio.

> *"To be a good coach at the college level requires the development of myriad capabilities and talents, but from my perspective, Coach Owens excels to this day at making each player better. He can see the potential in each one. Without a doubt, every player who ever played basketball for Ted Owens expanded his skills and became a much better individual player and team contributor. More importantly, every player under his tutelage became a better person."*
>
> — *Gerald Hertzler, Cameron College, forward, 1956-58*

Dreams fulfilled

In the early 2000's, I joined a Tulsa firm, First Capital Management, becoming friends with the senior partner, Clayton Woodrum. I treasure the days that I spend with him, Jake Whitely and the others in the accounting and investment business.

Returning to my native state has been wonderful. I had missed my friends and the few relatives who were still alive. I had missed talking and traveling with Mike Kimbrel and his son Michael to games in the Big Eight—now the Big 12, of course—where I had played and coached.

I have had the freedom to pursue a variety of things that enrich my life: time with my wonderful family; tutoring aspiring basketball players to develop their skills; continued reading and studying; playing golf at some of the best courses around the country and the world; following my favorite coaches and teams, including Bill Self's Jayhawks, Lon Kruger's Sooners, Scott Brooks' Oklahoma City Thunder, and Danny Manning at Tulsa University and Scott Sutton at Oral Roberts; spending time with former players and coaching colleagues, who mean so much to me; and enjoying our rock-solid, caring friends.

Scottish joy

In 2008, I fulfilled a dream playing golf on Scotland's legendary courses, where the game began, due to the generosity of my good friend Kent McCarthy. Along with a group of others, I was invited to play at Saint Andrews, Muirfield and Carnoustie. One night, we were having dinner in our hotel. The view overlooked the 18th fairway and hole and the first fairway, as well as the Royal and Ancient Golf Club. Our discussion focused on the life of one of the game's founders, Tom Morris. It seemed that old Tom had lived a long and healthy life, well into his 80s, and he attributed his health to swimming in the North Sea every morning.

Kent challenged the two youngest members of the group, Jay Hepler and Greg Gurley, to race to the sea and dive into the area where Tom, by tradition, had swam. The reward? $1,000. So Jay sped out of the restaurant door and flew down the stairs, leaving Greg, whose speed was never his greatest strength, behind. Jay left articles of clothing scattered over the 18th and first fairways, hurdled a fence, crossed the beach where *Chariots of Fire* had been filmed, and plunged into water that must have been frigid after day-time temperatures in the 40s. Now, this was a sophisticated restaurant, but everyone left their tables and rushed to the windows to watch. I am certain that anyone looking out from inside the Royal and Ancient Club would have been shocked to see such a thing happening on their sacred ground.

Somehow, though, I have to think that old Tom Morris was looking down with a smile on his face.

While that was one of the trip's most humorous occurrences, I experienced an emotional one the next day as we played the St. Andrews course. Approaching the 18th hole just in front of the Royal and Ancient Golf Club—a view I had seen often on television—I asked the caddy to hand me a special putter that I had brought with me. The putter belonged to my brother, Fred, who had died from Alzheimer's a few years before. An excellent golfer, Fred never had the chance to play at St. Andrews, and I wanted him to be a part of the trip by using his putter to finish the round.

As I started to tell my playing partners, Jay Hepler, Brian Wilkinson and Brad Shoup, what I was doing, I couldn't hold back the tears. Remembering Fred was such a special moment. He and my other brother, Quentin, had been my heroes as I grew up in southwest Oklahoma.

At the hang-up

My life hasn't turned out exactly as I thought it would. I have had my share of disappointments, but the rewards far outweigh them. Each disappointment has opened doors for me to accomplish things that I wouldn't have pursued otherwise.

As I turn 84 years old in 2013, I recall what my dad told me back in the cotton patch in southwest Oklahoma: "It's not what you have now that matters, but what you have at the hang-up." Too often, as my teammates, players and friends finish their journeys in this world, I am reminded that my remaining days are fewer and fewer. When the sum total of my life's experiences and accomplishments are weighed like cotton at the hang-up, it is my desire that I will have accomplished all God had in mind for me.

Chapter

The Trip Home

Coach's Life Lesson: *Be of service to those in need. Take time to do something helpful for others.Whether it is financial assistance or just words of encouragement, the warm feelings you receive will be reward enough.*

During the Great Depression, my dad and mother were quick to help neighbors and strangers. People looking for work would often stop at our house, which sat right along the highway, and rest on the porch. Mother would offer them food. I'll never forget the sharing spirit of those days.

In 2012, Coach Owens and Gerald Hertzler, a former player, took a trip to Hollis, Oklahoma.

Gerald Hertzler: The phrase "you can't go home again" has become a familiar saying across the American landscape. Its origin dates back to Thomas Wolfe's 1940 novel of the same name. Many people today experience this when they return to their hometown and realize that changes have altered all the things they held dear. I saw the reality of this on a recent visit to Hollis.

Ted Owens: *It had been several years since I had been back to Hollis and Harmon County, where my core beliefs were established. It was a community of people who overcame the difficulties of the Great Depression and the Dust Bowl Days. They sacrificed much, but they lived with a belief in the goodness of this country and a love for their families and their neighbors.*

Gerald: The call came on a Thursday. "Hey Gerald! I want you to go to Hollis with me next week." It was my friend, mentor, and former coach, Ted Owens. I had dodged that bullet once before when he had extended the invitation, but that time I had an honest conflict. This time I had no excuse.

Ted: *I had felt a desire to return to my hometown for several months and the trip didn't fit the schedules of any of my family members. Finally, I talked my former player, Gerald Hertzler, into making the drive. Gerald played on my first team at Cameron College and had retired in Edmond, Oklahoma, after a distinguished career as a navy pilot.*

Gerald: One has to know Coach to understand that he exudes the excitement, enthusiasm and curiosity of a kid for almost every endeavor. As we ate breakfast together the morning of the trip, he began to talk about going back home again. It is about a three-and-a-half hour drive from Oklahoma City, where I live, to Hollis, and some moments of silence would be expected, but the conversation never lapsed. We talked about the old times and the taboo subjects of women, politics and religion. Coach is a man of integrity and honesty, but he confessed to me once that he adheres to the Phog Allen theory: "Never let the truth get in the way of a good story." And can he ever tell a story.

On the way, we made a stop at Cameron University in Lawton, where we were met by Bud Sahmaunt. Bud and I played basketball for Coach at Cameron. We walked through the old gym where Owens began his coaching career, where we had endured long, grueling practices. We like to joke that if it hadn't have been for the talent, teamwork and abilities of the players on that team he would still be coaching junior college, or maybe junior high.

When we arrived in Hollis, we were met by Bill Cummins, Coach's longtime friend and former Hollis classmate. Bill, our tour guide, showed us the Hollis High School gym and the Darrell Royal football facility.

Owens: *As we drove down the street, memories of my youth came rushing back. I found remnants of the loving families I knew, along with their children and grandchildren. We met the superintendent of schools, Jennifer McQueen, who happened to be the granddaughter of my high school teammate, Willie Ray "Sprout" Seddon. Jennifer showed us the gymnasium where I spent hours and hours on summer days, making 200 or 300 two-handed set shots before stopping. I yearned for the smell of Jelly Moore's popcorn and to see his son, Monte, in the concession stand. I could almost feel the excitement generated by the crowds at the annual county tournament as I walked onto the playing floor. The dressing rooms actually had lockers so that players wouldn't have to hang their clothes on nails like we did.*

We drove to the stadium and as we parked on the asphalt outside, I remembered that this same parking lot had served as our football practice field, filled with sandburs and goat-heads. I could almost hear Coach Metcalf saying, "Let's run that play one more time." As we entered the stadium, I saw the plaque commemorating the Darrell K. Royal Field. Darrell, one of Hollis High School's greatest athletes and ambassadors, had passed away just a few days before.

I glanced over at the bleachers, remembering the hot summer days in the 1940s when we helped Coach Metcalf pour the cement for the seats. As I walked onto the field and felt that thick Bermuda grass, those feelings of Friday night football were aroused.

When we left the stadium, we drove by the nursing home to see my cousin

Johnny, my classmate, Sue, and my teammate, Paul. I could see the joy in the eyes of my friends, but their joy couldn't have been any greater than the personal blessing that I received.

Gerald: I knew the story of Coach coming home and being sure his dad wanted to show him off and brag. Instead, they went to the rest home and visited the room of every resident. Not once did Homer mention anything about his son's winning season.

Owens: *We drove to old farm about three miles north of town. Even though the farmhouse is not there anymore, there were enough landmarks to give me a sense of where the house, barn and smokehouse were located. The land was now irrigated and planted, cultivated and harvested by large equipment, and not by a father, his three sons and some mules and horses. As we drove down the road, in the distance I could see the cottonwood trees in the shade of which we kept our water jugs for a few moments of refreshment.*

Gerald: Coach pointed out the field where he and his brothers had worked. He loved the trees at the far end of the field, which would beckon him with shade and a cool drink of water. It was this setting that would later be the inspiration for his autobiography.

Owens: *We drove to the site of the Arnett Country School. None of the buildings remain; nothing but a sign reminds us where the buildings were located. But I could still see the old stone elementary school where I attended school for the first time.*

Gerald: We stopped at the Antioch Baptist Church and Coach climbed over an electric fence to approach an old fallen-down structure, most of it now on the ground. This was where Coach and his family attended church years ago.

Owens: *My grandpa, Miles Emerson Owens, helped to found that church. The brush arbor, where I walked down to the altar when I was 12 years old, has fallen in. Still, I could envision those sweltering summertime night revivals, the adults cooling themselves with hand-held fans.*

Gerald: At the Hollis cemetery, there was a moment of solemn silence as Coach stood over the graves of his parents, Homer and Annie Owens.

Owens: *I have always had great love and admiration for my beloved parents, but as I have aged, I have become more acutely aware of their wisdom, love and sacrifice.*

Gerald: Bill took us through the main street of Hollis while Coach pointed out the various businesses, many now closed, that his family had once frequented. Coach pointed out where cars used to double-park because of the Saturday crowds when everyone came to town to shop, visit and take care of business. It was the thing to do. Today the streets are mostly vacant on a Saturday afternoon.

Owens: *The main street is pretty much empty now. There is no J.C. Penney store, no Anthony's or Hill's department store, no City Drug with the ice cream parlor in the back, no grocery stores, no barber shops where you could talk about the Cardinals, and certainly no LaVista Theatre, where I sat and watched Westerns and shared popcorn and cherry limeades with my brother Fred.*

Gerald: The town may have changed, but the people there retain their proud heritage. One of the original buildings had been converted into the Harmon County Museum, which includes what could be called the Hollis Athletic Hall of Fame, paying tribute to Darrel Royal and Ted Owens. I joked with Coach that when they heard he was coming for a visit, they must have quickly scrambled through the storage lockers to come up with some memorabilia.

Owens: *I presented the museum with a painting of my Kansas All-Americans and me. I was privileged to see old friends and their families, and a couple of young men (actually not so young) who had attended my KU basketball camp years ago. They still had their camp uniforms, which they brought to the ceremonies. My heart was as full as it could possibly be.*

Gerald: There was a gathering at the museum, a small ceremony to honor Darrell Royal. Coach eloquently lifted up Coach Royal, his friend and former Hollis teammate, paying homage to his roots and those who had supported him and ended with a beautiful prayer.

Several days after our trip, I called Coach and told him what a good time I had had. He said, "Gerald, I can't tell you how much I, too, enjoyed that trip. I have been so energized ever since we returned. I want to go back and see everyone again, and maybe do a book signing after my book is published."

Owens: *When it was time for Gerald and me to go, I felt such warmth and fulfillment from being* home. *Hollis will always* be my home. *Memories of the trip warmed my heart for many days.*

Gerald: Maybe Thomas Wolfe got it wrong. Maybe you can go home again.

Conclusion

Coach's Life Lesson: *The ultimate challenge in coaching or leading is to prepare those you are training to perform successfully without you. If a player or a child can leave the nest and perform admirably, then you have probably done a good job.*

There is a temptation to not allow a child or a player to fail, a tendency to do things for them. Abraham Lincoln warned us about this when he said that we shouldn't be doing things for our children that they should and could do for themselves. In Allen Fieldhouse, the crowd noise is so great that it is difficult to communicate, and it is important that the players are so well prepared for every situation that they can respond without the coach's assistance. The same thing is true of preparing your children to do without you. The best thing that we can hope to do is to train them to think for themselves.

As I play out this last quarter in the game of life, I have found time to reflect on my experiences and try to come to some conclusion about its purpose and meaning. It has been a lifetime full of success and failure, joy and pain. I am grateful that the joy has far outweighed the pain, but I am also grateful for the pain because suffering has caused me to grow and mature and return my focus to things that are of lasting value.

Although I went through a period when I questioned my faith, in recent years I have recommitted to studying the Bible and books that deal with the creation of the universe and life itself. My examinations have reaffirmed my belief in a Creator and I have concluded that the Bible is a guide for how God desires a personal relationship with each of us.

I continue to count my blessings every day. My wife, Michelle, continues to be an inspiration to me, and it is so very special to have her, along with all four of my children and my two grandchildren, in my life. Working on her doctorate in Florida, Nancy continues her academic development as an educator and resides in Palatka with Charlie. At 17, grandson Arthur plans enrolling at Boston University. Kelly graduated from the Dumas Pere L'Ecole de la Cuisine Francaise in Glenview, Illinois, interned at a Ritz-Carlton hotel and resides today in Colorado Springs, Colorado.

> *"Upon graduating from the academy, I apprenticed at the Ritz Carlton in downtown Chicago. Soon I was the sous chef at Monique's, a popular restaurant, gourmet market and catering company. Several years later, I was attending some sort of a function with Dad. We were chatting with some old family friends and they asked 'So, Kelly, what are you doing these days?' Dad stepped in and answered, 'Well, Kelly is now in Chicago working as a stew chef.' I replied, 'No, Dad, I am a sous chef!' We all nearly fell over in laughter. To this day I wonder how many people dad told I was cooking stew for a living! The lesson is: You can take the boy out of Hollis, Oklahoma, but you can't take the Hollis out of the boy.*
>
> *— Kelly Fischer Owens, daughter*

Taylor is completing her CRNA (Certified Registered Nurse Anesthetists) degree and resides in Tulsa with her husband, Nick O'Connell. Teddy has continued the family tradition of coaching and teaching. After completing his master's degree and two years as a graduate assistant to Lon Kruger at OU, he has joined Tim Miles men's basketball staff at the University of Nebraska. He and his dear wife Ashley have given life to our second grandson Layton Bracket Owens. The bracket comes from having been born in March, of course.

In December 2012 at KU, I reunited with my 1966 Jayhawks team, which lost to Texas Western (or won, depending on whether you think JoJo stepped out of bounds on his game-winning shot). They were a remarkable group of

Playing golf at my alma mater, the University of Oklahoma, I was joined by Sooners basketball coach Lon Kruger (to my right) and (from left) my good friends Kyle Travis, Bruce O'Connor and Mike Kimbrel.

Conclusion

men—unspoiled, good students, great people. In my mind, they will always be one of KU's greatest teams.

"On Feb. 23, 2013, I sat among former KU players, coaches, broadcasters, telecasters, managers and trainers who had come back to celebrate 115 years of Kansas basketball. As I looked over that assembly of men, I was struck not just by their accomplishments on the playing floor but by their successes beyond their playing days. The room was full of businessmen, teachers, coaches, doctors, engineers, ministers and other professionals who had used the lessons learned as athletes to prepare for productive lives. More importantly, they had become great parents, providing love, care and guidance to their youngsters. I was reminded of what Dr. Allen said when he was asked to identify his greatest players and teams: 'Let's wait 25 years and see what they have accomplished in their lives.' It struck me that night that Dr. Allen would be immensely proud of the men who had worn Kansas across their chests."

— *Ted Owens*

Final Coaching and Life Lesson: *May God bless each and every one of you!*

I was honored to join a recent celebration of 115 years of Kansas basketball. (From left) Bud Stallworth, Dave Robisch, JoJo White, Al Lopes, me, Roger Brown, Coach Bill Self, Roger Morningstar, David Magley, Tommy Smith and Ron Franz.

255

Resources

Publications:

- The Holy Bible
- *Make It Count: The Life and Times of Basketball Great JoJo White,* by Mark C. Bodanza
- *Tommy's Honor: The Story of Old Tom Morris and Young Tom Morris, Golf's Founding Father and Son,* by Kevin Cook
- *My Losing Season: A Memoir,* by Pat Conroy
- *Presidents Can't Punt: The OU Football Tradition,* by George Lynn Cross
- *God Forsaken,* by Dinesh D'Souza
- *I Don't Have Enough Faith to Be an Atheist,* by Dr. Norman L. Geisler and Frank Turek
- *Systematic Christianity, Vol. 1: Introduction/Bible,* by Dr. Norman L. Geisler
- *Knight: My Story,* by Bob Knight with Bob Hammel
- *Does People Do It? A Memoir,* by Fred Harris
- *Kansas Jayhawks: History Making Basketball,* by John Hendel
- *Wooden's Wisdom, Craig Impelman,* www.woodencourse.com
- *Guardians of the Game—A Legacy of Leadership,* by Dr. James E. Krause
- *John Adams,* by David McCullough
- *A Coach's Life: My 40 Years in College Basketball,* by Dean Smith with John Kilgo and Sally Jenkins
- *The Case for a Creator* and *The Case for Christ,* by Lee Strobel
- *The Oklahoma Supreme Court decision, The Egg Case Story,* rights owned by Judge Mike Warren
- *The Purpose Driven Life,* by Rick Warren
- *The Basketball Man: James Naismith,* by Bernice Larson Webb
- *Dear Jay, Love Dad: Bud Wilkinson's Letters to His Son,* by Jay Wilkinson
- *Bud Wilkinson: An Intimate Portrait of an American Legend,* by Jay Wilkinson with Gretchen Hirsch
- *My Personal Best,* by John Wooden with Steve Jamison

Oral Interviews (in order of appearance):

- Ted Owens, author, December 2012
- Walter Wesley, University of Kansas, January 2013
- JoJo White, University of Kansas, January 2013
- Dave Robisch, University of Kansas, January 2013
- Isaac "Bud" Stallworth, University of Kansas, December 2012

Written Interviews (in alphabetical order):

- *Scott Brooks, head coach, Oklahoma City Thunder*
- *John Calipari, head coach, University of Kentucky*
- *Kelly Owens Fischer, daughter*
- *Ron Franz, University of Kansas*
- *Joey Graham, Oklahoma State University and NBA*
- *Stephen Graham, Oklahoma State University and NBA*
- *Gerald Hertzler, Cameron College*
- *Riney Lochmann, University of Kansas*
- *David Magley, University of Kansas*
- *Taylor Owens O'Connell, daughter*
- *Theodore "Teddy" L. Owens, son*
- *Dr. Bud Sahmaunt, Cameron College*
- *Nancy Owens Wilde, daughter*

Appendix A

Ted Owens' Coaching Records and Highlights

Cameron College, NJCAA

- Basketball record: 93-24
- Three consecutive trips to the NJCAA national tournament
- Three NJCAA semifinals appearances
- Baseball: 1958 NJCAA national championship

University Of Kansas

Year	Overall	Conference	League/Postseason
1964-65	17-8	9-5	2nd Big Eight
1965-66	23-4	13-1	1st Big Eight, NCAA Elite Eight
1966-67	23-4	13-1	1st Big Eight, NCAA 2nd (3rd Midwest)
1967-68	22-8	10-4	2nd, NIT quarterfinal
1968-69	20-7	9-5	tied 2nd Big Eight, NIT first round
1969-70	17-9	8-6	2nd Big Eight
1970-71	27-3	14-0	1st, Big Eight, NCAA Final Four
1971-72	11-15	7-7	tied 4th Big Eight
1972-73	8-18	4-10	tied 6th Big Eight
1973-74	23-7	13-1	1st, Big Eight, NCAA Final Four
1974-75	19-8	11-3	1st, Big Eight, NCAA first round
1975-76	13-13	6-8	tied 4th, Big Eight
1976-77	18-10	8-6	4th, Big Eight
1977-78	24-5	13-1	1st, Big Eight, NCAA first round
1978-79	18-11	8-6	2nd, Big Eight
1979-80	15-14	7-7	tied 4th, Big Eight
1980-81	24-8	9-5	tied 2nd, Big Eight, NCAA Sweet 16

1981-82	13-14	4-10	7th, Big Eight
1982-83	13-16	4-10	tied 6th, Big Eight

TOTALS 348-182   170-96

- 1978 National Coach Of The Year
- Five-time Big Eight Conference Coach Of The Year
- Six Big Eight Conference titles
- Nine Big Eight Conference Tournament titles

Oral Roberts University

1985-86	10-19	5-7	5th
1986-87	11-17	5-7	tied 5th

TOTALS 21-36   10-14

Appendix B

Professional Careers of
Ted Owens'
All-American Jayhawks

Dave Robisch
Boston Celtics (44th pick, 3rd round)
Denver Rockets/Nuggets, San Diego Sails (ABA), Indiana Pacers,
Cleveland Cavaliers, San Antonio Spurs, Kansas City Kings
10,581 points (11.4 ppg)
6,173 rebounds (6.6 rpg)
1,655 assists (1.8 apg)

Isaac Frank "Bud" Stallworth
Seattle Supersonics (7th pick, 1st round)
Seattle Supersonics, New Orleans Jazz
2,403 points (7.7 ppg)
861 rebounds (7.8 rpg)
213 assists (0.7 apg)

Darnell Valentine
Portland Trail Blazers (16th pick, 1st round)
Los Angeles Clippers, Cleveland Cavaliers (NBA), and Marr Rimini,
Burghy Medera, Regio Emilia (Italy)
5,400 points (8.7 ppg)
1,318 rebounds (2.1 rpg)
3,080 assists (5.0 apg)

Walter Wesley
Cincinnati Royals (6th pick, 1st round)
Chicago Bulls, Cleveland Cavaliers, Phoenix Suns, Washington Bullets, Philadelphia 76ers, Milwaukee Bucks, Los Angeles Lakers
5,002 points (8.5 ppg)
3,243 Rebounds (5.5 rpg)
385 Assists (0.7 apg)

JoJo White
Boston Celtics (9th pick, 1st round)
Boston Celtics, Golden State Warriors, Kansas City Kings
Two NBA Championships, NBA Finals MVP, Seven-time NBA All-Star, Two-time 2nd Team All-NBA, NBA All-Rookie first team, No. 10 retired by the Celtics
14,399 points (17.2 ppg)
4,095 assists (4.9 apg)
3,345 rebounds (4.0 rpg)

Ted Owens' Coaching Tree

John Calipari, University of Kentucky

Bob Hill, Seattle Supersonics

Gale Catlett, University of Cincinnati and West Virginia

Bob Mulcahy, University of South Dakota and Eastern Kentucky University

Tad Boyle, University of Colorado

Ray Giacoletti, University of Utah, Gonzaga University, Drake University

Scott Brooks, Oklahoma City Thunder

Kenny Natt, Sacramento Kings

Grey Giovannine, Lamar University and Augustana College

Appendix D

NBA Players Coached by Ted Owens

Player	Draft selection
1965 – George Unseld	Los Angeles Lakers, Round 8
1966 – Walter Wesley	Cincinnati Royals, Round 1
1966 – Al Lopes	Baltimore Bullets, Round 13
1967 – Ronald Franz	Detroit Pistons, Round 4
1968 – Rodger Bohnenstiehl	New York Knicks, Round 9
1969 – JoJo White	Boston Celtics, Round 1
1969 – Dave Nash	Chicago Bulls, Round 4
1969 – Bruce Sloan	Philadelphia 76ers, Round 11
1971 – Dave Robisch	Boston Celtics, Round 3
1971 – Walter Roger Brown	Los Angeles Lakers, Round 4
1971 – Pierre Russell	Milwaukee Bucks, Round 13
1972 – Bud Stallworth	Seattle Supersonics, Round 1
1972 – Aubrey Nash	Baltimore Bullets, Round 14
1975 – Rick Suttle	Los Angeles Lakers, Round 7
1975 – Roger Morningstar	Boston Celtics, Round 8
1976 – Norm Cook	Boston Celtics, Round 1
1977 – Herb Nobles	Detroit Pistons, Round 7
1978 – Ken Koenigs	Cleveland Cavaliers, Round 5
1978 – John Douglas	New Orleans Jazz, Round 6
1979 – Paul Mokeski	Houston Rockets, Round 2

1980 – Randy Carroll	Phoenix Suns, Round 10
1981 – Darnell Valentine	Portland Trail Blazers, Round 1
1981 – Art Housey	Dallas Mavericks, Round 3
1981 – John Crawford	Philadelphia 76ers, Round 7
1982 – Dave Magley	Cleveland Cavaliers, Round 2
1982 – Tony Guy	Boston Celtics, Round 2

Appendix (E)

Ted Owens' Favorite Expressions

a. "Walking in tall cotton" is an expression that I used when things were really going well. As a boy pulling cotton, my dad would tell us that when the stalks of cotton were taller, they would usually produce more cotton bolls and a better harvest.

b. If my players weren't communicating effectively, I would remind them, "Timid salesmen have skinny children."

c. When I wanted my players to be more aggressive, I would tell them, "Don't let things happen to you—you happen."

d. Before an emotional game, I would remind them, "Tonight, both teams will play with their hearts. The team that wins will also play with their heads."

e. Dr. Allen had a phrase that Coach Harp used, and then I used: "Men, you have a huge advantage tonight because you wear Kansas across your chest." I could never say that to my players without getting tears in my eyes.

f. If a player wasn't digging deeply and giving 100 percent, I would say what a coach once said to me, "Young man, you are trying, but you are trying too easy."

g. "It's not what you have now that matters, but what you have at the hang-up."

h. "Potential doesn't matter. It's production that counts."

i. "Play within yourself and don't try to be somebody that you are not."